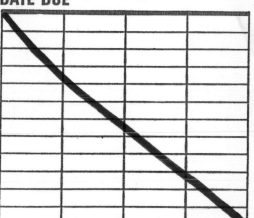

The Motorless Flight Series

MANBIRDS: Hang Gliders & Hang Gliding

THE WILD, WONDERFUL WORLD
OF PARACHUTES AND PARACHUTING

In Preparation:

THE GREAT AMERICAN BALLOON BOOK
HALF-A-MILE UP WITHOUT AN ENGINE:
Sailplanes & Soaring

The Motorless Flight Series

MANBIRDS
Hang Gliders & Hang Gliding
by **Maralys Wills**

Foreword by R.V. Wills,
Chairman,
Accident Review Board,
United States
Hang Gliding Association

Preface by Gil Dodgen,
Editor,
Hang Gliding Magazine

Book II: *The Education of a Hang Glider Pilot*, by Chris A. Wills, M.D.

Prentice-Hall, Inc., Englewood Cliffs, New Jersey

To Bobby and Eric, who fell out of the sky too soon

Address inquiries to Prentice-Hall, Inc., Englewood
Cliffs, N.J. 07632
Printed in the United States of America
Prentice-Hall International, Inc., London
Prentice-Hall of Australia, Pty. Ltd., Sydney
Prentice-Hall of Canada, Ltd., Toronto
Prentice-Hall of India Private Ltd., New Delhi
Prentice-Hall of Japan, Inc., Tokyo
Prentice-Hall of Southeast Asia Pte. Ltd., Singapore
Whitehall Books Limited, Wellington, New Zealand

10 9 8 7 6 5 4 3 2 1

Library of Congress Cataloging in Publication Data

Wills, Maralys.
    Manbirds.
    (The Motorless flight series)
    Includes The education of a hang glider pilot, by
Chris A. Wills.
    Bibliography: p.
    Includes index.
    1. Hang gliding. 2. Hang gliding—History. I. Wills,
Chris A., joint author. II. Title. III. Series: Motor-
less flight series.
GV764.W53   797.5'5   80-29253
ISBN 0-13-551101-1

Contents

Foreword

As a sophisticated and demanding sport, hang gliding has come of age in less than a decade. Anything prior was essentially experimentation and adventure.

As an art form and a sensory experience, hang gliding is known to the average person only through glimpses of flights in television commercials. The reasons for the artistic obscurity of such a spectacular sport are not immediately apparent, but two come to mind. The first is that the sport came early to be regarded as daredevil and death-defying by the media, which learned of it primarily through accident coverage. The other lies in the nature of the devotees the sport attracted in its early years. They were a combination of youthful adventurers and older aeronautical purists, neither aligned with—or even trusting of—the media or commercial sponsorship. The manufacturers, usually pilots and their patrons, knew even less about publicity and promotion than they did about making a profit, which was very little in the Seventies. The exhilaration of free flight was enough. Who needed public relations, commercial sponsorship, or even public acceptance? The goals were to build better "kites," to fly better, and to avoid governmental interference.

As a consequence, the public learned of the risks of hang gliding, but not its extraordinary beauty. Meets and competitions were barely public affairs, tucked off in selected pockets of terrain with no real publicity. Prize money was modest because of lack of commercial sponsorship. Photographers couldn't resist the sport, but the rest of the public stayed away in droves. Until 1975, spectators numbered in the hundreds.

Naturally, pilots fell to earth with increasing frequency in the early Seventies, and the media did take note of them. Fatalities make news, especially fatalities in an apparently high-risk activity that is novel or rare. Hang glider fatalities received coverage appropriate for an acrobat, a mountain climber, a sky diver, or an aerialist. Risky business. Too bad. . . .

Those of us watching the sport evolve from within lamented our fallen pilots no less. But we saw beauty and challenge and excitement possible in precious few sectors of life in our times. Between 1971 and 1975, flapping plastic on bamboo frames evolved into silent Dacron rainbows on polished aluminum skeletons, and ten-second glides down a grassy slope became unlimited soaring above ocean cliffs and mountain ridges. The transition in those four years could be compared to a telescopic leap from the Wright brothers' contraption to the early jets of the Fifties.

Since 1975, flights have strung out from twenty-eight miles to over one hundred miles, and thermaling pilots now require oxygen. From flapping plastic on bamboo frames to instrument panels on sleek gliders with a thirty-five–foot wingspan and a glide ratio of ten to one, in less than a decade.

Ironically, the new altitudes and cross-country flying reduce spectator exposure to the beautiful birds. Competitions are no longer confined to a visible flight path and landing area. Pilots launch far from home and hearth—without fascinated passers-by. A declining fatality rate even contributes to the lingering obscurity. Pilots are better trained and more experienced than five years ago. Gliders are better designed and constructed. Happily, the risks are known and taken into account.

Hopefully, the pages that follow will introduce the reader, aficionado, or uninitiated to a sport of incredible physical exhilaration, intellectual challenge, and visual beauty. The history of the sport is a story of adventuresome intellects, not daredevils. Brilliant men conceived and flew the rapidly evolving wings, not hippies and hot-rodders. The sport today is a triumph of both spirit and intellect, one in which physical prowess alone falls far short.

I personally will never forget the consummate thrill of watching two sons trail each other through the endless sky above the cliffs of Waimanalo, like gaudy gulls, back in 1973. Then stepping off the cliff and soaring through that balmy air myself, as a passenger, with one of those sons. The fact that he and another son were later killed while hang gliding gave us a tragic legacy from a backyard project of years before.

But our fallen pilots were victims of mistakes that others now avoid, one his own and one the carelessness of another. My wife and I still respect and admire the sport as before. Men now do fly like birds—huge, multicolored birds. My effort is to reduce their risks. Hers is to tell their story. I hope you will agree that she has done it herein with a special insight and with good humor.

Robert V. Wills, Chairman
Accident Review Board
United States Hang Gliding Association

Preface

Every so often an author discovers hang gliding. A hasty research project usually produces a superficial essay that doesn't accurately represent the sport. Books written by those from the inside of the sport are usually too esoteric for the nonflying reader.

In this book you will find a refreshing marriage of a familiarity with the sport that only someone who has been involved could have, and an understanding of what makes a treatise accessible to a general audience. The author's style has created a work that will be informative and entertaining for any reader.

The story of hang gliding is really the story of people. The dream of flight, having been realized at the turn of the century, was temporarily diverted by the recognition of its practical applications. The modern hang-gliding movement was triggered by the imagination and technology that made personal wings possible. The story of the realization of this dream is a true adventure story. No exaggeration, fiction, or sensationalization could improve on the true drama of the modern sport.

The story of hang gliding is the story of exhilaration and excitement, as anyone who has flown even for a few seconds can attest. It has been a humorous story, as Maralys demonstrates frequently. It has been a tragic story, as she who has lost two sons to the sport knows better than anyone. The history of the industry is a human story as well. Dozens of little businesses have blossomed and died, often sustained by nothing more than the enthusiasm of their owners.

Maralys has accurately and skillfully captured the drama, from the dreams of the ground skimmers to the excitement and challenge of today's one-hundred-mile cross-country flights. This is the story of where the world's most exciting sport has been and where it is going.

Gil Dodgen, Editor
Hang Gliding magazine

Acknowledgments

In writing this book I needed more help than I ever dreamed. Fortunately, I received more than I could have hoped for.

For those of you familiar with college term papers, this project became a dozen rolled into one, with research reaching across oceans and, at the end, around the clock.

My benefactors start at home and extend to scores I've never seen:

My husband, Bob, who brought me as many dinners as he did choice phrases . . . who also listened endlessly. He was always sure I could do it—even when I wasn't.

Chris Wills, who lent his years of experience to a part of the book I couldn't have done otherwise.

Betty-Jo Wills, who slaved away during the final push, and whose sense of fun made drudgery enjoyable. Lucky is the person who works with her.

Patty Teal, my agent and friend, who started it all—then fielded a relentless stream of phone calls with good cheer and sound advice.

The people who offered ideas and a keen sense of where the sport's at: editors Gil Dodgen and Tracy Knauss. Gil, living nearby, also offered critical review of the manuscript and sometimes suggestions for coping with the overwhelming.

The sport's early figures, who gave me lengthy interviews and added history—and charm—to the pages: Volmer Jensen, Bill Bennett, Francis Rogallo, Donnita Kilbourne, Paul MacCready, Willi Muller, and Taras Kiceniuk, Sr.

Pioneers and humorists Jack Lambie and Richard Miller, whose choice phrases needed no alteration.

Writer Carol Price, who captured some of the sport's big moments and big personalities.

Today's leaders, who gave thoughtful interviews, answered endless questions, and helped in a multitude of big and little ways: Chris Price, Don Partridge, Rich Grigsby, Ken de Russy, Mike Meier, Pete Brock, Dan Poynter, Jan Case, Dan Johnson (who let us use information from his *Whole Air Magazine*), Stein Fossum, Ed Vickery, John Harris, Mary and T. J. Young, Trip Mellinger, Bill Pregler, Joe Greblo, and Dean Tanji.

Others who filled in willingly: Carol Velderrain, Linda Liquori, Bonnie Nelson, and Karen Lambie.

Friends whose giving of pictures and words cost them much overseas postage: Minoru Hirata, Bjorn Myhre, Ken Messenger, Vincene Muller.

The photographers—both generous and skilled—whose photos cover so precisely all the things I was trying to say: George Uveges, Stephen McCarroll, Bettina Gray, LeRoy Grannis, Minoru Hirata, Bjorn Myhre, Rob Kells, Bill Allen, Richard Jenks, Hugh Morton, Jim Morton, Chris Wills, Vincene Muller, Betty-Jo Wills, Don Monroe, Ken de Russy, Carol Price, Ernst Furuhatt, Donnita Kilbourne, Greg MacGillivray, Ulvis Alberts, Clay Nolen, Floyd Clark, Ed Vickery, Steve Pearson, Bill Wood, and Don Whitmore.

Pete Suthard, from the Smithsonian Institution, who helped as if we were old friends.

Joe Linton, who did the drawings on short notice—and well.

Linda Bisignani, who not only typed like a maniac but decoded data in a sport not her own.

The hundreds of flyers all over the world who responded quickly and in detail to our questionnaires.

My good friends at home who cheered me on . . .

The warmth and helpfulness that came to me during these past months was by far the best part of doing the book!

Book One

The Mad, Magical, Many-Sided World of Hang Gliding

THE DINOSAUR'S ALIVE

On a cliff swept by a relentless wind a man stood under a hang glider ready to launch. He stood with feet apart, eyes intently fixed on the man facing him, senses keenly alert to the feel of the wind and the sharp flapping of his sail. When his wires were released he knew he would go up—straight up to perhaps five thousand feet—and from that moment he would be free to soar as long as his will and his body allowed. If it suited him, he might not come down for eight hours.

Thus has the sport of hang gliding developed from that time in 1970 when a man needed all his friends, pulling and pushing together, to launch him and his ungainly wing a foot or two off the ground for a trip that would last two or three seconds.

Even if we weren't there we know how it was because we see those early pilots in their home movies. They were always hanging by their arms from their odd craft, and almost always each had his own assemblage of launchers who pushed, pulled, panted, stumbled, and ran, trying to get him airborne. We see the crowds who gathered to gape. We see crashes, always crashes.

In those early days pilots flew so little and crashed so much it's a wonder they persisted.

But it seemed to come to a lot of people, all at the same time, that if they only tried hard enough they could experience basic, elemental flight. And so they tried, straining, crashing, laughing, while the crowds strained, gasped, and laughed with them.

And the idea grew.

It only took a few men flying a few feet on a few occasions to ensure that the new sport of hang gliding would survive. It was irresistible. One experience was enough to infect them. It got in their blood. If they flew at all they had to fly again. And they had to talk about it.

They had to involve others.

For euphoria was then—and still is—the predominant mood of hang gliding. People who try the sport do so because they want to fly (some say they *need* to fly) in the elemental, basic way that men have always wanted to fly—feeling the wind, moving their bodies freely in three dimensions, getting higher than *everybody*. It is a passion which has existed, probably, since the first man saw his first bird.

The excitement, the exhilaration of hang gliding remain in the eighties, but the sport is changing. Sophistication is the way of the world: It touches and changes everything. Nothing stays simple. Nothing remains pure. As much as men may wish to fly simply, in the way of the birds, they cannot do so. Improvements must be made.

If the Wright brothers were alive, they might very well say, "This is where I came in." They would know better than we that aviation began simply, became complex (it took computers, after all, to put us on the moon), and grew simple again with the advent of hang gliding.

When, in 1971, hang gliding was "discovered" as a new way of flying, it seemed a totally new experience. Only faintly did people realize that it had been done this way before, for it was not within anyone's memory. It was like rediscovering the dinosaur—alive and chewing.

But now, once more, the simple is getting complex. Hang gliding is changing, changing so fast and so relentlessly that its eight-year-old models are relics. Hang glider designers, with their engines, high-aspect-ratio gliders, and aerodynamic principles, are accused of reinventing the airplane!

We don't know where it will end—whether hang gliding as we now know it will become obsolete once again . . . only to be rediscovered, perhaps, in 2050.

But for now we have it.

We have flying in an almost elemental state. We have its beauty and freedom—the added fillips of soaring and thermaling—as yet unfettered by government regulation. We are limited today only by our skills, our mountains, and the state of the wind. The equipment is giving and forgiving. Instruction is everywhere. It is safe as never before.

Today is the day to *go for it!*

THE MYTH THAT EMBODIES THE DREAM

The flight ended in heartbreak.

But it was a chance Daedalus and his young son, Icarus, had to take. There was no other way to leave, no other means of escaping their imprisonment on the Mediterranean island of Crete. They could only go by air. Daedalus gazed wistfully upward beyond the walls and said, "Minos can indeed prevent me from going over land and sea . . . but at least the skies remain open to me."[1]

And so Daedalus, brilliant engineer-architect, prisoner of the cruel King Minos, began building wings for himself and his son. He would copy the birds. The wings would be built of feathers, secured in the middle with threads of flax, on the ends with wax, and bent slightly to give them a curve.

With such wings he and his son would escape the prison walls and fly to Athens, a feat that was surely possible—for didn't the birds do it every day?

"When he had put the final touches to his handiwork, the craftsman, with a pair of wings, balanced his body in the air where he remained suspended by beating them. He then also gave a pair to his son and said to him: 'I advise you, Icarus, to remain half-way between the waves lest they, should you go too low, make your wings heavy, and the sun, lest it burn you with its fires, should you go too high: Fly between the two. . . .

"And while thus teaching him how to fly, he adjusted these wings . . . on his shoulders. While he was working and giving his advice, the old man's cheeks became moist and his paternal hands trembled. He gave his son kisses that were destined to be the last, and then, lifting up with his wings, he flew off in front. . . . he beat his own wings, fixing his eyes on those of his son behind him. Some fisherman, bent on outwitting the fish with his trembling reed, a shepherd leaning on his stick, a farmer grasping his plough, who saw them, stood dumbfounded and thought that these beings who were capable of traveling through the air must be gods.

"The child began to savor the joys of this audacious flight, abandoned his guide, and, giving in to his desire to approach the heavens, flew ever higher. The proximity of the devouring sun softened the odorous wax that held the feathers. The wax having melted, the child only beat his naked arms and, lack-

Daedalus and Icarus try new wings. (Smithsonian Institution Photo No. 13440)

4 **The Mad, Magical, Many-Sided World of Hang Gliding**

ing henceforth all means of fending the void, he had no longer any support from the air; and his mouth was still screaming the name of his father when the bluish waters engulfed him. . . .

"As for the unfortunate father, who was no longer a father, he said: 'Icarus, where are you? Where must I look for you? Icarus,' he repeated, when he saw feathers upon the waters. Then he cursed his invention and shut up the body in a sepulchre, and this land has taken the name* of he who is buried within it."[2]

It is only a myth, this tale of Daedalus and Icarus.

Nobody can fly by flapping his arms—so why tell the story?

Today we ridicule such silliness. But for nineteen hundred years, perhaps longer, when men yearned after the birds, imagining themselves flying, they always supposed it would be with a flapping of arms. They conjured up Beethovian variations on the theme: Feathers. Hand-held propellers. Round discs. Umbrellas. But always those arms pumping up and down.

Two thousand years is a lot of man-years given over to false hopes: The dreams assume some importance.

Even today, at the Selsey Birdman Rally in England, there are the vestigial arm-flappers. The distances flown are minuscule, but nobody cares. It's all so funny.

LAWS AND FEATHERS

It was Leonardo da Vinci, genius of paint pot and Pythagoras, who finally expressed reasonably what the dreamers had only assumed: Logically, men can fly. But da Vinci, too, was from the arms-flapping school—with a twist. The arms would be used, but energy would come from the legs. "Man," he said, "has more strength in his legs than is needed by his weight alone."[3] He studied eagles, impressed with the great heights they reached by the mere beating of wings. And he observed sailing ships, heavily laden, yet moved by the force of wind alone. For Leonardo, both had significance; together, they meant men could fly.

It was all so simple to Leonardo. Birds were machines that operated according to mathematical laws. Potential birdmen had only to reproduce the machine to arrive at the same end result. For da Vinci, the differences between men and birds were laws and feathers. Nothing more. Nothing human intelligence couldn't solve. And to prove it he drew pictures, designed machines, wrote descriptions.

Today we know where da Vinci erred. The differences between men and birds are greater than he thought; in fact, insurmountable. Men have neither the

---

*The eastern part of the Aegean Sea was called Icarium Mare by the ancients.

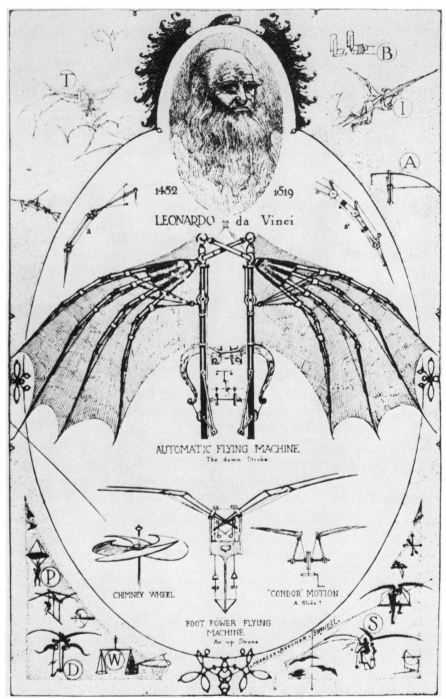

Da Vinci saw the possibilities. (Smithsonian Institution Photo No. A-4601A)

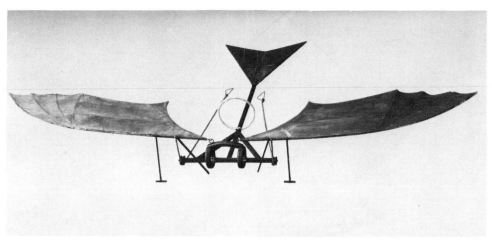

Da Vinci's ornithopter. (Smithsonian Institution Photo No. 30524B)

muscles, the heart rate, nor the breathing rate to fly by flapping—even with fabricated feathers! Our legs may be strong, but they're not strong enough. Our hearts don't beat fast enough; our breathing is too slow. The heart of a flying swallow beats eight hundred times a minute! A man's body, physiologically, would hardly fly him across the kitchen!

For all of Leonardo da Vinci's fascinating drawings, the ones concerned with man's going up remain the remarkable outpourings of a brilliant mind, revealing more of himself than of aeronautics. His plans for coming down are better: With a tent of linen, he believed, a man could throw himself from any height and come down unscathed. His design for a parachute does seem to resemble those of today.

Ah well, Leonardo . . . up isn't everything!

Da Vinci had his secretive side as well: One day painting a cryptic half-smile on the face of the Mona Lisa, and the next taking great pains to hide his inventions from discovery—by writing all his notes backward! There were five thousand pages of them, all unreadable. (Generations later, someone held them to a mirror and exposed his little game.) Thus did his theories of flight remain hidden from the world for centuries.

Meanwhile, people kept thinking they could fly.

Individuals less reasoning than Leonardo (who preserved himself for sixty-seven years by not attempting personally what his brain said was possible) jumped from various places. There are drawings of them everywhere. One leaves his tower with an open umbrella. Another attempts to fly with a virtual windmill resting on his shoulders. A third glues feathers to his arms and takes off. Some pump their arms; some blithely assume they are angels and none of the above is necessary. Most of them join the angels quickly.

The Mad, Magical, Many-Sided World of Hang Gliding 7

Da Vinci's notes—all written backward! (Smithsonian Institution Photo No. A-14753)

CAYLEY AND THE COACHMAN

How or why the transition from pumping arms to gliders came about is not clear—unless hot-air balloons had something to do with it. At almost the same time that excited English crowds were watching balloonists light their fires and fill their craft with smoke and rise miraculously, a young boy, George Cayley, was beginning to think of flying another way. In his head he conceived of gliders!

It was then the early 1800s.

In an era when men seldom lived past sixty, George Cayley (later *Sir George Cayley*) lived to the age of eighty-four; it was a good thing he did, because he needed the extra time. During his long life he discovered the principles of curved wings and propellers, constructed rudders and elevators, learned about varying tail surfaces and building wings in tiers. He spoke of flying with twenty-horsepower engines with weight limits of six hundred pounds.

Yet he worked in secret at first because he feared ridicule.

Like Leonardo da Vinci, Cayley theorized more than he flew, if he ever flew at all. Most of his craft, apparently, either flew unmanned or with someone else at the helm, and it is difficult to imagine some of them flying under any conditions . . . unless it's possible to get airborne in a small wheelbarrow with four windmills and two propellers.

By 1843 aeronautics must have become respectable enough so Cayley was no longer afraid of scorn. Writing long, pontificating letters to *Mechanics' Magazine* (published on Fleet Street), he discussed the intimate details of birds' wings—all you ever wanted to ask and a great deal more. Cayley was then seventy. At the end of a letter—theoretical and dispassionate in the extreme—he was finally moved to what, for him, must have been an emotional outburst:

I think it is a national disgrace, in these enlightened, locomotive times, not to realize, by public subscription, the proper scientific experiments, necessarily too expensive for any private purse, which would secure to this country the glory of being the first to establish the dry navigation of the universal ocean of the terrestrial atmosphere.

> I remain, Sir,
> Your obliged and obedient servant,
> George Cayley.
> Hertford street, April 2, 1843.[4]

Today it seems incredible that most of what Sir George Cayley learned lay fallow for nearly seventy years, and that the Wright brothers had to learn it all over again.

But go to Brompton Hall and see if George Cayley's been forgotten. . . . He hasn't.

Sir George Cayley. (Smithsonian Institution
Photo No. 76-17422)

Cayley's flying wheelbarrow! (Smithsonian Institution Photo No. A-36160B)

Immortality of the sort Britons love came to him at age eighty. By then Sir George had built a remarkable flying machine which he was too old to test. One can almost hear him lamenting, Now that I have this perfectly flyable glider I will never see it fly. But ah . . . surely someone . . .

And so Cayley approached his coachman. He persuaded the unsuspecting fellow to take the craft to a nearby cliff overlooking a valley.

By what means Sir George cajoled the coachman into taking off, nobody will know. But at any rate, the coachman departed the cliff, got airborne, cleared the hedgerows of Brompton for about fifteen hundred feet, and at the end crashed, demolishing the machine. It is said he looked back over his path of glide, realized where he'd been, and decided one such event was sufficient. He surrendered his cap indignantly. "I was engaged to drive," he said, "not fly."[5]

Go to Brompton Hall. They will gleefully tell you the story.

HE SWUNG LIKE A PENDULUM

And then what happened?

Nothing. Sir George Cayley, lone inventor, did not inspire anyone to fly what his coachman had flown or build what he had designed. He remained an oddity. Quaint. Interesting, of course, but more an example of the funny things that can happen in a man's head. Kind of a nut. People talked of his hapless coachman and laughed—how lucky the man was to have escaped with his life! But nobody dreamed of imitating him.

Who, then, would pick up the thread?

Perhaps Otto Lilienthal. Now *there* was a flyer.

In Germany, in the late 1800s, Otto Lilienthal became the world's first genuine pilot. Or, more accurately, the world's first pilot-showman, for he was

Otto Lilienthal. (Smithsonian Institution Photo No. A-39013)

both. He did what so many had yearned to do: He flew and he stayed up. And he did it repeatedly.

He would soon fly higher, longer, better than anyone before him (for who else had really done it at all?), finally even better than himself—always improving.

He wrote articles, he posed for cameramen, he directed camera angles. His was not the theoretical, untried logic of da Vinci nor the complicated theorizing of Sir George Cayley. His contribution was flying! Building machines. Finding hills. Doing it.

And telling people. Always talking, writing, poeticizing. Lilienthal was one to inspire others. He wanted to prove anyone could fly. He wanted to prove it visibly for his contemporaries and future men.

He was the original promoter.

In the beginning Otto had his brother, Gustave, to help him, and it isn't known whether Gustave persisted until the end because it was Otto who did all the writing and left all the pictures. We know Gustave was part of the scene, we just don't know for how long. It is curious that flying so often inspired brothers: the Lilienthals, the Montgomerys, the Wrights; and in hang gliding, the Arambides, the Braddocks, the Mitchells, the Willses.

Otto Lilienthal, the extrovert, and his brother, Gustave, found bird flight irresistible. Enough so that Otto wrote a classic book called *Birdflight as the Basis of Aviation*. In the introduction he wrote exuberantly, "with each advent of spring, when the air is alive with innumerable happy creatures; when the storks on their arrival at their old northern resorts fold up their imposing flying apparatus which has carried them thousands of miles, lay back their heads and announce their arrival by joyously rattling their beaks; when the swallows have made their entry and hurry through our streets and pass our windows in sailing flight; when the lark appears as a dot on the ether and manifests its joy of existence by his song; then a certain desire takes possession of man. He longs to soar upward and to glide, free as the bird, over smiling fields, heavy woods and mirrored lakes, and so enjoy the varying landscape as fully as only a bird can do."[6]

Yet when the desire took possession of the Lilienthals, men tried to dissuade them. Otto writes, "My brother and I, who were wholly without means, used to spare from our breakfasts, penny by penny, the money to prosecute our investigations. . . . While we were devoting every moment of our spare time to the solution of the problem, almost every one in Germany regarded the man who would waste his energies in such unproductive labor as a fool. Years ago the most distinguished professor of mathematics in the Berlin Industrial Academy sent me word that of course it could *do no harm* to amuse myself with such pastimes, but warned me earnestly against putting any money into them. A special commission of experts, organized by the state, had, in fact, laid it down as a fundamental principle, once for all, that it was *impossible* for a man to fly."[7]

Faced with such learned skepticism, the Lilienthals persisted, though they could hardly be called rash. Otto says, "My own experiments in flying were begun with great caution. The first attempts were made from a grass plot in my own garden upon which, at a height of one meter from the ground, I had erected a springboard, from which the leap with my sailing apparatus gave me an oblique descent through the air. After several hundred of these leaps I gradually increased the height of my board to two and a half meters, and from that elevation I could safely and without danger cross the entire grass plot. I then went to a hilly section, where leaps from gradually increased elevations added to my skill and suggested many improvements to my apparatus."[8]

His "sailing apparatus," in the beginning, consisted of a pair of enormous ribbed wings, "very like the outspread pinions of a soaring bird. . . . The frame is of willow, covered with sheeting; the entire area contains nearly 150 square feet, and the entire apparatus weighs about 45 pounds. . . ."[9] In the center a wooden frame circled his body, and his legs hung below, unencumbered and free for running. He steered by shifting his body weight. Supported thus by his armpits, Lilienthal's lower half swung like a pendulum.

As Otto and Gustave ran and took off from ever higher hills, they began to realize that in flying there is always a third factor present—the wind! Otto talked about it constantly. "It is an old adage that 'water has no rafters.' What, then, shall be said of air? . . .[10] I endeavor with every new trial to gain more complete control over the wind. . . . I have been at times surprised by a sudden increase in the force of the wind which either carried me upward almost perpendicularly or supported me in a stationary position for a few seconds to the great delight of the spectators. . . .[11] While the apparatus is supported by moving air, it is also subject to the whims of the wind, which often places it in uncomfortable

Lilienthal's biwing leaves the slag heap—the first true pilot. (Smithsonian Institution Photo No. A-48093K)

positions, overturns it, or carries it into higher regions and then precipitates it, headforemost, to the ground. . . . [sometimes] the apparatus becomes unmanageable, darts vertically up, turns about, comes to a stop, stands on its head, and descends with uncomfortable rapidity to the earth. . . . It is, on the whole, most advisable to follow the lessons of the birds, who ascend and descend into the wind. . . .[12]

"Anyone desirous of exposing himself unnecessarily to danger and of ruining in a few seconds the carefully constructed apparatus need only expose his machine to the wind without having familiarized himself with its management; he will soon know what it means to control an apparatus of from 10 to 15 square meters in area, where other people can but with difficulty manage an open umbrella."[13]

We may think Lilienthal is being funny, but he isn't. For all his virtues, he never exhibited a sense of humor. Whatever he says, he means to be taken seriously: "Each flight demands a rising from the ground and a landing; the former is as difficult as the latter is dangerous."[14]

Lilienthal isn't fooling.

Though Lilienthal at first stated adamantly he saw no usefulness in movable structures, he later developed elevators and a tail for his gliders. The elevator was connected to his head by a line, and he had merely to nod to make it work. To some of his craft he added second and third wings.

By now he had moved to his famous slag heap outside Berlin, a two-hundred-foot hill he built himself from the leftovers of canal diggings. He became famous in the area, the crowds growing as reports of his flying were carried farther and farther afield. He no longer seemed afraid of being overturned by the wind, and in fact grew so comfortable with his sport that he wrote, "The time has passed when every person harboring thoughts of aerial flight can be pronounced a charlatan. . . . It is a difficult task to convey to one who has never enjoyed aerial flight . . . the exhilarating pleasure of this elastic motion. The elevation above the ground loses its terror, because we have learned by experience what sure dependence may be placed upon the buoyancy of the air. . . . Resting upon the broad wings of a well-tested flying machine, which, yielding to the least pressure of the body, obeys our directions; surrounded by air and supported only by the wind, a feeling of absolute safety soon overcomes that of danger. . . . The indefinable pleasure . . . experienced in soaring high up in the air, rocking above sunny slopes without jar or noise, accompanied only by the music issuing from the wires of the apparatus, is well worth the labor given to the task of becoming an expert."[15]

In 1896, after more than two thousand successful flights, and having claimed—all too prematurely—that he'd made thousands of experiments without accident, except for a few scratches, Otto was experimenting with a movable elevator when a sudden gust of wind made his glider go into a spin. From fifty feet he dived into the ground and broke his back. He lived for a day, but he apparently knew he was going to die, for he said philosophically, "Sacrifices must be made."[16] We can almost see him shrugging painfully.

But he did what he had hoped to do. He proved that glider-type flight was possible—that in spite of capricious winds the machine would fly, supported; that once aloft fear vanished and that there was . . . well, nothing quite like it.

Otto Lilienthal inspired a generation of men to try newfound wings, and he started a passel of others theorizing about aeronautics. Men might have gone on flying as he did indefinitely—if the Wright brothers hadn't come along later to spoil it all.

THE FLYING PIANO

In England during the same period, another hopeful pilot had ideas. Hearing of Lilienthal, Percy Pilcher hurried to Germany to see for himself, then returned to Northamptonshire to tinker with variations of the Lilienthal gliders. Some resembled the early Lilienthal outspread wings, others were more like present-day fixed-wing hang gliders, except that the trailing edges were held firm with more than a hundred piano wires! Skeptical that the wind would do its job unaided, Pilcher attached ropes for towing. Bicycle wheels became landing gear.

As if they were children, Pilcher gave every glider a name. The Bat. The Hawk. The Gull.

Percy Pilcher—note the piano wires! (Smithsonian Institution Photo No. A-18261)

His sister was with him constantly, observing, and because she never attempted Pilcher's excursions into the air, she lived to write articles about their adventures later. In the *Aeronautical Journal* of July 1909, she wrote: "From Pilcher's earliest boyhood he was entirely wrapped up in the idea of flying, and from the time he was thirteen, when he joined the Britannia, he made small experiments. I remember when he was fifteen, a cadet in the Royal Navy, his explaining to me what he believed would be the shape and working of the flying machine of the near future. . . . During the winter of 1892-1893 he built the machine we called the Bat. The body piece was, as far as I remember, 11 feet 8 inches long and 2 feet 3 inches wide.

"The wings folded back like a fan. It was necessary to have it so, in order that it would pack easily, as Pilcher was obliged to live in the town on account of his work. In Glasgow he had the loan of a large room under the roof as a workshop, while we had to go down to the country for the experiments.

"The very first day of the experiments, which were made in the beginning of '93 near Cardross, from a slight elevation and against a slight wind, Pilcher was raised twelve feet from the ground, where he hovered without any forward motion for between two and three minutes, and then descended by tilting the machine forward quite successfully.

"But the next time he rose the wind caught the machine sideways, and his weight being insufficient to restore the equilibrium, it tipped forward and sideways in landing, breaking one of the front spars.

"After this he lowered the wing tips and had some very good results . . . starting from the top of a hill and gliding against the wind, the angle we reckoned, being approximately 1 in 10.

"We took a farmhouse with a very large, empty barn at Cardross on the Clyde, where we got nice, clear wind on the hills, and he was able to practice almost daily, his longest soar with no motive power being about sixty yards, and greatest height about twenty feet.

"At Cardross he built two more machines. One was never quite finished as the framework, which was built to carry an engine, proved too heavy for soaring. It was a monoplane, the wings being very square cut, and the body piece much the shape of the Bleriot short-span flyer.

"He then went to the other extreme, influenced, no doubt, by a month of very light winds, and the Gull was built with a wing area of 1-1/2 feet to the pound weight, and was so light as to be cumbersome and impossible to use for practice, except with the very lightest breeze.

"The Hawk—the most successful of all—was the last machine that Pilcher built. . . . With this machine Pilcher had many very successful flights, notably one at Eynsford, from the top of one hill to the top of the next across a valley, when as a substitute for power, he had a light rope attached to the machine, which was hauled in on a pulley on the far hill.

"The flight was . . . nearly 300 yards—and of course, in this case, across the valley, the flight was a high one."[17]

Percy Pilcher only lived to be thirty-three.

Toward the end he prepared to mount a motor to one of his gliders, not intending motorized flight, ironically, but only the use of an engine to get higher —for better gliding! But just before the great mounting he was demonstrating his craft to one Lord Brayes in bad weather. He crashed, becoming hang gliding's second fatality. The year was 1899.

ODE TO A VULTURE

The idea of flying seemed to appear everywhere at once in the late 1800's, for even in Egypt a man was observing vultures with an ecstatic eye, convinced that they held secrets humans could emulate. Louis Pierre Mouillard said, "The most stirring, exciting sight is to stand in the vulture roost on the Mokatan ridge near Cairo, and to look upon the tawny vulture passing within five yards in full flight. All my life I shall remember the first flight of these birds which I saw. . . . I was so impressed that all day long I could think of nothing else." Mouillard was convinced that vultures represented "a perfect demonstration of all my preconceived theories concerning the possibilities of artificial flight in a wind."[18]

Some believe Mouillard constructed a glider which carried him an astonishing 138 feet, that on getting airborne he was so startled he forget to test his control. Others make no mention of his actually flying.

Mouillard is remembered best for his classical contribution to aeronautical literature, *L'Empire de l'Air*, which he wrote in 1881.

Listen to nis passionate description of his beloved vulture: "The vulture's needs are few, and his strength is moderate. To earn his living he but needs to sight the dead animal from afar. . . . he knows how to rise, how to float aloft . . . to sail upon the wind without effort. . . . he has evolved a peculiar mode of flight; he sails and spends no force, he never hurries, he uses the wind instead of his muscles. . . . Beside him the stork is as a wren, the kite a mere butterfly, the falcon a pin-feather. Who so has for five minutes had the fortune to see the Nubian vulture in full sail through the air, and has not perceived the possibility of his imitation by man is—I will not say of dull understanding but, certainly inapt to analyse and to appreciate."[19]

With *L'Empire de l'Air* Mouillard may have brought a new understanding of wind currents to the dawning world of aviation, but he did just as much to gain appreciation for the soaring vulture.

A SIGHT "SUCH AS YOU'VE NEVER SEEN BEFORE"

San Diego in 1883. A small city near a harbor. Wood-frame houses bunched together along the beachfronts. A few homes on the nearest hilltops. But the hills farther south, bare. Tawny-colored and treeless. Wheeler Hill on Otay Mesa, a perfect place for boys with a sense of adventure to sneak off in the early dawn and practice flying. But careful . . . lest someone consider them crazy, hide the flying craft deep in the hay of the wagon. Take rifles to appear to be rabbit hunting. And go early so nobody's up. Crash in private. And fly— if you can—in private. See if it works, first. If it doesn't, nobody will know, nobody will laugh.

The ornithopter* of brothers James and John Montgomery, of course, didn't work. None ever had. But John Montgomery claims to have built a tandem-wing glider and launched himself into the wind on August 28, 1883, to become the first flying American. He said he flew six hundred feet, witnessed by his brother.

Montgomery wrote about the experience as fact, and his claims have survived.

Nonetheless, he quickly gave up flying and eventually became a professor at prestigious Santa Clara University. He didn't fly again until 1906, three years after the Wright brothers took it up.

In 1906, with his interest in the subject renewed, Montgomery found a young parachute jumper, Daniel Maloney, to fly what he designed.

Maloney was a showman: daring, coordinated, fearless, fond of performing for crowds. With Montgomery's glider he allowed himself to be towed by hot-air balloon to heights of four thousand feet, from whence he released the glider and returned to earth doing breathtaking dives, stalls, and spirals. His performances attracted large crowds and awed admiration. Maloney had his following, who came to see him week after week, and his mentor, Montgomery, always watching and dreaming of improvements to the craft.

On one occasion, in front of a large group of his friends from a military company, Montgomery sent Maloney aloft, promising everyone a sight beyond anything they'd ever seen before. Maloney would leave the balloon and spiral down in his usual spectacular fashion. But this day, as the balloon was rising, observers on the ground saw in horror that a piece of the glider's bracing had snapped apart, torn loose by one of the guy ropes. From the ground Montgomery and his friends shouted and waved, trying to make Maloney understand he must cancel the flight. But Maloney didn't comprehend, and cheerfully waved back.

---

*An experimental type of aircraft designed to be propelled by the flapping of wings.

John Montgomery and his aeroplane, the *Santa Clara*. (Archives, The University of Santa Clara)

From the moment Maloney released, the rear wings began to flap and the machine immediately turned over. Maloney and the glider floated peacefully down, inverted, with the glider acting almost as a parachute, and the speed of descent not much faster. When he hit everyone ran to him, but he was already unconscious, and died thirty minutes later. The six doctors who examined Maloney could find no cause for his death, the only apparent injury being a small wire scratch on the side of his neck. The answer might have been subtle: fear, shock . . . an overwhelmed heart.

For a while Montgomery gave up in discouragement. His friend was gone and he felt at fault. Then the San Francisco earthquake hit and distracted the populace from thoughts of flying. People had the horrors of a broken city to think about, the aftermath occupying them for several years.

But eventually Montgomery returned to his hills and his gliders. In 1911, having learned more about curved surfaces, he was aloft once more when a gust of wind hit him and one wing tip stalled and the plane tilted, fell to the ground, and struck sideways. Montgomery's head hit the side of the glider, ordinarily cause for a mere bruise. But it was his luck that a quarter-inch bolt protruding from the glider penetrated his skull, probably in the soft area behind his ear. At first Montgomery seemed unharmed, yet a short time later he fell into a coma and died.

A present-day hang gliding expert, Jack Lambie, determined to resurrect the Montgomery legend and bring this flying pioneer the veneration he deserves, studied Montgomery's early gliders, safely stored at the University

of Santa Clara. The more Jack pursued the matter, the more puzzled he grew: The 1883 gliders could not possibly have performed according to Montgomery's claims. There was doubt that they flew at all.

The evidence against Montgomery's 1883 flights grew: During a Montgomery Meet held in 1971 at the same Wheeler Hill, the best hang glider of the day, Taras Kiceniuk's Icarus, with its longest, flattest glide, stopped almost two hundred feet short of duplicating Montgomery's six-hundred foot flight.

James Spurgeon, a Montgomery expert in San Diego, has had an outstanding offer of two thousand dollars for anyone duplicating Montgomery's flight with a replica of his machine. Nobody has come close to claiming the prize, and in fact, the replicas don't get off the ground.

The final curiosity is that Montgomery never tried to repeat his own performance. He wrote no papers, never developed the design. The fact that he gave up flying altogether between 1886 and 1906—twenty years!—smacks more of failure than success.

So Jack Lambie, having devoted several weeks to intensive study and calculations, gave the man his due: "He *was* an early pioneer." But he decided to let the rest of the Montgomery legend rest in peace. "There was no purpose to be served," he said, "in debunking the man."

"NO MOTIVE POWER BEYOND THE WIND . . ."

Aviation was inevitable.

Like an ancient, buried treasure, this thousand-year-old dream, once exposed to public view, would prove irresistible. It wouldn't be left alone. It couldn't be left alone. Once people had seen it with their very eyes, flying would draw men again and again.

And so everybody got into the act. Octave Chanute—French born, but American since age seven, builder and railroad engineer—played at aviation as a hobby. At age sixty he built his first glider, and—understanding engineering somewhat better than the Lilienthals, Pilchers, and Montgomerys—he toyed with the problems of stability in his flying craft. On the sand dunes around Lake Michigan he invited young adventurers to fly what he designed. He braced his wings with a bridge-truss system of diagonal wires, a logical step for a bridge builder. He searched for materials that would add strength without weight. And always he was concerned with safety. He knew that flying had already claimed Lilienthal and Pilcher. He had no intention of being responsible for more deaths.

So Chanute designed and others flew and the newspapers reported it all joyously. According to a *Sunday Journal* of September 1896, "It is claimed that at last a machine which will really fly and carry a man without danger has

The Chanute flyers. (Smithsonian Institution Photo No. 80-465)

been constructed. The inventor is Octave Chanute, former President of the Society of Civil Engineers and a scientific thinker of pronounced ability.

"A run was made by Avery along the side of the hill, by jumping into the air and governing the apparatus in the wind gusts. The first flight carried the operator 50 feet and never less than two feet above the ground. This was considered an astounding result, considering that absolutely no motive power beyond the wind was used.

"After that first skim, the two assistants of Mr. Chanute made between 150 and 200 jumps, all without the slightest accident, either to themselves or the machine.

"In confirming these early experiments to jumping with the machine, Mr. Chanute has followed the line which he has long advocated, that the chief problem which is to be solved before man can hope to fly in the air is that of safety.

"He holds that this must first be worked out in a full-size apparatus, mounted by a man and exposed to the vicissitudes of the wind, before any attempt is made to soar or to apply a motor or propelling instrument."[20]

Occasionally the Chanute flyers meandered too far and bathed unexpectedly in Lake Michigan, sending Chanute back for revised calculations.

In 1910, having summarized what he'd learned in his *Progress in Flying Machines*, Octave Chanute earned a gold medal from the Royal Aeronautical Society. Yet his biggest contributions to flight may have been indirect.

Like Lilienthal, Chanute shared generously with others—not only ideas but money—and it was his aid to the Wright brothers that boosted them out of their humdrum bicycle shop and into the experiments which eventually led to airplanes.

And here we see "natural flight" come to an abrupt end.

THEY DID TERRIBLY DANGEROUS THINGS

The Wright brothers did it. Because of them, hang gliding ended for almost fifty years, not to be picked up in any big way until late 1960. Having learned all they could about gliding, the brothers used their knowledge only as a means to a powered end, and they can be deemed responsible for having "killed" hang gliding and kept it out of the memories of nearly all men now living.

Once Orville and Wilbur attached engines to their gliders, nobody cared any longer about flying any other way. Early airplanes were fun. They zoomed and darted around the skies, flew perilously close to the ground, slithered under bridges, scared farmers' cows, delighted clapping crowds who stood and watched.

Pilots were daredevils, darlings, macho men and women. They took chances; they did terribly dangerous things, like walking on each other's wings; they flew upside down and tried to see how close they could come to obstructions without actually hitting them. They were sportsmen, speed lovers, and maybe just . . . lovers?

Nobody dreamed then of going back to simpler forms of flight. Why should they? This headier stuff was too exciting. Anyone who had adventure in his blood wanted to be a pilot. Never mind that pilots were getting killed. A short, thrilling life held more appeal to some than a long, boring one.

In these days powered flight was everything.

Unpowered flight was nothing.

We all know what happened after a while. Aviation turned *serious.*

Not everyone took the deaths lightly; concerned men drew up regulations and laws governing the airspace. Airplanes were modified, cockpitted, cocooned from the elements. When men flew now they didn't feel the wind in their faces, they no longer seemed part of the great, abundant "upper freedom." Instruments did their calculations; buttons did the flying. Pilots became head only, not heart.

Flying had to be rediscovered. It was inevitable.

THE WORLD'S SMALLEST AIRCRAFT-DESIGN CENTER

Accounts vary as to who is really the "father" of hang gliding.

The truth is, the sport had many fathers.

It is no easier to pinpoint the real author of the sport than it is to decide who really discovered the West. Was it the Indians? The Mexicans? The missionaries? Lewis and Clark? The miners? The fur trappers? The pioneer settlers? The fact is, they *all* played a role. And so did numerous men in hang gliding.

But certain names stand out: Francis M. Rogallo, Volmer Jensen, Jack Lambie, Bill Bennett, Dave Kilbourne, Taras Kiceniuk, Richard Miller, Bob Wills, Paul MacCready. And before them, Otto Lilienthal, John J. Montgomery, Octave Chanute, the Wright Brothers. Before them, even, Sir George Cayley and Leonardo da Vinci—clear back to the legends of Icarus.

The lull that came to hang gliding after the Wright brothers spirited flying away on a gasoline engine lasted for almost fifty years. Only in Germany, where the development of powered aircraft was prohibited by the terms of the Versailles Treaty, was unpowered flight pursued. The Germans developed silent gliding to a sophisticated art, but even then men flew gliders in enclosed cockpits, away from the elements. Except for having no engines, German gliders resembled airplanes more than hang gliders.

Still, German gliding remains the single small thread of unpowered flight strung between the Wright brothers and Volmer Jensen.

What a singular man is Volmer Jensen!

For years, beginning in 1925, he kept the sport of hang gliding alive when nobody else in the world was doing it . . . or cared to.

Today, at sixty-nine, he stands trim, tall, sternly erect, and one could better imagine him as headmaster in a private boys' school, teaching math, than outside straining to push a hang glider up a hill. There is a cool distance to him—until he smiles. Then the sternness fades, replaced by gentle benevolence. Before your eyes he becomes approachable and warm.

With quiet pride he points to his latest project, the VJ-24 Sunfun, stretched across the yard in back of his house. It is another of his fixed-wing hang gliders, with rudder, ailerons, and elevator. But it is only the last of many accomplishments. For without a college education Volmer Jensen has built—with his two hands—almost every kind of small flying machine except a jet.

With help from his good friend Irv Culver (a Lockheed aerodynamicist), Volmer Jensen builds amphibians, sailplanes, and fixed-wing hang gliders; sells kits and plans—all from what may be the world's smallest aircraft-design center. Working in a shop the size of a two-car garage (it probably *was* a two-car garage), with a small backyard office a few steps away, he forges his links to the flying world right in the heart of residential Glendale, California. From the street he is Volmer Jensen, unobtrusive resident on a quiet tree-lined avenue. In the back he is pilot, designer, adventurer, famous innovator. A different sort of man might not get away with it. For Volmer Jensen it all fits perfectly.

Even about his flying he is modest, understated, as apt to give credit as

Volmer Jensen, whose backyard is just large enough. (Maralys Wills)

take it. He remains mildly surprised that the sport of hang gliding ever took off as it did, and he admits that he had very little to do with its rush of popularity.

While he may believe, privately, that his other home-built craft are more noteworthy, he concedes it's the hang gliding that made him famous.

In 1925, in Seattle, Washington, Jensen built his first monoplane hang glider, and for a long while new and improved versions appeared from his backyard yearly. Slowly he taught himself the rudiments of flying. His flying then consisted of "just prolonged jumps," and he admits, "it's a good thing I didn't know enough to fly in the wind . . . if there had been a wind blowing, I don't think I'd be here today." Ruefully, he adds, "It took me nine years and nine gliders to learn to fly turns," which may be an index of how fast the sport was moving in those days.

Actually, the "sport" wasn't moving at all: Only Volmer Jensen was moving.

During those nine years—almost as long as the current phase of hang gliding altogether—one would suppose "natural" flight might have caught on. But it didn't. Except for this lone designer and a few friends, laboriously pushing his large, rigid-wing craft up the hill for mini-flights down, nobody knew it existed. Even Volmer made his living elsewhere, working in small aircraft-repair shops.

Of those days Volmer says, "I had no idea anybody else would be interested in what I was doing . . . more or less just sliding down the hill. I didn't think there was any future." So Jensen did nothing to promote it: He flew only to please himself; and left to him, the sport of hang gliding might have died, unnoticed, of natural causes.

It was only much later, when a different kind of craft suddenly burst on the scene, that Volmer Jensen had thrust on him the notoriety he never really sought.

The cause of it all was a man named Francis M. Rogallo.

Francis Rogallo (left) and John Harris, operator of Kitty Hawk Kites, at Jockey's Ridge sand dune, North Carolina, a hang gliding school on the Outer Banks. (North Carolina Travel & Tourism Division. Photo by Clay Nolen.)

A ROGALLO FOR THE MASSES

During the Second World War, while Volmer Jensen was quietly pursuing his solitary pleasure, another thoughtful man—Francis M. Rogallo, Stanford graduate in aeronautical engineering—was mulling over a better way to bring flying to the masses. "I started working on it right after the war ended . . . having spent all the war years on purely military aircraft. I thought, by golly, now it's time to get back to something for people to enjoy." As he looked around him, he decided, "There has to be some way of reducing the cost and complication of personal-owner-type aircraft—that is, gliders and powered aircraft, either one."

For him, conventional aircraft had become inaccessible. "They were getting pretty complicated and expensive . . . getting out of my price range. I thought something could be done to make them cheaper and more practical, and I thought that since a slow-flying airplane had to have very large, light wings, it would be a help if you could fold them up for storage. So you wouldn't be subject to the problems I've often seen of small, light craft being destroyed in windstorms. . . . Because they're parked out . . . staked out in fields. So this led to a search for some way of building aircraft wings something like boat sails . . . so you could put 'em in a bag or fold 'em up. Also, something that would have a lot less pieces for fabricating . . . a simple structure . . . and it seemed to me also that very lightweight structures that are rigid are fragile—like eggshells—and therefore it would be better if they had more flexibility, so that when they were struck by some object they would just bend instead of breaking.

"All these things entered into it. And at first, for the first few years, I thought that the wings would have to look something like boat sails with masts and spars. . . . But then I got working on parachutes and thought, gosh, it might be possible even to make a wing with no rigid structure at all. So the first wings were made of cloth and a number of strings with a sort of parachute structure.

And they did eventually become parachute substitutes . . . what we call flexible wings."

Later, Francis and his wife, Gertrude, made a number of small kites with no sticks in them, because "it looked like a simple, easy thing to do at home . . . and of course no danger of manned flight involved there. So we started making kites which have been made ever since . . . for over thirty years now."

Out of his efforts had already come new forms of both kites and parachutes; yet the search for an "ideal wing," which might carry a man, continued —a search that mirrors the kind of person Rogallo is: intensely practical, down-to-earth, loaded with common sense. And of course enough of a genius to understand the importance of deceptively simple things. While another man might have turned to computers, might have thought only of embellishing already flying craft, Rogallo sought to reduce flight to its essence: to seek the heart of it, to find the obvious in the quite unobvious.

For most men of his aeronautical background such a search would have been inconceivable.

But Rogallo says, "I never believe in adding *any* additional parts or complexity to any piece of machinery if you don't have to have it. . . . My philosophy is to keep everything as simple as you can keep it. It's apt to be more reliable and less expensive."

The search went on.

The Rogallos experimented with all kinds of shapes and all kinds of materials, "Whatever we could get hold of at that time . . . paper . . . cloth . . . aluminum foil . . . cellophane. Actually, the first successful flexible-wing type we constructed was made of glazed chintz. It had been some sort of curtain on a cabinet. It was fairly light and airtight and had this coating on it. So it worked very well."

By 1948 the twin-lobed shape with a center keel and chintz-curtain covering had tested out satisfactorily in the Rogallo air tunnel—a fan placed at one end of their living room! In the names of Gertrude and Francis Rogallo a patent was granted in 1949.

The great excitement eventually stirred by Rogallo's flexible-wing idea did not happen all at once. In the beginning, when Francis Rogallo showed his limp wing to various government agencies, suggesting its possibilities in the space program, nobody was interested.

Then the Russians launched Sputnik.

In response, the government formed NASA, absorbing the National Advisory Committee for Aeronautics, where Mr. Rogallo had worked since 1936. The Space Race was on.

Among the problems of the day were bringing manned and unmanned space vehicles back to earth, and among the solutions was a flexible, triangular-shaped wing with Rogallo's name on it.

The government made tests and wrote reports.

The army snapped to attention. Other uses were found for Rogallo wings. The army wrote reports.

Private contractors jerked to attention. Ryan Aircraft wrote reports.

Enthusiasm for the simple Rogallo flexible wing grew.

Eager men with a yen for flying read the technical reports, none of them secret. They began to see possibilities. It all took ten to twelve years. But by early 1960 hang gliding under a Rogallo-type wing had begun here and there. Crudely at first. Awkwardly at first. Never very high.

And always isolated. A man here, a man there. None of them aware of the others.

At this stage the idea could easily have died and become a funny memory: "Do you recall that fellow who used to run down the hill under a kite kicking his legs?"

But the sport lived. And now, so do the names of the men who did it first. Barry Hill Palmer, a University of California student. Just as Rogallo wings became the hot item with the government and the military, Palmer built himself a personal kite of metal tubing covered with plastic. He made short flights by throwing himself off the nearest sand dunes; as far as anyone knows, there was no one earlier. Later Palmer moved to Miami, where he installed low-horsepower engines on his small craft, wrote a couple of articles for the likes of the Experimental Aircraft Association, and thereafter disappeared into obscurity.

Thomas Purcell, Jr. In 1961 he built a towing-type craft with wheels, then floats, which Francis Rogallo flew in 1965. It was Rogallo's first experience under the canopy that bore his name.

Here and there other early "nutters" picked up the idea. Jim Natland, a Californian, saw the potential, thought it could become an "addictive sport,"[21] and in 1965 paid to have a Dacron sail professionally sewn for his homemade frame. He kept running off hills near his home in Palos Verdes, California, taking short flights and hoping he'd attract someone with capital for a new venture.

Nobody took him up on it.

Later, having moved to Huntsville, Alabama, Natland flew some off the steep tenth tee of a golf course. About 1973 Jim Natland appeared back on the scene in California when hang gliding was in full swing. By then most manufacturers were too busy turning out hang gliders to pay much attention to this mild man hanging around reminiscing wistfully about the early days when he'd been the only one doing it. It was his luck to have been little more than an oddity at both ends of the story.

Still, in the sixties, the sport was at best a sporadic thing.

With so few flyers around, Francis Rogallo kept abreast of who was doing what and, though he never built a hang glider himself, he took a lively interest in everyone else who did. "Around 1965 or so, I was corresponding with John Dickenson [an engineer from New South Wales, Australia] and he came up with . . . anyway, he sent me photographs and drawings of kites he had made with the control bar." Though Mr. Rogallo didn't know it then—and John Dickenson might only have guessed—it was the marriage of ROGALLO SHAPE to CONTROL BAR that made the whole sport of hang gliding possible.

"THERE HAD TO BE A BETTER WAY TO DIE"

With all the innovations in the world, the sport of hang gliding would have come to nothing without its Great Promoters. And perhaps the ultimate promoter was Bill Bennett.

Short, energetic, with a twinkle in his eye and an Australian accent curling around every word, Bennett began an early career in flying with water skis hooked to his feet and an umbilical cord connected to a fast boat. He and his friends in Australia, for reasons he now wonders at, were engaged in the sport of flat kiting—"An invention of the devil," he says. Though even from the beginning the old flat kites were equipped with control bars ("We called them trapeze bars, because part of flying was doing acrobatic maneuvers on the bar"), control took place only in the horizontal plane, and great strength was everything. With a slight shrug he says, "You weren't controlling the monster . . . it was just being controlled by the speed of the boat." He laughs. "It was a requirement that you had to be strong in the arms and weak in the head."

The old flat kites had all the stability of a towing garage door, and Bennett knew it. "There had to be a better way to die," he says ruefully, but before this eventually caught up with him, friend John Dickenson had already seen the possibilities in the Rogallo shape and performed the famous marriage of twin-lobed Rogallo to flat-kite control bar. While at first the new Rogallo towing kite was not a perfect success—"and we have the scars to prove it"—Bennett and his friend Bill Moyes felt they'd been given a little longer to live.

Apparently neither of them considered the other alternative—giving up the sport.

Flying for fun, profit (they sold kites), and pure gutsy showmanship, Bill Bennett accidentally discovered the forgiving qualities of the Rogallo one day when his towing boat ran into a sandbar on the Hawkesbury River, stopped dead, and left him no alternative except to release at the top of the long line. To his relieved surprise, Bennett was able to guide the new Rogallo in a controlled, smooth glide back to the water. From then on, release at altitude became

Bill Bennett towing over Bridgeport, Texas, 1969. (Bill Bennett)

a scheduled part of the performance.

Though John Dickenson (dubbed Dr. Cyclops by Bennett and Moyes) seemed to play no further role in boat towing, he had done enough; Bill Bennett and Bill Moyes decided to expose their new skills to the world, departing in opposite directions. While Moyes went to Europe, Bennett came to America in 1969, the two of them having agreed, in effect, to "split up the world." Moyes would take Europe and Australia, Bennett could have America.

And "have America" is pretty much what Bennett managed.

Scheduling towing exhibitions—first in Berkeley, California, then in Cypress Gardens, Florida—Bill Bennett created so much hoopla with his spectacular show that he was soon snapped up by a land-development company who could see great possibilities in the Bennett act as a come-on for attracting buyers. On the artificial lakes the company developed around the eastern United States, Bennett gave towing performances that left people gasping. Nobody had seen anything quite like his controlled flights from the top of the magic rope. In a very short time his Rogallo kite had replaced the flat kites used at Cypress Gardens.

It was in Berkeley that Bennett first ran into disapproval for one of his antics. "We cut loose at a thousand feet over Berkeley, and of course not being accustomed to American traffic, I thought it was neat to go out and fly over the freeway, looking at the traffic coming towards me. I wasn't aware that if even one of those people had applied his brakes suddenly there'd have been the darnedest smashup!" When he came down, he was lectured sternly.

But he wasn't through bedeviling American authorities. On July 4, 1969, Bennett figured the greatest show of all would be a tidy little flight around the Statue of Liberty. The event was publicized on the radio—but too late to alert the New York Harbor authorities in time to stop him. By the time the Harbor Patrol was on its way, Bennett had flown around the outstretched arm and landed on the grass at the lovely lady's feet—only to be met instantly by an irate statue-keeper who hauled him into a building and lectured him for twenty minutes on the various city ordinances prohibiting aircraft from landing on Liberty Island—except for emergencies. Bennett protested, "But it *was* an emergency." Then, with Australian charm and entirely false innocence, he explained, "All I did was, I went around your beautiful statue and landed on your lawn."

The reply was, "Yeah, that's another thing . . . there's a sign there that says Keep Off the Grass."

By now the Harbor Patrol had arrived. A stern man charged up to Bennett and said, "Hey . . . is your name Bill Bennett?"

"Yup . . . yes, sir."

"I hear you're going to fly . . . fly all over this place and land on the grass."

Before Bennett could answer, the officer went on quickly, "My advice to you, young man, is to pack up your tent and steal into the night."

To which Bennett did a double take, nodded quickly, said "Yes, sir," and speedily got himself off the island.

"I don't know," he reminisces, "whether he knew I'd already done it and was just carrying out his official duties and being nice. . . . I'll never know, and I never, ever stopped to ask."

The Bennett act continued at fairs and shows around the United States. The towed form of hang gliding was being seen by thousands. When water and a boat weren't available, Bennett towed on foot, pulled aloft by a car. At night he carried flares.

He says now, "I believe I'm the first person to ever do a loop in America," but it was unintentional. He was performing at the Ontario Speedway in front of a quarter of a million people. Just as the kite reached maximum height, it hit the wind shear above the buildings and did a complete rotation, totally out of control, but for some reason put Bennett down right on the finish line. Bennett says with a little laugh, "The audience thought it was part of the act!"

By now Bennett had been joined by water-ski enthusiast Dave Kilbourne, who came along to drive the Bennett boats and learn the skills of tow kiting. Dave Kilbourne was to become a master of hang gliding in his own right, carrying the sport beyond where he'd found it with Bill Bennett.

But nobody can deny that Bennett, with his one-man whirlwind tour, fired up more excitement and exposed hang gliding to more unbelieving eyes than anyone had done before or since.

THE BAMBOO BUTTERFLY REALLY FLIES

What Bill Bennett was doing, mostly in the eastern part of the United States, others were doing elsewhere. But there were differences.

Bennett's flights were all towed. His flying machine was fairly sophisticated, but he never left the ground under his own power.

In California about the same time a few individuals were picking up the threads left dangling by Barry Hill Palmer and Jim Natland. With the simple triangular Rogallo shape luring them on, men like Richard Miller began experimenting here and there.

Miller came to the flying world via glider soaring; once an editor of *Soaring* magazine, he spoke rhetorically of the new forms of flight. "I alternately find myself a century ahead of the times and a century behind."[22]

With him it all began in Cape Cod in the autumn of 1962. He called it "an idyllic six weeks, much of it spent climbing on the great dunes that face the Atlantic. [Here] the urge to build a hang glider once again rose to the surface."[23]

In the late sixties, having seen the NASA reports, Miller built himself a hang glider with a bamboo frame and a covering of six-mil polyethylene sheeting, the sail being a mere three times the thickness of present-day garbage bags.

Progress! Richard Miller's Bamboo Butterfly, 1966. (© George Uveges, 1981)

His total outlay was nine dollars. On his first flight he flew straight into a briar patch, but wrote, "I can't say I regret the experience. Crashing is by far the best sort of experience a hang glider pilot can have, short of being broken on the wheel."[24]

This peculiar sentiment was no doubt a bowing to the inevitable: Early movies suggest crashing as the *only* experience!

Richard Miller inspired others to try his craft, among them both Lloyd Licher (later to be president of the United States Hang Gliding Association) and Paul MacCready (who eventually designed the famous Gossamer Condor and Gossamer Albatross). MacCready was unimpressed. After a few tries, MacCready ran down the hill with his arms outstretched and said, "I went farther and stayed up longer *without* the Rogallo, Richard."[25]

But Richard Miller persisted, and eventually he and his friends flew more than a hundred flights off the gentle hills around the Los Angeles beaches. In time they learned control, of a sort, by weight shifting alone.

But before hang gliding had reached this advanced state, another Californian, Jack Lambie, had ideas of proving—more likely disproving—the notion that self-launched flight was possible.

Unwittingly, Jack Lambie became the second of the sport's Great Promoters.

"THE MAYHEM BEGAN"

In 1970 Lambie was principal of Collins School summer session near Long Beach, California, and also taught a class in science and crafts. Always a nut about anything that flew, toward the end of the session Lambie inspired his students to help him build an original twenty-eight-foot biplane. They did—with glue, staples, clear plastic, and baling wire from the local newspaper distributor. Lambie christened their plane the Hang Loose, a name as suggestive of Lambie himself as his biplane. When they took their machine out to a nearby hill, the lighter students actually left the ground with it! Richard Miller was there, and so was photographer Bob Whiting.

Suddenly Lambie found himself the subject of articles in *Soaring* magazine and the Los Angeles *Times*. Men wanted plans for his Hang Loose, and Jack and his brother Mark, half in jest, created some. More articles were written, and the demand for Hang Loose plans grew. After an article in *Sport Planes* called, "The $24.86 airplane you can build in two weeks," Jack Lambie came home from a few months out of town to find three shopping bags full of mail waiting for him. Jack said, "Many had six- to eight-page letters, often from highly experienced pilots telling of their love of flight and how this seemed to be their long-sought dream. Some were from what were obviously twelve-year-olds.

The letters and orders poured in by the thousands."[26]

Among them was a letter from Richard Miller, suggesting they hold the world's first hang gliding meet on Otto Lilienthal's birthday, May 23. Jack thought it a good idea, and set about organizing it.

May 23, 1971. That is the date, perhaps, that hang gliding officially became a sport.

Before the Lilienthal meet, hang gliding was Bill Bennett towing for fascinated crowds. Richard Miller and a few friends galloping down to the beach.

Satellite flyers with curious wings hopping and skipping down mini-hills in crazy abandon—and sometimes even flying. Hang gliding was the oddballs, the nuts, the screw-loosers, doing their thing. But doing it solo.

Hang gliding was funny. Just watching the earnestness on the faces as they ran and came to naught was funny. The movies are as good as films of the early days of aviation. The man who runs pell-mell down the hill under a fat, cumbersome wing . . . and runs . . . and runs . . . and runs . . . and runs . . . and then at the bottom when his feet are still disappointingly on the ground, makes one tiny, hopeful jump—as if that might finally do it. And the girl who runs under her gossamer-wing glider, her legs churning like a bicyclist without a bicycle, getting a miniature distance off the earth, only to have one end of her wing suddenly collapse downward, like the dropped ear of a dog, taking her plane down with it.

The soloists were all there were.

Now Jack Lambie was bringing them all together as a *meet!* He thought there might be six flyers present.

Later, the names read like a roster of hang gliding's founding family. Richard Miller. Jack and Mark Lambie. Karen Lambie. Taras Kiceniuk. Bruce Carmichael and son Doug. Lloyd Licher. Joe Faust. Volmer Jensen and Paul MacCready, observing.

For Jack, finding the flyers was easy; finding the site, next to impossible. He says, "At the time it seemed we should pick a site that was not too dangerous and favored low sink and flat glide."[27]

But most of Orange County was owned by the Irvine Company, and getting them to cooperate was like trying to build a house out of marshmallows. You could set it all up, but it kept folding inward. The Irvine people were courteous, fine listeners, interested, but they had this little condition: a million dollars' worth of liability insurance, which Lambie found out from his agent would cost about twelve hundred dollars per day. "Why so much?" he asked. "They're just little featherweight devices that only go about fifteen miles per hour."

"Perhaps," the agent said, "but with no experience to go on we'll just have to put it at the same rate as a motorcycle race."

Terry Sweeney—note beer bottle wired upside down to wires at midspan, angled to whistle just before stall. (*Hang Gliding* magazine)

Crowd collects for first Lilienthal meet, Corona del Mar, California, May 23, 1971. (© George Uveges, 1981)

The Mad, Magical, Many-Sided World of Hang Gliding

How were the six possible competitors going to pay that, Jack wondered.[28]

Finally, after days of wandering the hills, and dozens of dead-end phone calls to find owners, Jack and his brother, Mark, found an ideal hill with no Irvine markings and no obstructions. With a single look they both got the same idea. Why not just come here and fly? The hell with trying to find the owner.

Jack says, "Having taught history for some years, I have been impressed with how whole civilizations have been conquered by just a few people. The Aztecs and Incas are good examples. Only four hundred Spanish soldiers did the job, the strategy of which was to capture the leader through some trickery and get him to surrender the country. Lesson: The more centralized the organization the easier it is to gain control of the whole. Another analogy: Highly developed life forms—that is, mammals—are dispatched with one well-aimed shot to the central nervous system, whereas some more primitive creatures such as the starfish can't even be killed when chopped into pieces."[29]

The group, Jack decided, would have no "heart." When confronted by the authorities, each man would have to be dealt with separately; there would be no leaders. Just a sort of multiheaded starfish.

On May 23 fifteen flyers—double what Lambie had expected—brought eleven Hang Loose-type craft and three Rogallo shapes. Taras Kiceniuk, a Cal Tech student, flew a version of Richard Miller's Bamboo Butterfly, called The Batso. Richard Miller had moved on to a Conduit Condor and Bruce Carmichael had a jib-sail Rogallo. The rest were Hang Looses.

Lambie says, "We had a brief meeting. No one was to say who any of the other competitors were, and there was no one in charge. A bevy of cute girls from the University of California, Riverside, were to time and measure distance . . . on their own, of course.

Lambie's portrayal of the day is a classic.

"The mayhem began. Many had never flown their gliders before this day. Launchers would grasp each wing tip. Another would hold the tail boom and the group would stumble down the hill. The tip men let go, the tail man kept shoving, and the machine climbed. The higher it got, the steeper the angle of attack, with the tail man still gamely shoving until he could shove no more; the glider was now in a full stall. The pilot was running and kicking as the machine flopped to the grass. In another variation one wing man would hold on and continue shoving after the other stopped, resulting in a spectacular ground loop. After a couple of stalls, ground loops, and backslides, the wiring became so tweaked that the out-of-rig biplane was insured of a curving flight no matter how deft the launch crew had become."[30]

Taras Kiceniuk later wrote, "The Bamboo Butterflies demonstrated [that day] that this design was capable of excellent control in the hands of a skilled pilot—and very limited in aerodynamic performance. The many Hang Loose

With enough assistance you might . . . (Karen Lambie)

. . . oops! . . . a Hang Loose pilot suddenly zooms upward during the Corona del Mar meet in 1971. (© George Uveges, 1981)

36 **The Mad, Magical, Many-Sided World of Hang Gliding**

Richard Miller's Conduit Condor, five years' fancier—May 23, 1971. (© George Uveges, 1981)

Volmer Jensen's Swingwing—a response to the Lilienthal meet. (Volmer Jensen)

gliders . . . showed the opposite face of the coin—acceptable aerodynamic performance and practically no control!"[31]

The hill, clearly visible from the road, attracted spectators, and soon hundreds—then thousands—of people strolled over to see the strange goings-on. Among the spectators was Paul MacCready, with a doctorate from Cal Tech and a lifetime enthusiasm for aviation. But what MacCready saw hardly qualified as aviation, for he remarked pleasantly, "What good is it? It's like rolling down-hill on a bicycle with the steering locked and seeing who can go the farthest before crashing."[32]

Volmer Jensen also felt it was all a little mad, funny but mad, especially the Rogallos. With the flyer dependent on his body and his buddies for every-thing—starting, steering, stability, and stopping—Jensen figured flight had gone one giant step—backward! He saw no future in weight-shift control—nor has his opinion ever changed: "Nobody who understands aeronautics would fly one of those things." Volmer Jensen's response was to go home and build his own VJ-12 hang glider, conventionally controlled from aileron to elevator. But he still grins when he thinks of the Otto Lilienthal meet.

In due time both the owner of the land and the police showed up, in that order. The landowner, cajoled by a friendly Russell Hawkes (writer, TV pro-ducer, and fellow Hang Loose builder), finally decided it was OK to proceed with the "good clean fun" about the same time a police helicopter appeared overhead and began bawling from the skies, "Will the organizers of the meet please report to the squad car at the bottom of the hill."[33] Over and over the command blared from heaven.

Nobody went.

Finally Joe Faust ambled down, but his peculiar brand of funny-speak only confused the police.

At last the landowner more or less convinced the authorities that every-thing was OK—and anyway, the police had been unable to pick even one genuine culprit from the mobs of people.

Defeated, the police gave up.

Jack wrote, "Mark and I took turns flying, and after one smooth launch Mark floated the length of the hill for 13 seconds, the meet's duration record. Taras made 23 seconds on a towed flight, including the towed portion, but this was not considered 'self' launched flight, so it wasn't counted for the self-launched prize. We had a batch of certificates of participation printed up—col-lector's items now—for each pilot and crew, with notation of the achievements.

"We picnicked under the wings of our planes and laughed and laughed at the flights and crashes. At one moment, forever frozen in my memory, one ship climbed straight up, stalled and collapsed in slow motion; another cart-wheeled in the background to the left, while another spun to the right.

"Although the Hang Looses did not turn in the flights I had expected, everyone was having such a good time it didn't matter. The simple joy of leaping into the air was enough."[34]

Jack Lambie's little meet became front-page news, television news, the subject of fourteen breathless phone calls the following week from writers and photographers asking when the next meet would be held for their benefit. The story was told by *National Geographic, Popular Science, Soaring,* and *Science and Mechanics.* In Germany, England, and France this crashingest meet stirred great excitement.

Interest in the event remained as strong with the participants as everyone else. "Two weeks later," Jack says, "when all our film was developed, a gathering was held in Mark's recreation room for movies and plans for the future."[35]

That first meeting was followed by others. From that day on, whenever flyers gathered to fly, they assembled later to talk about it. After a while the group gave itself a name: Coast Hang Gliding Club. In time the name changed, first to Southern California Hang Gliding Association, finally to United States Hang Gliding Association, but a little of the original purpose always remained —to refly in one's chair the best of what had already been flown off the hill.

Only three months later Lambie helped promote the Montgomery meet at the site of the John J. Montgomery Memorial in San Diego. But a second meet, so soon after the first one, brought an inquisitive shark from deeper waters. "The FAA called Mark and wanted a complete list of participants so they could charge them with flying unlicensed aircraft, flying close to people, flying after major structural damage and repairs without inspection, no type ratings for

Eddie Paul skimming—Playa del Rey, California (*Hang Gliding* magazine)

Taras Kiceniuk, Jr., airborne in the Icarus I, in a class by itself—East Los Angeles, California, 1971. (© George Uveges, 1981)

some of the flyers, et cetera. Mark said he had no idea who the people were and our own ship was tethered at all times, bringing it under kite regulations. We heard no more from them."[36]

For months afterward, shrewd hang glider pilots kept useless strings dangling from their craft to prove, if necessary, that they were nothing more than kites.

When Jack Lambie thinks about the great excitement generated by his first meet, he becomes philosophical. A licensed pilot himself, he says, "After World War II many thousands of people learned flying and the advanced era of personal flying came of age. . . . But now that everyone who wanted to was flying, there was a sense of disappointment. The kind of flying we were doing wasn't exactly what many of us had in mind. Grinding around in a light plane talking to center or the tower every few minutes—or sitting in an airliner watching a movie—wasn't it.

"The idea of launching oneself, running into the air like a bird, feeling wing lift body physically with the wind in one's face was more like it. The flyers were ready for that kind of flying. The days of purposeful flight had been achieved. Now it was time to get back to pure flying. The immense media coverage of the little meet attracted the attention of millions who had dreamed of self-flight."[37]

OUT OF THE COCOON CAME . . . A ROGALLO!

The dust raised by the first two hang gliding meets soon settled out in one of two camps—with the fixed-wing enthusiasts or the Rogalloists. Almost everyone aligned himself with one mode of flying or the other, and there were arguments for both.

Volmer Jensen looked on the Rogallo flyers as something akin to upstarts —"They even took our name," he said ruefully—and he still feels that way today. Though he admits, "We couldn't have done what we did with the rigid wings if the kites [Rogallos] hadn't come up with all the publicity and promotion," he still shakes his head in wonder at the number of people flying such obviously unmanageable craft. Without movable surfaces he is sure the Rogallo kites are little more than predestined accidents. "Not that we can't get hurt or killed in a rigid wing . . . but we stand a better chance. I'm real conservative. Irv Culver, John Underwood—all the fellows that have flown my ships—they wouldn't buy the kites. My friend Irv Culver—he's one of the top aerodynamicists in the United States—he just shudders when he sees those kites fly."

To Jensen, control by weight shift alone is as archaic as it is unreliable. "I mean, when you can sit there and take the control stick and move it *this much* for all the maneuvers you want to make . . . why fly by weight shift?" But Jensen is also fair-minded. "The Rogallos . . . it's another type of flying, I'll admit."

To Volmer Jensen the hero of rigid-wing construction is young Taras Kiceniuk. Although Taras appeared at the Lilienthal meet with his Batso and flapped down the hill on a diamond-shaped bamboo frame covered with plastic, by the Montgomery meet three months later Taras had constructed a graceful, tailless biwing. He named it Icarus. In October 1971 Taras and his Icarus cruised back and forth above the cliff at Torrance Beach, California, an event seen on television. By January 1972 Icarus had made the cover of *Soaring* magazine. The advantages of his biwing, and later the single-wing Icarus V, were obvious: In light or no breezes the Icarus could stay up and soar above the ridge, and the eight-to-one glide angle it boasted meant flights of long duration. The Icarus, and eventually Bob Lovejoy's Quicksilver, were simple, graceful planes that stood midway between conventional gliding and Rogallo hang gliding. Uncomplicated, easy to build at home, they could be

Taras (left) with Cal Tech Geology Professor Gene Shoemaker preparing to carry Icarus II back to the top of a cliff. (Floyd Clark, Cal Tech)

launched by running down a hill. They left behind forever the necessity of finding a plane to launch a plane.

Yet there were disadvantages.

When Jack Lambie noted, "The very slow speed Hang Loose was not to be the hang glider of the future,"[38] he could have been speaking for other fixed-wing craft as well—at least for the next six years. For while the Icarus and Jensen's VJ-12 series offered long, graceful flight, and Kiceniuk even caught a thermal in late '72, they hadn't solved the problems of portability, easy assembly, crash resistance, and restricted landings. They had left some of the problems of conventional gliders behind, but not all.

In the beginning the Rogallos had another advantage. They were different. What had failed to ignite enthusiasm when it looked like a familiar glider seemed to turn everyone breathless when it looked like a child's kite.

On this . . . this aberration, men were running down the hill—and flying! It was all so unexpected it somehow set people alight. It was like arriving on a flying saucer. While everyone accepted calmly the flight of a wing that looked like a wing, this funny, diamond-shaped contraption had all the crazy fascination of a flying umbrella!

So the early Rogallos got press that the fixed wings didn't get.

Volmer Jensen could have told reporters thirty-five years earlier that it was possible to run down a hill hanging by your armpits and fly. Only he didn't.

Now a different kind of man with a different kind of flying toy finally turned people on. The Rogallo shape . . . the promoters . . . and hang gliding . . . had arrived!

THE AVALANCHE ROLLED DOWN SEVERAL FACES

The Rogallo hang glider caught on incredibly. While the excitement it generated was not entirely reasonable, its practical success could be explained, which Jack Lambie did in part when he said, "Their secret was the hang-bar control and great crashability. The tyro could learn to fly before his glider was demolished."[39]

There were other things: The tyro didn't need to buy a trailer to haul his machine; he didn't need a tool kit for final assembly, nor a baseball field for landing. A Rogallo was truly a personal flying machine.

Potential flyers were quick to see these advantages, and by the end of 1972 and early 1973 the Rogallo rush was on.

When something begins everywhere at once it is often impossible to know who was first of the firsts. In Australia, in northern California, in Canada, in southern California, the same lessons were learned over and over, and numerous men were credited with the same "firsts."

The sport was like a series of avalanches begun at the peak of a mountain, each gathering snow as it tumbles down a separate face. At the bottom each would seem to have had a unique experience.

"IT WAS ALMOST MY UNDOING"

In Canada, in the winter of 1970–71, Willi Muller was skiing. Willi had come from Germany years before, and skiing was as natural to him as walking. A handsome man with dark hair and a smile so engaging he virtually radiates—people are immediately drawn to him—Willi became an early prophet for hang gliding in Canada.

His first look at the sport hooked him.

It was Jeff Jobe, a disciple of Bill Bennett's, who flew past Willi on the ski slope, flapping by overhead with abandon on his face and skis dangling from his feet. The minute Jobe landed, Willi skiied over to him; moments later, when Jobe wasn't looking, Willi covertly measured the Jobe kite with his own skis. A somewhat inaccurate yardstick, Muller's copy of Jobe's thirteen-foot, six-inch kite turned out to be eleven feet.

Willi Muller, April 1971. How else could one launch? (Murray Yeudall)

For two years, not knowing any other kind of flying, Willi Muller flew only in the winter, launching with skis, and the second year built himself a fifteen-foot kite.

Then in the spring of 1972 Muller met Terry Jones, who was just back from Australia with a Moyes tow kite. Interestingly, Jones knew only boat launching, and each was surprised to learn that kites were taking off another way.

Jones and Muller traded skills.

But for Muller the trade was a poor one, "almost my undoing." During his first towed launch, behind a car, the rope broke and catapulted Muller onto the pavement, breaking both his back and one leg. He was on crutches for three months, and one might expect he'd give up any further flying. Quite the opposite: He spent part of his recuperation building an eighteen-foot kite.

Muller now calls that kite "the world's first short-keel glider," and it came about, as so often happened, by accident. His sailmaker's shop wasn't big enough to accommodate the sail for anything larger.

Muller says, "I test-flew the kite while still on crutches. But my wife carried it up the hill for me."

In February 1972, Muller reports, two men got together to ski-launch their Jobe kites down a slope at Kelowna, Canada (Willi wasn't one of them), declaring themselves "the World's First Snow-Kite Championships." Bob Jones and one other man comprised the whole event, and the records don't say who won it.

It wasn't until the fall of 1972 that Muller first learned another part of the world was foot-launching these ski-borne hang gliders. The news of a record two-hour flight from a young Californian, Bob Wills, at Palmdale, California,

Willi Muller, January 1972. (Hälle Flygare)

had reached far into Canada; and in January 1973 Willi Muller and Terry Jones came down to Palmdale to see this new kind of flying for themselves.

Muller remembers standing at the top of the hill with Jones, saying, "I'll let you try first, Terry," while Terry responded, "You go ahead, Willi." Finally Bill Bennett arrived and the two saw their first foot launch, though Muller says, "Bennett crashed about sixteen times that day."

Bennett wasn't accustomed to foot-launching, either.

When Willi Muller became the first hang gliding manufacturer in Canada, some time later, he laid an accurate claim to being one of the very first men in his part of the world to try it.

"DAVE'S MACHINE FLEW BETTER UPSIDE DOWN"

The scene shifts to Marine World, near San Francisco. To the first exhibition of Bill Bennett's spectacular flying behind a towing boat. Dave Kilbourne, water skier and flat-kite flyer, is so impressed by Bennett's show that he tries to get Bennett to sell him a Rogallo kite.

Donnita Holland, Dave's girl friend (now Mrs. Dave Kilbourne) recalls, "Bennett wasn't manufacturing kites at that time. . . . He was just here to do shows. So, from photographs, Dave tried to copy the kite, and I guess that fall of '69, Bennett came back around again, and now Dave had a monster machine that flew better upside down. Some upholstery maker had sewn the sail. Bennett took pity on him and sold Dave the sail from one of his Deltas, and Dave built it and started flying it for Marine World . . . and of course for fun, too."

Shortly afterward Dave and Donnita joined Bill Bennett to drive the Bennett boat and become part of his whirlwind promotion around the United States. Dave learned to fly with Bennett's professional Rogallo, and he taught Donnita to fly too, which she did "mostly so I could get out of driving the boat. I wasn't a very good driver."

Although a few others such as Palmer, Natland, and Miller had foot-launched crude Rogallos hanging by their armpits, Dave Kilbourne was the first to take off, foot-launched, under a Rogallo with control bar. Donnita recalls, "It was the Labor Day weekend of 1970. Dave took the water-ski kite to Yosemite, with some photographers who wanted to see him fly off Glacier Point. What he intended to do was tow from the parking lot, release the line, and fly down. In his memory of how it was set up, this was a feasible thing to do. So we drove all the way to Yosemite, and of course the parking lot was way far away and there was no way to follow the plan. Instead he stood there on the edge of that thing looking down and thinking about it: . . . I wonder if you could just run off. . . . Luckily he decided not to do it.

"On the way home from that weekend—we had almost gotten back to San Jose—we were going through a pass around San Luis reservoir, and the

Donnita Holland Kilbourne. (© George Uveges, 1981)

Dave Kilbourne. (© George Uveges, 1981)

wind was blowing there about thirty miles an hour down this kind of ravine. So we stopped along the freeway, and took out the water-ski kite, a little thirteen-foot standard, and hiked up this little hill, and that's where he foot-launched it. And of course it was almost soarable. None of us knew any better. He foot-launched and the other fellow that was with him flew. They were just making little hops off a one-hundred-foot hill, something like that . . . and flying down. I tried it myself but I only went backwards . . . it was that windy, even in a thirteen-footer. Of course I didn't know how to penetrate, so they'd hold on to me, and they'd let go and I'd just kinda run backwards up the hill. So I was fairly unsuccessful.

"After that, Dave took the thirteen-footer and tried to fly it several times here in Milpitas at the same hill they're flying today . . . and he had some pretty unhappy experiences in no wind, trying to launch a thirteen-footer, though he did it successfully on a few occasions. However, after one really unhappy crash, that's when he decided to scale it up and build a sixteen-footer."

Donnita thought about Dave's first foot launch again and laughed, "You know, the only reason Dave did the foot launch in the first place is because he'd been told Bill Moyes had already done it off a mountain in Australia. So he said, 'Oh . . . OK . . . They said it was possible. . . .' so he did it. Later on, talking to Moyes, it turned out Moyes flew the mountain, all right, but he'd been *towed* up and released!"

Though the records mainly credit Dave Kilbourne with that first foot-launched flight, Dave himself values a different contribution. Unique among early flyers, Kilbourne soon came to understand the risks in what they were doing. He observed beginners rushing headlong into the sport without care or thought; he saw accidents, sometimes caused solely by unbridled enthusiasm.

But Kilbourne felt flyers who built their own kites were dedicated to flying, readier to understand the risks and assume them.

There were few plans around then for home builders. So in Joe Faust's little magazine, *Low and Slow*, Kilbourne published plans for a good standard sixteen-foot Rogallo. And he never took money for it. He considered it a public service.

"I'M GONNA HAVE A VERY SHORT, FAMOUS CAREER"

Donnita Holland stands alone as the first woman involved in hang gliding. For a long time she was the only woman flyer with any degree of proficiency. And she still flies today.

But for her it was never easy—partly because of what she views as her own athletic deficiencies, but even more because of the demands made on her by others. She says, "I wasn't an athletic individual, I wasn't a real sportsman; I didn't pick this up easily. It was very difficult for me, I had to struggle with it. And of course at first no one paid much attention to us because they didn't even understand what we were doing. But suddenly it starts coming out in the news and in the papers, and suddenly here I am the only female . . . And all this notoriety comes and the big ego trip starts invading. I was real scared because I knew I wasn't an exceptional person . . . I wasn't a real showman. I was the type of person who does better on my own than if somebody's watching me.

"So I really had to make a conscious decision about what to do. I started feeling like, gee, if I let this get to me, if I let them . . . you know how they come across—'Hey! Wow! You're really great, you're really special . . . You're the only woman . . . Wow! . . . Let me see what you can do,' kind of thing. . . . I just thought, boy, I'm gonna get killed. If I respond to that and try to show off to that and play up to that . . . I'm gonna have a very short, famous career."

When the cameras came around, and the newspapermen with their pads, "I'd just kinda slink off into the background." With relief, she adds, "I've never been sorry that I did."

Yet Donnita Holland got in trouble with her male counterparts. "My famous quote, which I really wished I hadn't said at that time . . . in my youth . . . was that the most dangerous thing in hang gliding is the male ego, which is a very sexist thing to say. But at that time it was true. There was so much outside pressure for our flying. 'Hey, there! You're a real hero, you do this dangerous thing' . . . Yet you know yourself that what you're doing—it's an evolution and you've gotten to this point slowly and you know you're not great. But it's difficult to keep it in perspective when all you're getting from the outside world is this, 'Gee! You're really great, you're really special.' It does, I think, affect your judgment. I'd watch guys on the spot, where they didn't want to fly but the camera was there, and they would literally risk their lives to make that flight because they didn't have the nerve to tell the cameraman, 'Hey, look, I'm not gonna do this today . . . this isn't right!'" She adds sadly, "Some of them didn't make it through."

Of those early days, Donnita says, "There was so much unknown, so much high risk. Of course I think that's how we all rationalized it. Like . . . well, I don't know if it can be done . . . but I *think* so. I was pretty conservative, yet I remember things that *I* did in those days, especially when we were towing. I'm just horrified. I feel so lucky that I survived."

"AS USUAL, NO ONE LISTENED"

Though the Rogallos had the lion's share of the world's attention in early 1972, persistent fixed-wing lovers clung to their craft, hoping perhaps for that one miraculous, sustained flight to come along and compensate them for the thumps and knocks they were taking. Most gliders, one had to face it, had minds of their own and were constantly out of control.

Richard Miller came upon such lingering enthusiasts, which he describes in the October 1972 issue of *Ground Skimmer:* "Dr. Pritchard, of Vista, is now practicing acupuncture and is also preparing to move, and while neither of these would appear at first glance to have anything to do with hang gliding, the reader is advised not to be hasty. Your reporter, while having a treatment with the doctor one Monday recently, was informed that he, while looking for a house the evening before, had seen a hang glider in a field adjacent to Gopher Canyon Road. Some lads had apparently been flying it earlier on Sunday and had left it to shift for itself. Dr. Pritchard described it as a very large and heavy biplane of roughly the Hang Loose variety, with interplane rudders actuated from the cockpit and returned to neutral by strips of surgical tubing. Why not, your reporter said to himself, just mosey on over to Gopher Canyon Road and see what was what.

"And sure enough, precisely in the advertised spot, was the glider. It *was* large, had interplane rudders, surgical tubing, and all. It also had a builder, if that's the proper term, one Tom Burnett of West Lilac Road, Escondido, who was busy making some repairs. On Sunday a pilot had bailed out and the glider, left to its own inclinations, had reared up and landed on the left wing tip and tail, breaking a few members here and there. These fractures were now being repaired with spare sticks and baling wire, although such was the state of things that once a repair was finished it was impossible to tell where it stopped and the rest of the glider began.

"Tom said this was his fourth glider and that it had been assembled, more or less, from parts of two of the earlier ones. These two had been biplanes; the ship unaccounted for was a bamboo and polyethylene Rogallo of which there were still some remnants scattered about. The finished product, to put the matter as kindly as possible, made very few concessions to aesthetics. The only noticeable bit of decor was a brace of three small letters painted on the surface of the upper wing. These, I was informed, stood for Bonsall Air Farce.

"Presently one of Tom's buddies, Don Fischer of San Luis Rey, arrived and began stapling loose ends of polyethylene to the framework. When this job was finished we carted the glider up the slope for test flights. Not to find how it would fly, mind you, but *if* it would fly. Your reporter, who considers himself something of an expert on crashing gliders in general and the crashing Hang Loose in particular, delivered his usual harangue about the necessity of getting the weight well forward and keeping up a good head of steam once in the air (if one hoped to avoid the inevitable side slip and ground loop), but as usual, no one listened.

"There was a good wind on the slope, into which Tom and Don made some attempts. The best of these, with Tom flying, if that's the proper term, gave me a chance to observe the control system and its method of operation. Wonder of wonders. From the inside corners of the aforementioned interplane rudders, lines run to the leading edge of the wing in the area of the cockpit. Yet other wonders, too diverse to be mentioned, had obscured curiosity as to just how these small triumphs of advanced technology were intended to be used. I was to find out, however, on Tom's final run.

"For this, as on the earlier ones, Don took the right wing tip, I took the left, and we set off down the hill. Perhaps it was the effects of the acupuncture, perhaps advancing age, but I reached V max [maximum velocity] somewhat earlier than the rest of the organization and announced in a loud voice that I was letting go. Don, of course, was unprepared for this and held onto his tip a bit longer. As a result the biplane veered slightly to the right and, when Don let go, began a lazy zoom. From my position just behind the glider I had an excellent view of what happened. As the ship reared up, the pilot appeared to be climbing out of the cockpit. Perhaps, I thought, having tried everything else in vain, he's simply going to walk out the left wing tip till it drops, an approach that did not seem at all unreasonable under the circumstances. But no, he was only after the first of the wood cross pieces on the control line to the rudder, which was several feet from the hang bars and which, I was informed later, needed a pull of some three feet to be effective. With this left piece of wood in his right hand, the pilot dropped back in the cockpit, the ship righted itself to some extent, and a landing, if that's the proper term, was made.

"Earlier in the day Tom had expressed the desire to have the biplane in pieces small enough to stuff into the back of his camper by closing time. Closing time had now arrived, however, and the glider was still in one piece. It was therefore decided to stow it head-on into a nearby clump of trees and try again some other time. Who knew, perhaps a windstorm would come up in the night and Tom's worries would be at an end.

"Something came up. Just what it was, we don't yet know, but the following Sunday when I took Bruce Carmichael and Bill Hannan over to show them the hill, we found what was left of the Bonsall Bomber strewed about the landscape. Ah, Lambie, what hast thou wrought?"

"FROM THAT MOMENT ON WE HAD TO HAVE ONE"

Early in 1972, while Taras Kiceniuk was just beginning to find lift for his Icarus, two men in Santa Ana, California, were reading about that first Lilienthal meet and Taras's Batso in *National Geographic*.

One day in February, Chris Price burst into the family room of his best

Chris Wills. (© George Uveges, 1981)

friend, Chris Wills, waving the *Geographic* and saying, "Ya gotta see this, Wills, here it is! What we've been looking for!" Excitedly, Price, six feet three inches, with curly hair and an irresistible grin, spread the magazine out on the family-room table. Together, Wills and Price studied the pictures, read the text. The story said only that a man on a bamboo rig could fly; it gave no dimensions, no physical descriptions of the kite.

Immediately the two felt themselves getting carried away.

Both had wanted to fly for as long as they could remember, and though Chris Wills had built several near-airplanes, the closest he'd ever come to really leaving the ground was at the end of a tow rope on an old home-built plane, the Red Baron. Chris Price had flown it, too.

It wasn't safe and it never went very high. But there was nothing better they could afford.

Wills studied the *Geographic* pictures, grinning. When he smiled like that his eyes became mere slits. "I can't believe this, Price!"

For the first time, flying was held out to them as an immediate possibility.

Wills said later, "From that moment on, we had to have one."

Together, Price and Wills measured with a ruler: The man in the picture, at two inches, was probably six feet tall; therefore his kite, at four inches, must be about twelve feet wide. With such inexactness they began construction,

Chris Price. (© George Uveges, 1981)

learning only six months later they'd been off by four feet—the kite in the picture measured sixteen feet across!

But never mind. Such details did not concern them.

They read the article on a Wednesday. On Thursday they scrounged successfully for bamboo, duct tape, and a huge roll of clear plastic. By Friday they'd finished the hang glider and on Saturday were flying it unsuccessfully. "Our style," Wills says, "has always been to build everything fast and start enjoying it."

But before taking it to the hill they tested it in the back of a pickup truck. While Price drove down the Wills's street, Wills stood in back holding the hang glider, trying to decide if the thing had any potential for lifting off. They were only halfway down the block when Wills yelled down to the cab, "It wants to fly, Price! It's trying to lift off!"

All this time the oldest Wills boy, Bob, watched with only half-interest. Perpetually barefooted, intensely serious, his passion was motorcycles, and he not only figured that weird-looking contraption would never fly, he didn't much care if it did.

A neighbor, aeronautical engineer Leo Pfankuch, also watched. When the boys started hopping up and down with excitement, Pfankuch observed dryly, "You know, boys, even a patio table will fly if you get it going fast enough."

Next day, believing their hang glider might fly better than a patio table, Wills and Price packed their craft on top of Bob's pickup and headed for San Clemente. With the hang glider's frame poking into the air and the plastic sail drifting off the edge of the truck, they rather looked like they were going to the dump.

At the foot of a moderately gentle hill they unloaded their machine and trudged it to the top.

Confidently, they expected they'd run a few steps and be airborne. Neither had seen anyone else fly; neither knew what to expect. But both were determined. Chris Price tried it first, grasping the frame with both arms, lifting the clumsy thing over his head and running—sort of—a few steps down the hill.

Nothing happened.

Wills tried next, ran a little faster, still found himself inexplicably bound to earth. The two sat down to mull over their situation. "We're not gettin' anywhere," Price said.

"Maybe we have to run faster."

"Yeah. But I'm not sure I want to." Price scratched his head.

"Me neither."

Wills stood up after a while and tried again. This time he ran hard, foolishly, all out, taking his chances on disaster. Suddenly, in the middle of his running, the ground left him. Feet churned on, but they met no resistance. Beneath his shoes, the earth shrank away.

He was flying!

The abrupt, nose-down stop that followed was of little consequence to Wills. The two of them clapped each other on the shoulders, yelled, laughed exuberantly. Chris Price and Chris Wills knew they'd arrived at a goal they'd sought since they were kids.

In time Bob Wills, then twenty-two, joined the two Chrises. Half-bored at first, after one flight he caught the spirit of what they were doing. With no

Bob Wills. (© George Uveges, 1981)

timidity he galloped down the hill full out, his huge bare feet taking him straight to disaster. At six foot three he was a ludicrous size for the small hang glider, but he got airborne anyway, sailed downward a few yards, and plowed into the earth magnificently. From out of the crushed remains he rose with an ankle that wouldn't support him. Bob's flying days came to an end just as they were starting.

But he healed fast.

In a few weeks Bob Wills was back on the hill, this time insisting that they all build a bigger hang glider. "With a bigger one, I know we can go clear to the bottom."

Bigger and better, longer and higher—but mostly *different*—were to be the trademarks of Bob Wills's life. "I never want to do anything that's been done before," he said, and he lived as though every mountain was a new goal, every limitation to the hang gliders a temporary problem to be figured out.

For a long while the crowds that came to see the Wills brothers and Chris Price flying down in San Clemente failed to tell them that around the beaches near Los Angeles other nuts were doing the same thing. The boys assumed they were alone, that perhaps the Lilienthal meet had been a once-only thing.

Then two things happened to end their bamboo days forever. Leo Pfankuch, their engineer-friend, suggested it was time, now that they were flying higher and further, to build something more substantial. And they saw a picture in *Soaring* magazine of a kite made with metal frame, Dacron sail, and

Bob and Chris Wills—no plans, no seat, but they fly. (Richard Jenks)

Uphill transportation made easier. (Richard Jenks)

control bar. It was obvious, then, that not only was flying being done elsewhere, it had reached a level of sophistication far beyond their crude bamboo kites.

They immediately cast aside the bamboo-and-plastic.

With Pfankuch buying the aluminum through his factory, and Chris Wills going down to a sailboat supplier for Dacron, they began putting together their own version of a professional Rogallo kite.

For days Price and Bob worked on the frame while Chris Wills sat at a sewing machine seaming panels for the sail.

Then, with a kite whose center of gravity was off by several inches, on July 4, 1972, Bob flew off mile-high Saddleback Mountain; he was the mountain's first hang glider pilot, and only the second man in history to attempt such a feat. (Unknown to them, Bill Bennett had earlier gone off Dante's View.)

While the current state of hang gliding was mostly limited to sand dunes and tiny hills, Bob—and an hour later, brother Chris—entrusted their lives to a mile of nothingness; they ran off the mountain with a kind of ecstatic ignorance they would later find appalling in anyone else. "We knew so little," Chris said later. "Our center of gravity was way off, our nico-stops [the fasteners that secured the cables] were pounded with a hammer, we knew nothing about mountainous winds—we were just lucky, I guess."

It was a historic day not only for the two Willses (Chris Price had a broken leg and was in a cast), but also for the California Highway Patrol, the Forest Service, and the Orange County sheriff, who took turns pursuing the boys on and around Saddleback Mountain trying to confront them with the various sins they'd committed. Among them were leaving a main road, driving too fast in

The Mad, Magical, Many-Sided World of Hang Gliding 55

O'Neil Park, and being on the mountain during the fire season. When they finally got a fire ticket, Bob grinned, "It was worth it."

A few weeks later, after the brothers flew from Crestline in the San Bernardino Mountains to the valley floor below, they collected a crowd of ten Forest Service rangers and three San Bernardino sheriff deputies, complete with helicopter, because of the fire-closed area and reports of a "downed aircraft." There followed a powwow on the desert floor near San Bernardino State College. The two quickly learned that (1) law enforcement people did not major in spirit, adventure, or creativity; (2) people in general don't know how to deal with anything novel or unusual; and (3) once law enforcement people see that you aren't cocky or defiant, they will usually suggest that you stop doing whatever it is you're doing, but apologetically.[40]

One day Bill Bennett showed up on their hill. "When I first saw Bob Wills," Bennett says, "he was flying a dreadful machine with exceptional ability."[41] Bennett asked Bob if he'd like to try a *good* hang glider, and Bob said he would; then, according to Bill Bennett, "He straightaway took the damn thing and almost made it talk."[42]

In time, Bill asked Bob to sell kites for him, an arrangement which later included the two Chrises.

It was Bob, now flying for Bill Bennett, who decided one day a hang glider could possibly hold two people instead of one. "Make me a tandem seat, Bill, I'm gonna try it." So Bennett constructed a heavy, two-place swing seat,

Bob Wills, pilot, Robert Wills, Sr., copilot. (Chris Wills)

56 **The Mad, Magical, Many-Sided World of Hang Gliding**

One . . . two . . . together now. (W. A. Allen)

and in August 1972, Bob and his brother took the world's first foot-launched tandem ride at Palmdale, California.

Side by side they charged down the hill under a protesting sail, their excessive combined weights suggesting they might end up running the whole way. Finally, picking up speed, they literally *forced* the kite to fly.

But the flight wasn't a perfect success.

Each had his own idea of where he wanted to go, and the two found themselves trying to out-muscle each other all the way down. When they arrived at the bottom, Chris's arms ached as though he'd been trying to push over a building. They came to a unanimous conclusion that day: Two equally good pilots would never be able to fly together.

Yet three years later the tandem flying they initiated became the basis for a major studio movie, *Skyriders*, a Twentieth Century-Fox release which starred James Coburn and Robert Culp.

It was about this time that Bob stunned other pilots and spectators by swinging around in his seat and flying backward, and also hanging upside down, controlling the kite with his knees. Chris eventually appeared on the cover of a magazine with his head and arms waving at the ground and his knees locked on to a flying hang glider.

In January 1973, an informal meet for Rogallo wings was held in Coyote Hills in northern California. By then, Bob had learned to make 360-degree turns with a minimum loss of altitude. Bill Allen, second editor of *Ground Skimmer*, said, "I remember Wills telling in January 1973 of his repeated attempts at three-

Bob Wills, flying by his knees. (The Wills Family Album)

Chris Wills, stunting. (The Wills Family Album)

Dave Kilbourne—Coyote Hills, southeastern San Francisco Bay, February 1973.
(W. A. Allen)

sixtys, trying to learn how not to fall out of them. . . . he was a real pioneer."[43] Until then, a 360-degree turn was mostly a diving maneuver.

Few people at Coyote Hills had seen Bob's new technique, nor had anyone from the north seen stunting. Donnita Holland (now Kilbourne) who was at the Coyote Hills meet, met Bob then for the first time. She said, "Bob's whole technique of flying was entirely different than anything we had ever seen before. We were all in a state of the art where we were pretty much making straight gliding flights with minimal coordinated maneuvering. What he introduced to us was the soaring turn.

"We have films of that day. Even now, Dave [Kilbourne] will say the same thing—he came up and showed us how to fly."

Bob Wills, who would one day be called "the pilot's pilot," had already begun his unique contributions to the sport.

THE WORLD CAME KNOCKING

In January of 1973 there were four companies making hang gliders. One year later there were nearly fifty. Most of them were in California, one in the East; the rest were scattered randomly. Outside the United States hardly anyone knew the sport existed.

The small companies making hang gliders were faced with strange phenomena: At the same time they found themselves inundated with enthusiasm ("I've always wanted to fly—send me all your literature." "I'm dying to do it. Please tell me how." "Where can I go to learn? I can't wait." "Your kites must be the best!"); most of it was naive, and few of these early enthusiasts ordered kites. Letters poured in—ten, twenty, thirty a day, sometimes before the company had done any advertising. But checks did not pour in. The letters had to be answered, yet almost none of them came to anything. The writer wasn't putting his money where his heart was. Everyone wanted to fly, it seemed. Nobody had thought it through. The companies were struggling.

One company, after two years of eager inquiries (and probably two thousand letters answered), found it had sold no more than a half dozen kites as a result of its correspondence. Clearly, the mail came to naught.

Yet occasionally the unexpected happened.

A California company received a letter from an accountant in Louisiana, a laboriously written affair with the tiny handwriting of a medieval monk. By squinting, the company secretary deduced the man was excessively nervous—eager to fly, but apprehensive about what might happen to him. Wearily, she answered two pages of anxious questions and sent her response off, glad to be through with him. Among all her dead-end letters this was surely the least promising.

To her surprise, the accountant wrote back—another microscopic letter, three more pages of questions. "Just how dive-free are these kites? Sure would hate to go into a dive. . . . I understand the nineteen-footer will be a slower descent. How much slower? I am for the slower speed. . . . Be sure and let me know of any pitfalls I might have overlooked. I am sure I have missed something." Then, as an afterthought, "Have to watch the winds around here, could end up in Texas."

By now the company secretary was exasperated. How much time should she spend on this fellow? The man was so timid that corresponding with him was an obvious waste of time. Yet something drove her to answer his questions . . . just once more.

To her complete surprise the accountant, in his third letter, sent a check!

The correspondence went on. All the time the company was building his kite, the edgy accountant did his nail biting on paper. The secretary figured he'd get his kite but never fly it. He even wrote once (she could almost hear the nervous giggle), "I'll bet you think I'm worried. . . ." Why, she thought, whatever gave you *that* idea?

They shipped the kite, and a month later another of those letters arrived. The secretary could hardly wait to open it. *What* had he done with his hang glider?

To her disappointment, the letter was just like the others—a full page of little bitty questions. She scanned them quickly, hoping for an answer. Had he ever flown his kite?

At the end he admitted it; he hadn't flown it once. He said defensively, "I haven't had the time."

You mean, she thought, you haven't had the *nerve*.

By now she was fascinated. For months afterward she searched the mail for the envelope labeled Dilly's Accounting Service. But she never heard from him again. In the end she figured he must have sold his kite. One thing was certain—he hadn't gotten hurt on it. His fainthearted legs would never carry him down the slope fast enough to get airborne.

Along with letters from wishful aviationists came letters from opportunists: "I'm writing a book. Send me all your pictures." "I'd like to do an article. Please tell me all you know about hang gliding." "I've got a great idea for a movie. All I have to do now is sell it to someone and then I'll be back to see you." Most of the opportunists never got beyond writing their first letters. Yet a few—like Dan Poynter, who wrote several excellent books—did. And the companies could not afford to ignore any of them, lest they bypass the one man who might bring them publicity. It was a heady and hopeful time.

Of them all, the ultimate opportunists were the people going into business making hang gliders. Build one for yourself and one for a friend and suddenly you're a company. Like the gold-rush days, everyone hurried to "get there before the others." If just one man had picked up a nugget—if one company had struck it rich manufacturing hang gliders—the phenomenon might have made sense. But nobody did, not in those early days. They were all working for a dollar an hour and hoping for two. After a few months, most were thinking survival. Those who persisted stayed in the game for the love of hang gliding, not the love of money.

Yet new companies continued to enter the field daily, blindly, even as older ones closed their doors. Chandelle, Pliable Moose, Free Flight, Concepts, Pacific Gull—all flourished for a time and disappeared. Still, each one that lasted saw itself as a budding General Motors.

The dealers and distributors (in those days nobody distinguished between the two) who soon began to sell for the hang gliding companies were equally naive. They sold kites out of the backs of their trucks, out of their garages. They were given discounts by the eager companies merely for selling two or three items. And simultaneously the companies competed with their own dealers, sometimes even undercutting them. But then the "dealers" never had storefronts or overhead, so they couldn't squawk much. It was several years before the first substantial dealers arrived—businessmen with phones, desks, and spare parts.

Sitting in an office under siege from eager would-be flyers, it was hard for manufacturers to believe that a very large part of the world had yet to hear of hang gliding. Even in late 1973 flyers drew disbelieving crowds wherever they went. Talk to your local barber about what you were doing—chances were he'd never heard of it.

Chris Price, skimming the grass in early Rogallo. (*Ground Skimmer* magazine)

Even the world of advertising saw no possibilities in the sport. One hang glider company, thinking they might advertise commercial products on their sails as the "Beetle billboards" were doing, sent out a thousand letters to all the ad agencies in southern California, offering themselves as flying billboards. For a large number of hours' flying over populous areas, the price would be a thousand dollars.

Only two agencies even responded. One, a compassionate sort, took time to write a letter explaining that their clients would expect a great deal more from a thousand dollars than that; the other scrawled a brief message on his letter and sent it back: "Are you kidding?"

Hang glider manufacturing was a juvenile. It behaved like one and it was treated like one.

"THINK WHAT LILIENTHAL WOULD HAVE THOUGHT . . ."

By 1973 Jack Lambie's Coast Hang Gliding Club had become the Southern California Hang Gliding Association and had left its members' living rooms for a meeting hall in downtown Los Angeles. Lloyd Licher became president. A slender man, serious and mature, he came to hang gliding from soaring and lent the association some of the respectability it needed.

By late '73 the group's name had changed again, to the United States Hang Gliding Association, accommodating the thousands of members living outside California.

Toward the end of that year the group decided it was time for Francis M. Rogallo to come West and see what he had wrought. They arranged a meet in his honor at Escape Country and planned to award him the Ed Gardia memorial trophy. (Ed Gardia was modern hang gliding's first fatality.)

Though Escape Country was so blanketed in fog that day that nobody could fly officially (a writer renamed it the Fogallo meet), Mr. Rogallo saw the antics of a few daredevils who took off in zero visibility, flew by some kind of internal radar, and homed in at the last minute to music broadcast from the speakers' stand. Before the music began, one adventuresome pilot flew in high over the landing area yelling, "Where am I?"

"Down here," somebody shouted back, whereupon the pilot executed a few fast turns and suddenly appeared on the field. Later the fog crept down so low that even after landing, a pilot could still wander off in the wrong direction.

Nobody worried much in those days.

A lot of people who might otherwise have been flying introduced themselves to Francis Rogallo that Saturday. He was easy to spot. He was the tall man wearing the Russian cossack hat. At close range, with his head cocked slightly in an attitude of listening, his eyes sparkling, and an almost impish smile on his lips, he had the appearance of a rather large leprechaun.

Dave Muehl accepts the winner's trophy from Francis Rogallo. (Jim Morton)

In this period, when nobody had really profited financially from hang gliding, it was surprising to learn that neither had Mr. Rogallo. His patent expired in 1968, long before hang gliding took off.

For just a little while justice touched him. Because the government felt Rogallo had made such a significant contribution to flexible-wing flight, they gave him a rare and substantial award. Unfortunately, ten years later they decided numerous taxes and interest were due on it, and they began proceedings to extract their pound of flesh. By the time the legalities were over, they'd taken it all back.

Mr. Rogallo laughs about it. "One learns to expect that kind of thing. It was two different branches of the government, you see . . . that makes it all right, doesn't it?" When told he was unusually philosophical, Rogallo replied, "Well, you see, money was no object in the first place. The whole idea was to come up with an improvement in aircraft . . . something that people could afford to fly and enjoy, and we thought we *did* that . . . so that was a success. Now the fact that we didn't get any money for it was sort of incidental." Quietly he added, "Fortunately, we had other means of making a living."

Today Mr. Rogallo is as spirited about flying as ever. He still flies hang gliders off Jockey's Ridge, the sand dunes near his home, and he still stops by to watch others. "In fact," he says, "a couple of weeks ago one of the instructors— for the first time—foot-launched off the dunes and got a thermal and climbed to over a thousand feet and flew about four and a half miles!" Excitement alters his voice. "He flew from Jockey's Ridge to the Wright brothers' monument. *That distance!*"

Rogallo was interrupted. "Think what Lilienthal would have thought . . ."

"Oh, my goodness, yes," he said. "Well, think what we thought! There was a group of us there. My wife and I just happened to stop by . . . and we couldn't believe it. Because heretofore the only place to fly was just in front of the dune. And he kept circling and got above it, and pretty soon he was behind it and still climbing and still circling. And that was real weird.

"And he kept circling and going higher and higher, and finally he just disappeared from sight. And then we got in our cars and started chasing down there to find him."

Rogallo at sixty-seven, with the enthusiasm of seventeen, jumps in his car to chase a soaring hang glider . . . the excitement in his voice trails off a little. "We didn't find him, but he landed down there, and called in where he was."

It is Rogallo himself who sums up his life best. "Although I worked on these flexible wings, the greater part of my professional career has been devoted to conventional aircraft—and particularly the control of them. The first patent I ever had awarded to me was on a spoiler type of control system to enable aircraft to use full-span, high-lift flaps—which are pretty common now and are used on most jet aircraft. And I have also worked on slotted flaps, single and double, and so on, that are in use now." Conventional aircraft were the focus of his life. Yet his immortality would lie elsewhere.

The irony of it doesn't escape him, and even he is amused by it. He recalls the first hint of what lay ahead. "When I was working at NASA," he says, "I used to give talks once in a while to local clubs. About that time, also, but with no connection with NASA, I was getting a little publicity for these flexible-wing kites. One evening I was going with the public-information officer down to give a talk to a club, and he said, 'Wouldn't it be funny if, after all the things you've done in aeronautics, you became known for a man that invented a kite!'" Rogallo chuckles, and one can almost see his rueful smile, long distance. "And I think that's just about the way it's turned out. Now, neither I—nor anybody else—remembers anything else I ever did!"

HE'S UP, HE'S STILL UP!

A race began. When Taras Kiceniuk found lift and stayed up for five minutes in his Icarus it was news. For those who had never seen a foot-launched flyer ride the air currents along a ridge, it seemed incredible. Everyone thought it was a first.

Yet a few months earlier Dave Kilbourne had flown an hour and four minutes on his own Rogallo design, the Kilbo Kite, at Mission Ridge near San Jose, California. The date was September 6, 1971. His record sparked wild enthusiasm and spurred a competition that was to last for years.[44]

On July 2, 1972, Taras Kiceniuk, now nineteen, foot-launched his Icarus

Bob Wills sets record—above Torrey Pines, 1973. (Richard Jenks)

off the 340-foot cliffs overlooking the Pacific at Torrey Pines, California. For an hour and eleven minutes he soared back and forth in the winds that blow off the cliffs and go straight up. These cliffs were to be the source of three more records in the next few years. But Taras was the first flyer to bring a fixed-wing hang glider to this dramatic spot.[45]

After hearing of Taras's record, Bob Wills decided to earn one himself. Whereas the old record had been beaten by a mere seven minutes, it was characteristic of Bob that he'd go for the largest possible increment. On September 7, 1972, he flew a nineteen-and-a-half-foot kite—barefoot, as usual—and stayed up two hours and sixteen minutes.

It was only a month later that Taras took the record back.

On October 29, 1972, Taras Kiceniuk returned to Torrey Pines equipped for battle. He wore a sensitive hiker's altimeter, attached airspeed and rate-of-climb indicators to his Icarus II, and brought two witnesses with stopwatches. When he came down, after two hours and twenty-six minutes, he'd bested Wills by ten minutes.[46]

Wills came to Kiceniuk's own lair for his next foray. The first man to fly a Rogallo from Torrey Pines, Wills was also the first flyer to land back on top. On December 7, 1972, flying for three hours and three minutes, he tried to put the record to rest once and for all. In later years, when as many as twenty kites sometimes flew Torrey at once, he recalled the joy of having had the site, that day, to himself.

The record remained for a while. Then on April 13 it was Tony Kolerich, a nineteen-year-old student at Northrup Institute of Technology, who beat Wills's record by six minutes. Tony hadn't intended any such feat. Flying his home-built black-plastic-sail Rogallo at Torrance Beach, California, he was up after school, for fun. It was Friday the thirteenth. Four of his friends had come to see what hang gliding was all about, and they, rather than Tony, seemed determined he'd make his mark. Though the flight began at 4:21 P.M., the friends hung around, shouting encouragement to Tony.

It got dark. Tony flew past a house where a couple was eating dinner by candlelight. He waved down and talked to them. The time went on. Some curious onlookers (including a policeman) tried to follow Tony's flight with spotlights, but his black sail blended into the black sky, and they found they could *hear* the rippling plastic better than see it. Freezing and exhausted, with deep bruises on his shoulders from the seat ropes, Tony could not distinguish the ground in the dark. His legs went limp as he crash-landed on the cold black beach.[47]

It took extraordinary determination for Pat Conniry to claim the record for himself on July 15 at Torrance Beach. Because lifeguards felt hang gliding interfered with swimming, flyers were prohibited from launching before five P.M. in the summer. But Conniry knew the wind died at sunset. The attempt had to start earlier.

One day a light storm blew in, making soaring possible, so Conniry snuck his Seagull III past the lifeguards and assembled it before anyone noticed. Safely launched, he ignored the lifeguards who suddenly spotted him and blared over their loudspeakers for him to come down. When Conniry persisted, the lifeguards summoned police, who barked additional amplified threats. Conniry flew on. Short of shooting him out of the sky, there was nothing anyone could do. Eventually the boy outlasted them all and flew for three hours, thirty-six minutes. He reported later that all the commotion below "helped pass the time."[48]

Mike Mitchell, later to become a champion flyer, next stayed aloft for three hours and forty-five minutes at Torrey Pines. Mike was light, too light for his Seagull III, but conditions at Torrey Pines were marginal that day, and it was only a flyer with superior skill and extraordinarily light wing loading who could have accomplished what he did. The day was August 13, 1973.[49]

On September 1, 1973, Bob Wills and his brother Chris performed the strangest feat of all. Determined to set a new duration record together, they planned an assault from the cliffs above Waimanalo Bay in Oahu, Hawaii, where Chris was honeymooning.

Pat Conniry, holder of two records, with Seagull III and sailplane variometer. (*Hang Gliding* magazine)

The Mad, Magical, Many-Sided World of Hang Gliding

Flying above Waimanalo is unlike anyplace else in the world. The wind rushes against the eleven-hundred-foot cliffs and pushes upward beyond the top for another thousand feet. The body of upward-moving air is so strong that sailplanes once set records there.

The mighty wind on top is awesome, but the cliff's edge is more so; to look over is downright terrifying. One young spectator, unwilling to trust her legs, crawled to the edge on hands and knees to look down.

Until Bob had launched his hang glider there a few days earlier, the site seemed unfit for hang gliders.

That day Bob and Chris quickly learned one does not *launch* off these cliffs; one is held down until a state of equilibrium is reached between sail and wind. Once released, the hang glider pops straight up like a helium balloon out of a child's hand.

Now, while a crowd of TV cameramen, newspaper reporters, and spectators watched, Bob and Chris made final preparations: canisters of apple juice tied to belt loops with kite string, Hershey bars in pockets, stopwatches set.

If anyone had mentioned taking a jacket, they would have laughed. Nobody gets cold in Hawaii!

So, bare-armed—and in Bob's case, barefooted—the two launched, Chris holding Bob's wires and younger brother Eric helping Chris. The cameras whirred and clicked.

But Chris's takeoff was almost a disaster. Eric held on to Chris's wires an instant too long, and the hang glider, instead of going up, veered crazily to one side and for a split second threatened to spin back into the cliffs.

Chris wrestled for control.

Nobody could know that these cliffs would soon take human sacrifices—so many that hang gliding was nearly banned in Hawaii forever! The spectators watched unconcerned.

Perspiring, Chris threw his weight to the right. And slowly, gradually, the glider turned away, came back under control, and headed out to sea.

For almost two hours Chris flew near the takeoff, swooping toward the cameras on the rising ridge of air, turning back toward the ocean to lose altitude.

Conserving his energy, Bob departed for a distant cloud and sat there. From a thousand feet away he didn't appear to be moving at all.

The drama continued, and soon became less dramatic than wearisome. The time seemed so long.

One by one, the news media departed, asking to be notified when the record was broken.

To relieve his legs, Bob climbed into the triangular control bar and squatted there like a gibbon, with his knees under his chin. Holding onto the sides, he peered out awkwardly. But those on the cliff at first saw only the

Off Waimanalo, Hawaii, Bob and Chris Wills attempt time-aloft record, 1973. (The Wills Family Album)

empty seat hanging below the kite, and for a moment they panicked. My God, had he fallen out of the kite?

Suddenly Chris swooped low over the cliff and shouted to the spectators, "I'm cold! Pick me up!" To everyone's disappointment, he slowly disappeared in the direction of the beach. Now the record, if any, would be up to Bob.

Chris's story was astonishing. Up there, sitting in one spot, unable to move or stretch, the air no longer caressed the skin with its feather-light touch. After two hours at two thousand feet up, the wind was *cold!* He shook his head. He couldn't see how Bob would continue.

And twenty minutes later, Bob, too, was calling down that he was cold. Any minute now he'd probably give up. The spectators realized the attempt had failed—for want of a jacket!

Yet they refused to quite accept it. Surely, Chris thought, a jacket could be given to Bob. But how? Two hang gliders couldn't fly close to each other. Bob couldn't land to get one. And—why dream—nobody up here had a jacket, anyway.

But an interested spectator quickly spoke up. "I have a friend at the foot of the cliff. We'll borrow one from him." It was only a glimmer of hope. How would they get the jacket to a flying hang glider?

Still, Chris shouted to Bob, "We're getting you a jacket!" He had to shout twice, and nobody was sure Bob even understood. Even more, nobody knew how they'd do it.

The obstacles were endless. After the spectator and Chris's father drove fifteen minutes down the mountain to find the friend and his jacket, the friend wasn't home. So they knocked on a neighbor's door, quickly explained their mission, hurried back up the mountain with the jacket from a complete stranger! They also borrowed a Windbreaker for Chris.

Bob Wills flies this kite eight hours, twenty-four minutes. (The Wills Family Album)

Next they pondered the uselessness of what they'd done so far. The jacket was in their hands, but it wasn't in Bob's.

Finally Chris or his father thought of the kite string they'd bought for tying juice to their belt loops. Slowly the plan emerged.

Chris laid out all the string and doubled it once. Then he wound one end around the jacket, shaping it like a sausage, and all the rest back on the spool. The spool he stuffed in his pocket and the sausage inside his Windbreaker. Both hands were now free for flying.

By now only a few people were left on top. Once more called to duty, the spectator stood courageously with his back to the cliff and released Chris's wires a great deal better than Eric had done.

Rising precipitously, Chris turned the craft toward the sea.

The two flyers could communicate poorly at best. Chris only hoped his brother would understand what they were doing.

Slowly, gradually, Chris fed the jacket into the airstream behind his kite, trying to manage it so the string wouldn't snap. But he quickly realized he'd have to reduce flying speed because the jacket was trailing straight out behind him. Out there, Bob couldn't get it. From the cliff the watchers saw the bundle following Chris's kite like a puppy, the string invisible, no perceptible link between Chris and the object trailing him.

After a while they saw Bob's kite flash by underneath Chris with great speed, a bird of prey, one quick motion, then Chris drifting slowly away and a dark object trailing Bob's kite. The jacket had passed from one kite to the other!

In that great ocean of air, Bob had intercepted a string the size of a spider's thread.

Yet it wasn't over. Endlessly, the bundle followed its new master. For a moment the spectators thought they perceived the object falling into the ocean.

The Mad, Magical, Many-Sided World of Hang Gliding 71

Not so.

Slowly, agonizingly, the tiny black thing moved closer to the kite and finally blended with it. Then, like a billowing parachute, the jacket suddenly opened up and threatened to sail away. Its flapping took on an energetic life of its own. The spectators gasped; somebody murmured, "Hang on to it!" The jacket ballooned ominously. It was obvious Bob only had it by part of one sleeve. But gradually the billowing subsided, then stopped, and the spectators knew the man was wearing the jacket.

A great cheer came from the top of the cliff.

Chris flew back over the top, shouted, "He's got it! Pick me up!" and everyone screamed and waved.

The rest of the time was dramatic for its very lack of drama.

Bob flew for another hour and a half, and in the end was up five hours and six minutes. The evening news showed him flying on film, even as he circled to come down, and those nearby could see him on their screens and rush outside to see him still in the air.

Next day his kite appeared on page one of the Honolulu *Advertiser*.

For Bob Wills, disappointment followed almost immediately. The victory was hardly celebrated before the news reached the mainland, and Pat Conniry two days later began scurrying about, checking the local wind conditions. The wind was reported to be twenty mph from due west at Palos Verdes, California. Perfect! At Buff's Cove—a steep, three-hundred-foot slope where the wind becomes quite vertical—Pat took off, and once aloft began shouting down to the Labor Day crowd that gathered beneath him. He flew over a backyard barbecue where the surprised partygoers toasted their flying friend. But Pat's troubles began when he was still thirty minutes short of five hours. The wind was beginning to die, the conditions becoming barely marginal. Would all his efforts be in vain? Pat hugged the cliff and made tight turns to squeeze every single inch (and second) out of the lift. He battled the dying wind until he had beaten Wills's record by fifteen minutes![50]

The Wills family came home to a dilemma. Bob had remained in Hawaii, and now they debated whether to tell him his record had lived a mere two days. Perhaps, they thought, they should just let it drop. The feat had been horrendous; it seemed almost sadistic to suggest he try again.

Finally Chris called his brother. "Just thought I'd let you know, Bob. You do whatever you like."

Bob considered letting it go. But in the end he couldn't.

When he decided to set a new record that was unbeatable, filmmaker Carl R. Boenish flew to Hawaii to document the event.

For several days conditions were unsoarable. Finally the wind came up, flung itself against the ridge, and bored upward in its usual pattern toward the heavens.

This time Bob was prepared with water and sandwiches. And a jacket! He also had padding on his seat and a rope attached underneath so he could stretch his legs. Further, he had equipped his kite with an altimeter. He flew out to sea in a cloud streak until the altimeter started to drop. His highest point was 2,220 feet, or 1,070 feet above takeoff. Bob set two records on that flight: duration and altitude gain.

When he finally came down, he'd flown for eight hours and twenty-four minutes! Wearily he said, "If anyone wants to try and break that, let them. I don't think it's important anymore."

It wasn't to be the end of duration attempts, though Wills's record lasted for six months. It was just the end for him.

Months later John Hughes stayed up for ten hours and five minutes at Waimanalo, not really intending to do it, and flying an old trainer kite that had carried two hundred people on their first flights (and crashes). He had mended the broken control bar by sawing off the worst part and bolting a broomstick in its place. On this relic Hughes hung on to marginal lift until eleven o'clock at night.[51]

New records were set periodically until 1980, when Jim Will stayed up on this same soarable ridge for twenty-four hours, thirty-one minutes!

Today flyers speak disdainfully of such heroics. Carol Price (flyer and editor) says, "Flying for ten or more hours now has about the same significance as pole sitting. Such marathon flights only prove that the wind blows for a long time in certain places."[52]

What flyers yearn for today is *distance*. And Eric Raymond may be their new hero: In July 1980, in the Owens Valley, Raymond flew 121 miles!

"IT WAS AS IF I WERE GOING INTO COMBAT"

In 1973, when flyers were leapfrogging over one another for time-aloft records, a race was also on for altitude drop. Bill Bennett started it two years earlier with his flight from 5,727-foot Dante's View down to the Death Valley floor. The flight lasted almost 12 minutes and covered 6.2 miles.

Foot launching was then almost unheard of, Dave Kilbourne being one of the few who'd done it, and Donnita Holland Kilbourne remembers that "Bennett was on the phone, here, to the fellows in northern California . . . like ten-thirty the night before, just scared to death, asking them, 'What should I do?' And they're trying to tell him over the phone." But he accomplished it, a landmark in foot-launch flying!

In August 1973, on their same Hawaiian trip, Bob and Chris Wills stared at ten-thousand-foot Haleakala on Maui and wondered if they could fly off the top for a new world record. Trouble was, the peak was never visible. A permanent cloud circled it like a protective veil. Even Dick Eipper, a well-known pioneer hang gliding pilot who lived on Maui, had never attempted to fly from the top.

Still, the brothers thought, there must be a way.

They went to the local weather station and asked questions and studied contour maps. They finally concluded that such a flight was possible only at dawn. But when the time came, all their fellow vacationers balked at getting up at four in the morning to drive them *anywhere*. It was Bob, with water-dripping-on-stone persistence, who finally coerced two family members into sacrificing a night's sleep.

The two caught the shy peak at six in the morning, momentarily naked in the dawn mist. With confidence they ran two steps off the top, dropped straight down for an agonizing split second, caught the wind, and headed for the ocean.

Though they were breathless over the unparalleled view of island and Hawaiian water from ten thousand feet, the flying was uneventful until they were ready to land. Increasingly, they found themselves battling a head wind, until at the end it became so strong they had to land flying backward! Chris said, "It was exactly like backing into a parallel parking space!"

On the twenty-sixth of October, that same year, thirty-one-year-old Rudy Kishazy—an electrician from Plymouth, Michigan—tackled Mont Blanc, Switzerland. From the start the weather seemed against him: There was rain, snow, wind. Three days before he gave up, the Geneva meteorological station announced lessening winds for the first time in weeks. As Kishazy waited for the helicopter to take him up he nervously chewed an entire pack of gum.

At three in the afternoon Rudy took off from Chamonix and landed on "the roof of Europe." The helicopter dropped him off and went back to get the cameraman while Rudy waited uncomfortably—in five-degree temperature!

At four o'clock everyone was ready. Kishazy says, "I grabbed the trapeze bar; I wasn't afraid, but it was as if I were going into combat. All I had to do was win. At takeoff time I wasn't seeing too well. I was rushing down the northeast wall, faster and faster. A sharp noise suddenly told me that the sail was correctly spread and I had reached takeoff speed. I pushed the trapeze. Nothing, no response. My mind raced: Was the air perhaps not dense enough to take off? That was my last thought. Suddenly I felt a jolt, like when a fast elevator stops abruptly; the wind was blowing in my face and I heard myself shouting, "That's it, that's it!"

Rudy fought turbulence all the way down. There was cloud below, too, but just as he approached it miraculously thinned, giving him the visibility he needed. Shortly afterward he landed at Servoz, 13,008.6 feet below the summit he'd just left. "There I was, under my wing, trying to dream a moment longer; I wasn't sure it had all really happened. But I was immediately awakened by the crowd that surrounded me. To celebrate, a man handed me a glass of wine."[53]

"I'LL WRITE IT ON YOUR HAT, KAZ"

The first United States Hang Gliding Championships in 1973 excited everyone like no championships have done since. Hang gliding was then new. It carried a mystique. Anyone brave enough—or crazy enough—to jump off a mountain was a hero. Danger was sensed and always lurked as a possibility, and there'd been a few deaths, but nobody recoiled at promoting the sport.

The manufacturers all believed then that winning a competition would give them a sales edge that couldn't be bought at any price. Almost everyone skilled at the sport was associated with some manufacturer. The competition among manufacturers was tense to the point of lunacy. Win or wither, they believed.

Partly because of commercial sponsorship and partly because of the novelty, even the news media reacted with fervor. Before the competition they followed the flyers around with cameras and notebooks, especially those who had already achieved some notoriety. *Sports Illustrated* sent Coles Phinizy to cover the story and Bob Wills. The first nationals were a BIG DEAL.

Before the first flights Kaz de Lisse, the meet director, asked flyer Chris Wills who was going to win. Chris said, "I am, Kaz."

"Oh, yeah?" Kaz stared at him quizzically. A former circus clown, he wore an outsize hat covered with pins and slogans.

"I'll write it on your hat, Kaz." Chris took a pen and printed, "Chris Wills, Champion."

Kaz grinned at him, and Chris laughed. Then he strode off to catch a truck up the mountain.

Four days later, having led all the way, Chris became the first United States champion. But the drama went to second place, where brother Bob—after a floundering start—came from behind to take runner-up. When asked how he felt about his younger brother winning the contest, Bob said, "I'm glad as hell."

In two months, when the December 10, 1973, issue of *Sports Illustrated* came out, acceptance of hang gliding by the established media seemed official.

Coles Phinizy summarized both the history and current state of hang gliding with elegant prose. A former Time-Life writer, he said, "Just now, when a new breed of primitive birdmen is emerging . . . East and West and in between the new breed is proliferating and quietly enjoying the sky at a dirt-cheap price." He spoke of Rudy Kishazy's record flight and noted, "Using an identical Rogallo wing, a less-enterprising duffer can have a perfectly safe and larky time casting himself off low sand dunes into a sea wind."

The focus of Phinizy's story was Bob Wills. Phinizy said, "Many of Bill Bennett's records have been exceeded and his antics duplicated by disciples, notably 23-year-old Robert Wills, a Southern California barefoot folk hero of elfish bent and Bunyonesque proportions. Since boyhood Bob Wills has walked the world in a friendly way, doing what comes unnaturally. He once [said] 'I don't know what I am going to be when I grow up, but it won't be what everybody else is.' And how true, how true."[54]

The *Sports Illustrated* story brought letters to Bob Wills addressed simply, "Bob Wills, Santa Ana, California."

The following year, when Bob and Chris won the nationals again, in reverse order, their prominence in hang gliding was assured. That second year

USHGA president, Lloyd Licher, and first U.S. champion, Chris Wills.
(© George Uveges, 1981)

76 **The Mad, Magical, Many-Sided World of Hang Gliding**

Chris Price finished third, and now the three—who had formed a small manufacturing company—figured riches would flow to them automatically.

But it wasn't to be that simple. Tragedy would stalk them as readily as fame, while money seemed forever on the distant horizon.

In those days money eluded nearly everybody.

A NEW DESIGN EVERY SIX MONTHS

In 1974 hang gliding changed so fast nobody could keep up with it. While half the world was still ignorant of the sport, those who were living with it daily had a new idea for every day the sun shone. Instrumentation came first. The first nationals saw a few kites with crude variometers taped or screwed to their control bars. The variometers whined shrilly, the pitch changing up or down as the kite experienced lift or sink. Since a hang glider any distance from land moves in the vertical plane imperceptibly, the flyers soon found variometers a necessity for heralding their ups and downs.

Altimeters came next. Only with an altimeter could pilots tell absolute altitude. Some kites carried wind meters, and eventually a manufacturer dreamed up a "flight deck," which was a complete, fancy instrument panel. A cockpit without the pit.

Almost immediately manufacturers homed in on kite designs.

Restless and always dissatisfied, Bob Wills was the first to abandon the ninety-degree nose angle on his conical Rogallo kites and to design—with help from Chris Price—a higher-aspect-ratio hang glider. The sail curved inward on each side of the tail, and because of its characteristic shape, was named the Swallowtail. Within a year the name Swallowtail became a generic term worldwide for that kind of hang glider. The significance of the design change lay in the kite's ability to fly farther and stay up longer, while actually improving ease of handling.

At the second United States Nationals, where the Willses and Price did so well on their Swallowtails, another young designer, Roy Haggard, appeared with a different version of a high-aspect-ratio kite. Called the Mark I Dragonfly, it further revolutionized flying. The trend was toward wider spans and narrower chords (the average distance from leading to trailing edge); the startling effect was that now flyers caught minimal rising air and went *up* where previously they'd only gone down.

The new Rogallo designers were beginning to combine the best of two worlds. Taras Kiceniuk's Icarus V and Volmer Jensen's VJ-23 were the original high-aspect-ratio hang gliders. But they lacked the portability and one-man handling of the Rogallos; they could seldom land on a spot. Most flyers still preferred the lower-performing delta wings.

The Swallowtail—first improvement on standard Rogallo. (Chris Wills)

The trouble with the rapidly changing designs was that manufacturers felt obliged to come out with a new kite about every six months. It brought havoc to their shops. They scarcely got themselves organized for the latest innovation before one of their pilot-engineers dreamed up something new (or a competitor dreamed up something they felt obliged to copy). They dared not ignore improvements lest buyers all flock elsewhere.

Manufacturers designed their sails on the shop walls, wrote frame measurements on scraps of paper tacked over the workbench, carried critical numbers in their heads. One metalworker wrote three years' worth of changing tubing lengths on a single piece of paper—in his own code—and when he left his company in a huff, the company was out of business for a week. It took a genius from outside to come in and break the code to reveal the critical dimensions.

An engineer from outside the hang gliding world would have found such practices inconceivable. A new design every six months? No blueprints? No exploded drawings? Nobody with an engineering degree?

Well, no. And hardly any profits, either.

"WHAT ABOUT HIS TWO FRONT TEETH?"

In a small way, hang gliding began to reach across the two oceans. An American from Garden Grove, California—Mike Harker—brought it to the pop-eyed stare of Europe. Mike was suave and understated, spoke perfect German, and flew dramatically. He so impressed the Europeans that he soon had a chain of hang gliding schools established in Austria and Germany. Jumping from one American manufacturer to another, he enticed each in turn into believing Europe was "sewed up" for themselves. He also very nearly put together a grandiose international competition—flying would take place in several countries, each site more exotic than the last—which fell through when sponsors backed out. Before he suffered a bad accident, Mike had introduced hang gliding to a continent, to become the Bill Bennett of Europe.

Tentatively, novice flyers from elsewhere sniffed about to see what was happening in America; they arrived to buy kites and wheel and deal for exclusive distributorships. Seldom announcing themselves in advance, they just showed up at the manufacturers' doors.

One company found itself entertaining two Japanese who barely spoke English. They seemed eager to make a deal, though, if one could judge by the "interpreter" . . . who needed an interpreter himself. With childlike pride they passed around pictures of themselves hang gliding in Japan. Intended as proof of intent, the variety of ungainly postures only confirmed that the men couldn't fly.

After a while the owner of the company began to observe that the interpreter did not only all the talking, but all the smiling and laughing as well. The other hardly opened his mouth.

Finally, in a careless moment, the reason came to light: The sober one was missing his two front teeth!

Over drinks that evening the American ventured to inquire about the missing teeth, and the interpreter explained with hand gestures and a wide grin that the man had knocked them out hang gliding.

"Really?" asked the owner with some concern. "And why doesn't he get false ones?"

"His dentist refuses. He's waiting for Mr. Yamamoto to knock out the rest."

Clearly the world had some catching up to do!

SANER HEADS GOT OUT

It happened: The first wave of deaths. Dave Sizemore died in late '73 when his cable, with a baling-wire splice, broke during a radical maneuver. A Western Airlines pilot flying his hang glider overhead saw Dave struggling to reopen the collapsed wing. Twice Dave wrestled it apart, only to have it close in on him again. Dave was on top of the sail, falling.

After Dave's death the commercial pilot left the sport. He had no heart for it any longer.

It seemed like a freak occurrence.

Then in early November Chuck Kocsis, an officer of the United States

Not a recommended landing . . . (Stephen McCarroll)

The Mad, Magical, Many-Sided World of Hang Gliding

Hang Gliding Association, shocked the hang gliding world by dying during his first prone flight. The force of Chuck's crash didn't explain his death from a broken neck. Flyers shook their heads in stunned surprise.

Dave Gibas, an expert and Chandelle's best, dove in on an altered kite during prototype testing in late November.

In quick succession there were three others: James Foster ("dived in hard"), Gary Smith (flipped after tow release), and Thomas Williamson (hit high-tension wires.)

Flyers grew wary.

In March of '74 Eric Wills, twenty, turned his second-ever three-sixty into a spiraling dive, hit the ridge of a mountain when a few more inches would have saved him, catapulted through the control bar, and broke his neck.

The Wills family, shocked, considered leaving the sport. Its malevolent side was becoming all too apparent. "Deadly butterflies," Eric's father called the hang gliders. Yet, because brother Bob's whole life was hang gliding and he had already become an expert, they chose to remain. For Chris alone, they wouldn't have stayed in the sport; as a pre-med student, his ultimate goals lay elsewhere.

The Wills family rationalized. Eric's death was explainable: a novice doing an expert's thing. The family wrote articles to forewarn others.

Yet flyers continued to fall, one after the other. Eric had died on March 16, Steven Ervin died on March 17, and Michael Phillips on March 18. 1974 was terrifying. By December 31 the sport had claimed fifty people in the United States alone, ten more in Europe. The media and the public began backing away. Though each death had an "explanation," nobody needed to have a "killer sport" explained. There were moves to ban it.

By then hang gliding had come too far, was beyond banishment. The flyers who understood hang gliding best vowed never to give it up, though each fatality was a new personal blow, and almost everyone suffered a loss that was close to him. A few good flyers did leave, temporarily. Others took steps.

Eric's father, Robert Wills, Sr., formed the United States Hang Gliding Association's Accident Review Board to study, record, and disseminate the causes of accidents. Only then, he felt, could their reduction begin. Only when people knew what was happening and in what numbers would the industry find the means of responding. Slowly it began to work as he thought it would.

Pete Brock, a flyer and manufacturer, had long since decided it was time to form a Hang Glider Manufacturer's Association. The purpose was to set standards for hang gliders and become a self-enforcing body. Yet he found resistance. He was accused of being "political." He says, "I think, perhaps, I was a little ahead of my time. We had fancy hardware and most of the other manufacturers felt we were trying to legislate everybody else out of business

The ultimate test—five on an SST! (Chris Wills)

Note extreme flexing of leading edge—count the legs. (Chris Wills)

The Mad, Magical, Many-Sided World of Hang Gliding

Solitude *(Ernst Furuhatt, Norway)*

Two's Company *(Rob Kells)*

Midnight Sun *(Ernst Furuhatt, Norway)*

Yosemite
*(Highster Aircraft, Bill Wood,
photographer)*

Grenoble *(© Bettina Gray)*

Lift Off *(LeRoy Grannis)*

Airborne *(Ultralight Products, Don Whitmore, photographer)*

because they didn't have all the trickery that we had. There was a lot of resistance to any sort of certification or standards at the time, and my persistence in this area always seemed to make matters worse, so we let it die. Later, when the accident rate began to climb, we all began to see the reason that an industry group was needed."[55] Eventually two others, Gary Valle and Tom Price, were able to make the HGMA work.

In the meantime, flyers and manufacturers took steps. Bob and Chris Wills stopped stunting; it wasn't for everyone. Both began wearing helmets (though Bob never capitulated to the extent of wearing shoes).

A general indignation at unsafe practices ensued. "Hey, you turkey, you shouldn't fly this hill—get some air time first." "C'mon, man, you could get killed doing that!" Occasionally flyers got physical, prevented others from taking off. (More than one pilot was coerced into not flying his Chandelle Competition, a hang glider with fatal flaws designed into it.) Purely selfish, non-altruistic motives often prompted the watchdogs. Everyone knew what might happen next: Get yourself killed and you'll wreck it for me.

In lieu of formal new-model testing, manufacturers devised their own tests: measured the breaking point of tubing, stretched cables till they snapped, hung six flyers off a hang glider to see if it would break. A lot was learned.

A lot more remained to be learned.

Some companies doggedly test-flew every kite they sold, believing this to be the only sure means of quality control; a few dirt-smudged sails for proven flyability was a fair exchange, they believed. (Today factory test-flying is an industry requirement.)

Sadly, Pete Brock lost his own son, twelve-year-old Hall, in 1975; and Chuck Stahl, commercial airline pilot and safety director for the USHGA, suffered the loss of his boy, Curt. Three sons, now, of families intimately connected with the sport.

Before hang gliding turned the corner on safety in 1975, there were 110 deaths in the United States, 23 foreign. The deadly butterflies weren't deceiving anyone!

THE GREAT SCORPION HUNTS

Hang gliding entered center stage, smiled, bowed, and took its curtain calls in 1975. That was the year Twentieth Century-Fox spun a yarn about terrorists and an incredible hang gliding rescue of a captive lady and her kids from a monastery located atop a mountain pinnacle. The movie was called *Skyriders*.

The setting was Greece. Chris Wills, one of the five flyers in the film, described what took place backstage while making the movie.

"We had four helicopters (one to take us up the mountain, one to film us, and two as actors in the movie), four helicopter pilots, four VW minibuses, and a total of thirty-four people just to complete the filming of the hang gliding portion of the film. This was called the second unit (action unit). In most films the actors and acting are part of the first unit, and the action and stunt work are done by the second unit. Often it is necessary for both units to work together to film certain scenes. This is known as a mess.

"We found we worked very efficiently when we worked as a second unit, but when we worked together with the first unit, miracles happened. It was a miracle if anything went smoothly and according to plan! It was a miracle if the weather was right for the particular scene we were filming. Through good luck and some important decisions by the producer, Sandy Howard, we made some good shots that work well on film."

Chris and wife, Betty-Jo, left for Greece on June 10, 1975, to meet with the local people and scout locations. With them went three Swallowtail kites. They were joined later by four more flyers; equipment manager Roy Hooper; and fifty-four pieces of baggage, which included eleven additional Swallowtails, one motorcycle-kite combination, one fixed-wing Quicksilver and one Icarus II. By the time the group arrived in Kalambaka, the first filming location, all the flyers were restless and anxious to fly.

"We found a suitable one-thousand-foot cliff overlooking our hotel and proceeded to take five thousand miles off our VW tires getting up the five-mile paved road. Bob [Wills] had flown the site once before, six months earlier, when he'd traveled to Greece with the director and others to scout locations. *I'd* had a nice twenty-minute soaring flight, one thousand feet above the cliff in a rainstorm, before the others had arrived. Both Bob and I had been mobbed by everyone within sight of the area when we landed (I swear it was in the thousands; only with police protection could I take my kite down). Now the others were ready for the onslaught.

"With this on our minds we began feverishly to set up our kites and prepare to fly. Roy Hooper decided he would fly also and began to set up his kite. He had the double duty of taking abuse from us for not having the equipment better organized and acting as our baby-sitter, finding the right control bars and kites, while also setting up his own kite.

"One by one we began piling off the one-thousand-foot vertical cliff, losing our thoughts to the bliss of being airborne again. I was first, Bob second, Curt Kiefer third, Chris Price fourth, Dix Roper fifth, and Roy sixth. I landed in the motel parking lot, pointed my kite into the wind to signal the wind direction to the others, and proceeded to answer questions from the British helicopter pilot. As I watched Dix make a turn, the pilot asked, 'Did that pilot intend to do that?' Not noticing where he was pointing, I said, 'Sure; he turned on purpose by shifting his weight.' The Britisher looked at me and said strangely, 'Not him, *that* one.'

"At this point I saw a horrible sight. The last kite off had stalled, turned back into the cliff and proceeded to hit, tail-side backward in a slight turn, drop the nose again to fly, and then hit the cliff again. He hit about six times before he stopped on a ledge halfway down the sheer face. The kite began to blow off the ledge. I watched in horror as a gust caught the kite and took it the remaining five hundred feet to the rocks below. I then observed a miracle. The pilot had managed to unhook and was clinging to the ledge halfway down the mountain.

"After everyone else had landed we discovered, by a frantic process of elimination, that the pilot was Roy Hooper. Dix reported he'd encountered quite a lot of turbulence as he took off and had to dive to regain airspeed. We also decided Roy was still alive since he had unhooked his prone harness before the kite went the rest of the way down.

"We now had to formulate a plan to get him off the cliff. It began to dawn on us that we were in Greece, which was not exactly California in sophisticated search-and-rescue techniques. Luckily, we had a large number of Motorola walkie talkies for air-to-air communication; they had great range and clarity. We sent our Greek interpreter into town with a radio to get as much rope as he could buy, sent someone else to get some form of ambulance, while we went to try to get Roy off the cliff.

"To make a long story short, the ledge was about two feet wide, and fortunately ran along the cliff to a spot toward which we could hike. Roy was hurt but coherent; he had unhooked his carabiner in spite of a dislocated shoulder, and expressed the wish that he were not in Greece. We managed to get him out with uncanny assistance from the Greeks, who ran along the ledge in sandals! We put him in an 'ambulance' (a half truck, half van with absolutely no springs or suspension of any kind) and drove him—or rather bounced him—to the hospital.

"On one of the 'up' bounces, Roy glanced out the window and saw the hospital. He began to realize he was in for trouble. A hospital in the Greek hinterlands is a place where they take you to die. It looked like a concentration camp, with no screens to keep out the flies, no lights at night, not even any doctors. We were met at the entrance by 'Igor' who would not let anybody else carry Roy. 'Igor' delighted in banging Roy's broken leg against his back as he carried him in. Roy spent a terrible night there before we could arrange a helicopter to fly him to a more modern hospital in Athens.

"Roy spent six more weeks in the hospital in Athens before he could be put on a plane to the U.S. The film company went to great effort and expense to take care of him in Greece, including bribing doctors to look at him during a doctor's strike. Robert Culp, one of the stars of the film, was on Roy's plane coming home and made sure he had first-class service, along with four seats to lie down on.

"Roy is now up and around with a pin in his leg. To look at him, you'd not suspect he nearly lost his life on a ledge in Greece.

"Kamina Vourla, two and a half hours north of Athens by car, is a plush resort town where many Greeks go for their vacations. It is located on the Aegean Sea and offers great waterskiing and fantastic hang gliding if you have a helicopter to take you to the launch site.

"The only way to get to the top of our three-thousand-foot mountain was by helicopter. The landing area was a nice beach that the movie crew designed to look like a circus location. We were amazed to find that every day at dawn crowds of Greeks gathered on the beach to watch us fly.

"We quickly learned that as long as the camera helicopter was moving forward with a reasonable amount of airspeed there was no problem flying hang gliders above, under, or next to it. We all had radios with boom mikes and earphones built into our helmets so we could communicate with each other and the helicopter pilot, Frank. We had confidence in Frank, and besides, there was the somewhat useless consolation that if we got tangled in his rotor blades, he would go down also. At least that kept him honest.

"The circus-sequence script called for all kinds of outrageous stunts, but was flexible enough to let us do all the crazy things we'd been wanting to do in a hang glider. We flew in the control bar, flew backward, flew upside down, jumped out of the kites at sixty feet above the water, and decked our kites with banners and Mylar strips fifty feet long. We flew wingovers, whip stalls, and spins. Suzie—Bob's wife—even flew tandem, undid her seat belt, climbed down a rope ladder, and hung upside down from her knees while Bob did tight three-sixties.

"We tried to get the fixed-wing Quicksilver to wingover without much success on its one and only flight. We were notified that the Icarus was in a truck, being transported from France across country. It finally arrived one day before we left Greece for good and one day after we were finished filming. So, after three months of traveling from California to Greece, it was taken to the dump and broken in pieces. The cost of shipping it home exceeded its value, and it couldn't be sold in Greece because of import limitations. Color one Icarus *gone!*

"Flyer Dean Tanji arrived weeks after the rest of us, since he didn't know he was coming until I called him from Greece. On his first day of flying they shaved off his mustache, made him up like a girl, put him in tights, put a wig on him, had him fly seated for the first time, with radios for the first time, and filmed him stripping for the first time on the way down—all on his first test flight. They reasoned that as long as he was flying, they ought to film him.

Dean Tanji's an excellent pilot; a stripteaser he's not. (Chris Wills)

Chris Wills—the dashing Captain Marvel. (Betty-Jo Wills)

"On one of my early stunts (made up as Captain Marvel) I hit some really good lift as I came over the face of the mountain. Following my instincts, I turned in the lift to gain altitude. Altitude, of course, means more time to do stunts on the way down. As I began my second pass, the director began yelling on the radio. He said he didn't want me to soar way up in the sky as a little speck. He wanted me to soar fifty feet above his head so he could get hours of film. He also wanted me to do stunts at fifty feet, dive down and do a touch and go, take off again, and fly three hundred feet to a spot where I was to land left foot forward and right foot back on two spots he had placed next to an umbrella in the sand. After several minutes of heated discussion, we decided it could not be done in one flight, much less the first flight, and we reached a tentative understanding on what could and could not be done.

"We flew the circus portion for a week. The helicopter, with Frank flying and photographer Jim Freeman hanging out the door with his feet in the air, wrapped around the vibrationless, free-floating camera, could make hang gliders look like the Blue Angels. I would love to make a movie out of the film they left on the cutting-room floor.

"Kalambaka, the attack-sequence location, was a small village about five hours north of Athens by car. It was located on the Thessalian Plain and was well inland. It is very popular with tourists because of the fantastic monasteries in the area, known as Meteora.

The Meteora monastery. (Chris Wills)

"The Meteora monasteries are brick, rock, and cement communities built atop huge pinnacles, some with one-thousand-foot vertical drops. Built by monks around the twelfth century A.D., they are an inspiration to look at. Initially, the only way to get to the actual buildings was to be born there . . . or to go up in a rope basket, hauled up by hand. In the 1920s stairs were built with bridges and paths so that tourists could see them. The monasteries are almost all still being used by monks, so all male visitors have to wear shirts and shoes, and female visitors must wear skirts and cannot have bare arms.

"This was the setting of the escape and attack. The 'family' was held hostage in a particularly precarious monastery perched atop a single vertical rock. A bridge gapped this rock and the side of a nearby mountain. We would fly over the bridge while being machine-gunned and would drop grenades and generally make it look like we were raising havoc. The terrorists would also make it look like they were raising havoc with us, which the fake explosions sometimes did.

"The pinnacle was the place where we spent many a day. One thousand feet straight down on all sides, slightly rounded on top, with barely enough room to land a helicopter and have four kites set up, the pinnacle was the hell of hang gliding. If you fell in any direction, you could roll off the edge. If you sat down anywhere, a scorpion would climb out of the rock you were sitting on. If you stood up in the shadeless one-hundred-degree heat you would tire in twenty minutes.

"This was the highest peak overlooking the monastery, and was the theoretical launching point of the rescue party of hang glider pilots. Supposedly, we mountain climbed our way to the top with ropes and our kites. It was right in the middle of the biggest thermal generators in miles. Huge thunderheads formed most afternoons, and the winds were nothing short of treacherous. Our flight path to the monastery from this point led through a row of other rocks which looked like shark's teeth. The gaps, as we called them, were less than seventy-five feet across and were subject to terrific turbulence. We had to have almost absolute calm to fly through the gaps safely. At times, in perfect weather, we got as many as three kites abreast through the gaps with a helicopter buzzing around us.

"Once we were through the gaps, the worst still lay ahead. The landing area was in a very small box canyon, so that any way the wind blew, it blew turbulence. To make things harder still, the landing field was only big enough for one kite at a time, so when more than one flew, the others had to land on a road with a bank on one side and a cliff on the other. The road dropped away in one direction right at our glide angle and the other direction was usually downwind. The box canyon was too tight for much maneuvering, so the land-

The pinnacles . . . (Chris Wills)

Through the gaps. (Betty-Jo Wills)

The Mad, Magical, Many-Sided World of Hang Gliding

ing had to be judged perfectly. With three kites and a helicopter in the air at once, it was scary.

"With this kind of flying to contend with, we spent many long days sitting on top of the pinnacle waiting for the right weather. We became masters at backgammon.

"We did have one consolation if we should miss the landing area—there were nice soft bushes everywhere. The only problem was the nice soft bushes had two-inch sharpened thorns. You might think maybe one variety of bush had thorns. This was not the case. ALL the bushes had thorns. Even the house plants had thorns. In fact, Chris Price asked a local why all the bushes had thorns, and the man answered in surprise, 'You mean the bushes in California don't have thorns?'

"On one occasion we were preparing to throw a dummy off the pinnacle rigged in a kite so the kite would fly at first and then go into a screaming dive. The road to the monastery had been blocked as usual when we were filming, so a large number of tour buses were stuck at the bottom. The tourists were informed that hang gliding was taking place, but were not told about the crash or the dummy. The dummy in the kite did as was expected and crashed into the ground with a tremendous impact. The road was then opened and everybody in the film crew left to film another scene. The tourists must have been shocked to see that nobody went to help the 'pilot.' Later we talked to one French gentleman who said, when asked about the flight, that it looked perfectly normal to him. He said all the hang-glider pilots he had seen in France landed like that every time.

"Since the script called for actors flying hang gliders, and since none of the actors were trained to fly hang gliders, we needed to find some way to get shots of the actors' faces while they 'flew.' This was accomplished with a crane.

"From the very beginning we had insisted that the only way to get pictures of actors in hang gliders was to teach them to fly. For a while it looked like we'd get our way, since all the actors were willing and able, and the producers were mildly sympathetic to our cries for realism. In the end, the production insurance company won the battle, and it was decided the only way the actors would fly was firmly attached to a crane. Thus the actors would be perfectly safe—or so they thought.

"The set designer went out and rented a crane big enough to lift a Sherman tank, and we set about testing it. We rigged a Swallowtail so that it was attached to the crane by a bracket under the king-post bracket, connected to a lead cable which looped over the thousand-pound hook of the crane. We then spent a day driving the crane to an area with a suitable backdrop.

"The crane operator did not speak English and we did not speak Greek, so we spent lots of time arguing with him over what to do first. For all we knew,

The crane "flys" the glider. (Chris Wills)

James Coburn rides the crane. (Chris Wills)

92 **The Mad, Magical, Many-Sided World of Hang Gliding**

we could have been agreeing with him! Finally someone yelled 'Shut up,' and we used sign language to get him to go to the cab and lift the kite up.

"I sat in the swing seat as the crane lifted me twenty feet in the air and started to turn in a huge circle to try to fill the sail. The first part of the turn was downwind and did not do the job. As I came around into the wind, the sail started to fill. Suddenly the sail was not only filling, but the kite was also flying. Just as I climbed the twenty feet to smash into the three-thousand-pound hook, we were going crosswind again, so I was no longer flying. I then dropped the twenty feet I had gained and smashed to a stop at the end of the slack in the lead cable. About this time the crane operator started to realize my wildly flapping arms did not mean to keep going. He could not hear my screams of terror over the noise of the crane. As he lowered me to the ground, I knew I would never again be strapped to a hang glider on a crane.

"Since the set designer wanted to try one more test with a little more speed, and since *my* career as a crane pilot was over, we went over to a Greek gopher who also had not heard my screams of terror over the crane noise. Smiling broadly, the set decorator and I motioned how much fun it would be for the gopher to try our fun ride. He must have interpreted my wild arm motions as signals of delight, and he readily strapped himself to the swing seat. After two revolutions of similar back-breaking 'fun,' he was also lowered to the ground and hobbled off smiling, since this is what he thought I had done. At this point, I decided the crane would never work—just as the production people decided it was perfect.

"The crane was then driven the five hours from Athens to the crane location near the pinnacles of Kalambaka, where we spent a week with the actors helping them fly, one by one, on the crane. Since it was only possible to film them on the small part of the revolution when they were going directly into the wind, they'd have to go round and round in circles for hours at a time to collect enough footage. It is hard to imagine how incredibly boring it all was.

"We flyers took turns on instruction duty, escaping whenever possible to fly for fun. One of our primary functions on crane duty was to decide when the actor's life was really in danger and when it was just possibly in danger, as was the case at all times. We had the right to stop the filming at any time if we thought it was too dangerous. At first we exercised this right with every revolution, but the production personnel decided that wouldn't work. In the end we were allowed this right only if the wind speed exceeded twenty mph or if the kite blew into the crane hard enough to possibly break it. On several occasions the actor was being blown about, twenty feet over our heads, listening to us argue with production about how he might be killed. Usually about then the actor inserted an opinion that was in agreement with ours, and they'd lower him down until the wind subsided.

The Mad, Magical, Many-Sided World of Hang Gliding 93

"Early in the filming we'd agreed to take several of the braver members of the production crew up tandem in our kites. Bob was the first to actually do it, and as soon as the passenger landed, word spread throughout the crew that it was the most fun thing you could do and seemed safe enough. From this point on, we were literally swamped with requests to fly tandem. Every day after work we would go up to the thousand-foot pinnacle overlooking the hotel and fly members of the crew and cast tandem until it was too dark to see. Almost every day we had more people ready to go than we had time to take up. Since we flew them from the spot where Roy Hooper had crashed, we called the takeoff point Hoop's Hop.

"After about a week, we had taken up all the actors except Coburn, Culp, and Susannah York. Coburn was excited to try it and was scheduled to fly with us the day after next. The following day MacGillivray and Freeman talked him into actually hanging on the skid of one of the helicopters and flying around at two thousand feet while they filmed him. When the film came back, the insurance company won another battle and it was decided that he could not fly in the kite. We protested, saying we would sneak him off to do it anyway, and nobody would know. They argued that sneaking off still counted, so we couldn't do it. They won.

"As time went on, we began to take up almost anybody who wanted to try, but Chris Price carried it a little too far. He decided to take up the Greek headwaiter who served us breakfast, lunch, and dinner at the hotel. Bob had taken up our Greek interpreter the day before, and she briefed the headwaiter on what to do. The headwaiter—whose English was confined to 'milk,' 'peas,' 'soup,' and other assorted food items, seemed ready to go. Price had no way of checking the man's level of enthusiasm, so he buckled the man in and started to run off the cliff. The waiter took three steps, sat down, skidded his feet along the ground like brakes, and pushed the bar all the way out. They were moving off the edge, so Price had no recourse other than to try to fly. They cleared the edge just as the kite totally stalled and ended up ten feet from the ledge, pointed straight at the ground. At this point the waiter pulled the bar all the way in and held on for dear life as they accelerated to about sixty—straight down. Chris Price tried pushing out, with little response, before he noticed the death grip the waiter had on the bar. He shouted, slugged the waiter, shoved out all the way, and pulled the kite out, just missing a jutting rock below. The rest of the flight was uneventful, but you could tell by the green tint of the waiter's complexion that he did not care to do it again.

"Chris Price seemed more excited about how long we were able to see the top of his sail than worried about his narrow escape from the protruding rock. The rest of us knew they'd been plain lucky, and soon thereafter the tandem rides stopped.

"About eight weeks into the filming, we had our second accident. Dix Roper was flying through the gap with two others and was assigned to land on the road. As he was landing, one of the typical gusts blew up the canyon. He was about twenty feet up, trying to mush the kite down on the road that dropped away right at his glide angle, when it hit him. Instantly it turned him ninety degrees to the right and slammed him into the bank on the uphill side. Since he was wearing painted-black tennis shoes (an integral part of any commando's high-temperature, high-protection outfit), he cracked his heel in the impact.

"Dix was in considerable pain, so we loaded him into the helicopter and took him to the same hospital where we'd taken Roy. The hospital could do no more for Dix than it did for Roy, so next day he was flown to Athens. His wife, Dee, went along, and next day we sent their six-year-old daughter, Tessa, by film car. A film car drove to Kalambaka every day to pick up the latest exposed film, take it to Athens to be processed, and bring it back on the next trip. The film-car drivers drove like maniacs, as did everyone else in Greece, and Tessa's ride was the occasion they picked to have a car wreck. Tessa was unhurt, but one of the other occupants had a heart attack, so she was taken to the hospital too. Tessa was transferred to another car.

"The production man who went to the hospital to check on the heart-attack victim was run into by a motorcycle rider on his way out of the hospital, and went right back in again as a patient.

"It took weeks to untangle the mess.

"When the movie came out, it was a good one. And in spite of our predictions, all the crane shots worked. We looked back on the Greek days as an incredible adventure, but none of us want to be away from home that long again. By the end we could have killed for a taco!"[56]

Though *Skyriders* was the first full-length feature film expressly about hang gliding, other movies had short flying bits.

Much earlier Bill Bennett had done a flying sequence for a James Bond movie; Anheuser-Busch had included hang gliders in its bicentennial film for Busch Gardens, *The Eagle Within* (using the cast from *Skyriders*); the Smithsonian Institution commissioned Greg MacGillivray and Jim Freeman, cinematographers for *Skyriders*, to produce a feature film *To Fly*, for the oversize screen at the Institution (Bob Wills did the hang gliding portion); and, wonder of wonders, hang gliding was finally shown in a television commercial! When Marina toilet paper moved to the sublime with a soaring hang glider, they elevated both hang gliders and bathroom tissue to new heights of respectability!

A PASSENGER THAT . . . BARKS?

Aberrations were bound to come to a sport which conventional aviationists themselves considered an aberration. Not content with merely flying hang gliders off mountains, some flyers had to find different ways of doing it. Men like Moyes and Bennett had themselves boat-towed on longer and longer lines until Bill Moyes finally towed to 4,750 feet over Lake Ellesmere behind a jet boat doing seventy miles an hour. He must have put the lid on rope towing then, because subsequent record flights involved balloons.

The first balloon-launched hang glider flight apparently was made by Bob Kennedy in 1970, over Lake Elsinore, California. Next Dave Kilbourne balloon-launched from 9,200 feet in 1971; other height lovers followed until, on November 22, 1976, Bob McCaffrey, an eighteen-year-old flyer, was dropped from a hot-air balloon at 31,600 feet, breaking the existing balloon-drop record by 7,000 feet! Gil Dodgen, present editor of *Hang Gliding*, notes, "With that, the balloon mania ended. Flyers would be getting into pressurized suits next, and they lost interest."

The largest number of hang gliders ever dropped during a single balloon launch was eight! *Hang Gliding* magazine reported, "The event was master-minded by associates of balloon builder George Stokes and Eipper-Formance, Inc."[57] In the summer of 1976, after much careful planning, eight Cumulus VB hang gliders were attached by cables to the world's largest hot-air balloon. The cables connected the kites' king posts to large triangular patches sewn on the balloon's equator. In their hands the pilots held stabilizer lines running to the balloon basket. The purpose of the lines was to keep the glider noses pointed away from the balloon's center, preventing a collision between gliders during launch. For additional safety, the gliders were hung at staggered levels.

With gliders and pilots attached, the balloon slowly climbed to altitude.

Spectators at Escape Country, California, were bedazzled as, four by four, the hang gliders released first their stabilizers, then their suspension lines, and flew smoothly away from the balloon.

The only bad moment came when a hang glider carrying a passenger immediately went into a dive past vertical, partially inflating the wing negatively. But it quickly recovered, "no doubt to the relief of pilot and passenger (on his first hang glider ride!)"[58]

It was in 1974 that engineer-inventor Douglas Malewicki, whose interest was motorcycles, approached Bob Wills with the idea of a flying motorcycle. Bob said later, "I'd often thought of putting a sail on a motorcycle, but now I had a reason for doing it." Together, Wills and Malewicki designed a sail and support mechanisms for Malewicki's motorcycle, and toward the end of '74, Bob

Historic balloon drop at Escape Country, California (*Hang Gliding* magazine)

finally tested the strange contraption. To the delight of onlookers at Mirage Desert, the cycle took off from a low ramp, soared briefly, and stayed airborne long enough to travel about one hundred feet.

Because Wills was a champion motorcycle rider in the days before his hang gliding, he was able to coax the motorcycle into longer and longer distances off the higher and higher ramps Malewicki kept building. The next year, after a falling-out between the two men, Wills put his higher-performing Swallowtail sail on his own motorcycle and, in spite of an injunction thrown at his feet by Malewicki's henchman moments earlier, rode the flying cycle to a record 323 feet! From that moment he was never allowed to fly it publicly again. Malewicki threatened Twentieth Century-Fox into abandoning footage of the fly-cycle, and when the various injunctions were finally lifted, after three years, it was too late. Bob Wills was dead, blown down by a filming helicopter.

It wasn't Burke Ewing, exactly, but a "friend" who made him one of the sport's oddities. Burke's specialty was tandem flight, but his passenger wasn't your usual two-legged Homo sapiens: He was a dog!

Bob Wills ready for motorcycle-kite jump at Mirage Dry Lake, California (Ulvis Alberts)

He's off . . . (The Wills Family Album)

98 **The Mad, Magical, Many-Sided World of Hang Gliding**

And higher . . . (The Wills Family Album)

(Ulvis Alberts)

Burke Ewing and friend. (Hugh Morton)

Curtis has earned the pilot badge around his neck. (Stephen McCarroll)

Burke never exactly intended to fly with friend Curtis, but the dog intended to fly with him, for he kept running down the hill every time Burke launched, chasing the glider frantically until it was clearly out of range. One day Curtis tumbled over a cliff and broke his leg. When his canine friend had healed, Burke made him a harness, and thereafter dog and master flew together. The dog took no time adjusting to flight; in fact, Burke says, "He leans and shifts his weight whenever I do." The dog rides on Burke's back, "and I can feel him, half-flying the kite!"

THE COMPETITIVE EDGE

The very first hang gliding competition, as Willi Muller described it, got right down to the basics. In 1972 two men in Kelowna, Canada, flying from a ski launch, declared themselves the World's First Snow-Kite Championships. No one disputed them. They were, after all, judge, jury, and sole adversaries. As far as anyone knows, they were pilots numbers one and two in the universe.

It wasn't one of your hotly disputed events.

Competitions have changed since then, but it took time. The very next year a second competition was held at the "old Kelowna site," and this time there were perhaps fifteen times as many contestants. The event was won by Bob Wills, not so much for having swept it in any formal way, some claim, but more because he demonstrated with tricks, stunts, and tandem rides that he was the best pilot there.

Along the way the exact points seem to have become obscured.

But Bob brought home what may be hang gliding's biggest trophy, a multitiered extravagance crowned with a winged goddess supplicating toward heaven. "People kept doing double takes when I carried it through the airport," Bob reported, "and the stewardess couldn't think where else to put it, so she gave it its own seat on the plane." Bob also won a barrel of wine and five hundred dollars. Such exorbitant winnings would not be seen again in hang gliding for three or four years.

That second Kelowna meet had both towed and free-flight portions, and it was during the free flights that a most bizarre event transpired. Dick Eipper—one of hang gliding's earliest pioneers—was ready to launch, and as Willi Muller describes it, "He stood there with long hair and a Fu Manchu type beard, thin and scraggly."

The temperature was twenty degrees below zero. Dick Eipper, waiting at the top on his skis, held above his head an aluminum-frame Rogallo with a plastic sail.

Finally he pushed off, and as he came skiing down the hill—going faster and faster, yet not quite flying—the spectators suddenly heard a gigantic "CRACK," and looking up, they saw Eipper's sail part like a fat weight lifter's pants and the two parts rise straight toward the skies on either side of him.

But by now Eipper was well under way. The frame was in his hands, the skis on his feet, the sail formed into a sort of flapping windscreen on either side of his head. Even to the most naive, his prospects of flying had suddenly dropped to zero—but what was he to do with this thing in his hands?

Nothing, apparently. For he came on, clinging to his worthless apparatus, while down below the spectators became convulsed. He skied the entire way with the skeletal remains in his hands and the defunct sail boxing him on the ears. He never left the ground!

Eight years later, Willi Muller still considers it one of the funniest sights he's ever seen. He also says, "It was the last time a plastic sail was ever seen in a competition."

By 1974, 127 people attended the Kelowna Championships, and Willi Muller hired a Greyhound bus to transport his twenty competitors.

Competitions were held with increasing frequency, and new events

Bob Wills, lined up for the bull's-eye. (© George Uveges, 1981)

.. and in—without shoes, of course. (© George Uveges, 1981)

The Mad, Magical, Many-Sided World of Hang Gliding 103

Dean Tanji and fellow flyer at the U.S. Nationals in Heavenor, Oklahoma. (© Bettina Gray)

The Mad, Magical, Many-Sided World of Hang Gliding

sprang to life every year: The first World Meet at Escape Country, California. A year later, the first Aerial Ballet at the World Meet. The first Telluride meet in Colorado. The first Masters at Grandfather Mountain, North Carolina. The yearly United States championships. The first international meet in Kossen, Austria. State and local meets everywhere.

But as the meets proliferated, pilots grew increasingly critical of the whole competition scene. More and more, winning a meet seemed dependent on luck instead of skill, with weather the capricious deciding factor. The wind, it seemed, was always "wrong for me and perfect for you."

Dean Tanji, a flyer-businessman who has competed in most of the major United States competitions since 1974, and whose consistently high placements seem to belie a luck factor, nevertheless says, "Hang gliding has always required a lot of luck for the consistent winner. I don't think there's ever been a consistent winner in *all* the different types of contests. Contests have been anything from bomb drops—which demonstrate no flying skills—to something like the Owens Valley, which requires the best cross-country flying. Between these two extremes are hundreds of different types of contests. And in the majority of them, I'd say ninety-five percent of them are mostly luck. Maybe some opportunity. And the rest skill."

Though Dean Tanji accepts luck—or the lack of it—as one of the facts of competing, other pilots have found the luck factor galling. Among the complainers, Chris Price was perhaps the most vocal. He decided ultimately that

Tom Peghiny flys in 1976 World Meet, Escape Country, California (W. A. Allen)

Start of a cross-country task, British Hang Gliding League in the Yorkshire Dales, May 1980 (© Bettina Gray)

The Mad, Magical, Many-Sided World of Hang Gliding

the only fair means of determining the one best pilot in any event was to have multiple eliminations where pilots flew one-on-one—two men leaving the hill at the same moment and thus flying in identical weather conditions. Ideally they would be scored only against each other.

Price fought long and steadily for the kind of meets he envisioned, and in 1980 he was elected to run the Southern California Regionals, which Dean Tanji called "probably the best competition I've ever seen. I think it was one of the top small meets—whether anybody realized it or not. It was along the lines of the Owens Valley Classic. Here we had pretty close to eighty or ninety of the most competent flyers, flying a one-on-one task, over twelve miles. Going anywhere from four or five thousand feet above takeoff to ten, twelve feet above the terrain, and completing the course in a little over half an hour. And we had competition on *that* level, flying every day for two weeks. But there was only one task, and it was designed so that you had a winner and a loser, no matter what the conditions were—on any flyable conditions, from a no-wind to a twenty-five-mile-an-hour gale. The task was flexible enough to accommodate the full situation."

Dean Tanji did not finish well in this competition; he had been too busy to do much practicing. From his usual position in the top five or ten he dropped to number nineteen.

Yet from Tanji, Chris Price drew the ultimate praise—a loser lauding the contest which has just done him in. "Next time," Tanji added, "I'm going to be prepared."

In the Owens Valley in July 1980, a competition was held which represented the highest aspirations of hang glider pilots for the next decade. As such, it belongs in a later chapter, because the meet clearly looks ahead.

THE WING BECOMES A BIRD

The inevitable happened. Hang gliding changed . . . and then changed some more. The chunky little triangles of its earliest days were no longer seen. The "standard" was dead—long dead. In its evolution, even the name changed. In the beginning everyone called hang gliders "kites." In the end it was a mark of being out of it to do so. Subtly, around 1976, the accepted word became *glider.*

Perhaps it was just as well; the new gliders hardly resembled the old kites. The things were wider now, and thinner. They had spread, and spread more, until those that sported scalloped edges became the wings of eagles.

Francis Rogallo could have predicted it. "When the hang glider people started, they started with these very simple types, which we also had started

On the wings of an eagle—Bob Wills. (Stephen McCarroll)

The Mad, Magical, Many-Sided World of Hang Gliding

World Cup, Grenoble, France—
Nisaino Mitsuo. (© Bettina Gray)

with. But we had done experiments and published reports on a full range of aspect ratios. We had some very high performance wings."

It was perhaps lucky that the hang gliding industry repeated Rogallo's steps, else they might have arrived too early at a level of performance no one was equipped to handle. For those killed in bewildering '74, the sport had already moved too fast.

THE LAST OF THE "KIDS' STUFF" IMAGE

The sport was a grown man. It had a deep voice and it shaved. It was treated with respect. No longer was there talk of punishing it, of sending it off to its room. Or sending it away altogether. Hang gliding was master of its own destiny, in control of its affairs.

The sport was self-regulating. The rules it made for itself were respected. It monitored its own, decided who could fly and where, who could teach and in what manner. It set up standards and expected its manufacturers and flyers to live up to them.

Because of these things hang gliding became safer. In fact, its outstanding achievement was its improved safety record. The year 1979 was the safest one since 1973, considering increased participation. Only 1975, with an identical fatality rate of forty-six deaths worldwide came close to 1979. Yet the sport's participation was perhaps three times greater in 1979!

Rich Grigsby, a trim, soft-spoken man who is one of hang gliding's most respected flyers and teachers (and an early editor of *Ground Skimmer*) notes, "Instruction in the past four years has developed rapidly to the point . . . well, as an example, in our school . . . we've taught approximately thirty-five hundred students how to fly and we've had no significant injuries except one that occurred about two days ago. Now these students . . . not all of them have continued. But the ones who *have* continued went on to fly at the intermediate levels and advanced safely. There were no subsequent accidents—even after the learning period."

Grigsby defines the reasons clearly: "Two major reasons for the accident rate going down are the HGMA [Hang Glider Manufacturer's Association], which forced manufacturers to design better gliders, and the great instructional program, which has meant certified instructors and that sort of thing."

Chris Price—who by hang gliding's standards is now an old-timer, one of the few flyers left from the 1972 days—echoes Grigsby's observations: "There are a number of instructors now that train you . . . and Ken de Russy is one of them. Ken de Russy [a long-time flyer with his own school in Santa Barbara, California] trains his students so that from the very first time on the hill they have a successful flight. He *never* lets his students crash, through the whole training experience. At the same time, he fills them with caution. De Russy is probably one of the best, if not *the* best instructor there is.

"In that way these people are learning to fly in a totally different way than we did. There's no trial and error involved. They're all programmed, practically, to become successful pilots; and then finally, when they're out on their own and can start experimenting, they know the parameters, so they do it safely.

"As late as 1978 there were still an awful lot of people crashing on the training hill, breaking gliders, but it just doesn't happen any more. They've got it all figured out. You can go out and just learn, learn, learn, and the instructors know—maybe it's because they've had so many students—but they *know* how to keep the slowest student from crashing as well as the guy that has no respect—the guy that wants to go really fast—from crashing.

"It's totally different than when I was training." He laughs, thinking back to 1973. "Then, every other student crashed on his first flight. We didn't have any idea. We thought crashing was just part of learning." (Price himself even said, years ago, "I always let my students crash. *Then* they will pay attention!" But his attitudes have matured with the sport.) "Nobody crashes now. They just don't."

He pauses reflectively. "There still are a number of instructors out there, though, I'd say fifty percent, that *do* let their students crash, and there's just no need for it. So it's up to the student to get a hold of these teachers—the right ones. They should know to look *very* carefully for an instructor—check how

Beginning student reaches elevation. (Ken de Russy and Bonnie Nelson)

many years he's been doing it, and just ask him how many broken legs and arms has he had. After training for five or six years, the instructors have learned, through trial and error, how to train people without hurting them."

Chris Price, in fact, has a concern that might surprise a lot of people. The sport has changed so much, he feels, that the peril to its future lies in quite a different direction. Its very image of safety can lull pilots into false security. "It's kind of like putting your head in the sand. Joe Blow stands up in front of his classes and says that he could never get killed in a hang glider. He might break a leg someday, but that's all. And I think that's an underlying problem. I think what you have to do is convince people that it's OK to *do* this sport even though you *can* get killed at it. I think that this is not a good enough reason *not* to do it. You can get killed in cars, too, but that's no reason not to drive.

"There's a very high turnover in hang gliding. It's unbelievably high. People get into it, they take a couple high flights, they start to learn how to thermal and quit.

"What is happening, then, is people that have been in the sport for about a year and a half, two years, get into some bad turbulence or have a scare, and then they realize how easy it is to get hurt—how easy it would have been to get killed as they were learning. Then they quit, because they're scared."

Strong grip . . . and soft landing. (Ken de Russy and Bonnie Nelson)

Price deplores the turnover, which takes pilots out of the sport just as they're becoming expert. "If there are more better pilots out there, it's going to force *me* to be a better pilot, and that's what I'm in the sport for—to be a good pilot."

SAFETY TO THE FORE

Parachutes.

Certified gliders.

Factory test-flying of all production gliders.

Certified instructors.

The industry groped for each of these, hesitantly at first, and found itself rebuffed. "Who needs parachutes?" people scoffed. "You don't get into trouble till you're practically on the ground!"

But this wasn't always the case. Pilots *did* get into trouble thousands of feet up. Hang gliders came apart in severe turbulence. Midair collisions occurred. Gliders failed aerodynamically.

Suddenly, when a couple of lives were saved by parachutes, the mocking voices grew quieter. Now almost everyone wears a parachute. And though

Note parachute, front of Ken de Russy's harness, and variometer on control bar. (Ken de Russy and Bonnie Nelson)

cold statistics are missing (who keeps track of all the near misses?), among fifteen of hang gliding's better-known flyers, the consensus is that parachutes are one of the most important developments in the sport.

Pete Brock states it categorically: "I think that parachutes in general have pretty well saved hang gliding. Over here, we've saved at least thirty people, and from talking with the Europeans I know that on some weekends they have three and four parachute deployments a day!"

Certification of gliders, first required back in 1977, meant tough new standards. Manufacturers grumbled. It was a costly process, certifying a glider. It meant purchasing several cameras, testing rigs, measuring devices, big and powerful cars with testing towers.

It meant deliberately destroying thousand-dollar gliders. Sometimes it even meant risking the test pilot's life.

Yet the certification process pointed up weaknesses, highlighted what might have been fatal design flaws.

Has it been worth it?

Most pilots would shout a resounding "You bet!"

In the last two years only one certified glider is known to have been in-

Glider undergoing positive-loads test to find out the number of g forces the design will withstand. Note the glider, badly distorted and near failure. (Wills Wing, Inc.)

volved in either a turbulence-induced mishap or structural failure. The glider in question was doing radical whip stalls and broke only after it slipped onto its back and the pilot crashed into the keel. Yet the pilot spun into the ground and walked away.

Chris Price says, "The HGMA's standards seem to be working well. The gliders *aren't* breaking in midair like they used to. Someday they'll figure out that these standards weren't strict enough."

When asked if that isolated failure didn't prove adequate standards now, Price hesitated, than argued, "Well, you *can't* say that, and I'll tell you why. I made a statement in a letter to *Hang Gliding* magazine saying gliders were virtually tuck- and tumble-proof. And yet we *know* they can be broken in flight if you do certain things. And if you fly in the wrong conditions. You don't want pilots thinking they're indestructible when they aren't.

"Eventually the weakest part of the airplane will be the pilot himself; he will pass out from too many g's or break his body by hitting the glider before the glider breaks.

"I think that's where the HGMA will take these things. Because the turbulence the pilots fly in sometimes just takes the glider and tumbles it. In fact, supposedly in a recent meet some guy tumbled twice and didn't hurt the glider one bit. He tumbled once, and was trying to figure out what happened when he tumbled again, and *then* he realized what had happened because the second tumble was definitely a tumble and it was just like the first.

"But the image the sport had in the beginning, of gliders falling apart and tumbling to the ground . . . the new gliders, the last two years, that just isn't happening."

Factory test-flying of all production gliders came hard. Right from the beginning, a few manufacturers test-flew routinely, at great cost in time and money: Every hang glider went out to a hill to be flown before it was shipped.

But most companies resisted. Their dealers checked and test-flew their gliders, they said. Spot-checking in the factory was enough. Yet the companies who test-flew every glider knew it wasn't enough. Human beings put gliders together and human beings made mistakes. Small mistakes, perhaps, but did the industry want human lives at risk on small mistakes?

A battle began. The companies who test-flew regularly insisted that *all* companies ought to share the expense. The companies who didn't felt that unreasonable demands were being forced on them. For perhaps three years it was a hot and bitter issue among manufacturers. To support the resisting companies, no one could prove nonfactory-flown gliders had actually caused accidents.

Letters, accusations, and quarrels disrupted the Hang Glider Manufacturer's Association. In the end the protracted struggle culminated in a requirement for factory test-flying of all gliders.

Most of the buying public never knew the difference. But the exceptional hang glider integrity record of the last few years must be due in part to industry-wide test-flying.

There was no such struggle over the certification of schools and instructors. Schools such as Chandelle, in San Francisco, found themselves teaching under close public scrutiny even in the early days, and co-owner Jan Case, among others, led a move to legitimize what they were doing.

In increasing numbers, partly as a matter of survival, hang gliding schools sent their members to classes to learn the latest methods for teaching flyers. More and more, schools proudly proclaimed that their teachers were certified.

Even without public pressure, professionalism in teaching was sought almost from the beginning. Out on the hill the drama of failure was all too clear: Nobody wanted any part of anguish-laden trips to the hospital.

By itself, without government regulation—without FAA intervention—the hang gliding industry got its act together and imposed its own strict standards. On itself!

UP THERE WITH THE BIG BOYS

"Never fly higher than you care to fall" is an old hang gliding cliché—as out-dated and laughable as: If men were meant to fly, God would have given them wings. Even pilots who once stayed within a few hundred feet of the ground hardly consider themselves flying any more unless their altitude is measured in *thousands* of feet.

Flights in the regions above ten thousand feet have become common-place. Twenty thousand feet may be rarer, but it happens. Hang gliders fly so routinely in the national airspace that when they are sometimes called air-planes, nobody contradicts.

Tracy Knauss, publisher of *Glider Rider*, says, "We are interfacing today with regular aviation. Right now I can show you a picture of a hang glider above an airliner. We're really *up* there.

"In the beginning the FAA said, in effect, 'We'll turn our backs as long as you're gliding down the hill . . . we don't care. But when you get up a couple of thousand feet you're in the national airspace, where other aircraft have to obey our rules.'

"The federal government's concern isn't really that we're in the airspace, it's the knowledge of the user, they call it. How did he get that knowledge, and how is it tested? Do hang glider pilots really know that eighteen hundred feet and above is federal airspace? Do they know where the restricted areas are?

"They just wanta make sure because they're charged with protecting the public safety.

"Pilots need to know the applicable FAR—Federal Aviation Regulations —ninety-one, subpart B, pertaining to the airspace they fly in. It has to do with controlled areas, restricted areas . . . in fact, most of the rules that pertain to hang gliders.

"The USHGA has just incorporated these regulations in the Pilot Pro-ficiency Ratings. Hang ratings have become Pilot Proficiency Ratings now."

And so hang gliding, in its new, sophisticated era, has gone beyond its earlier lessons. Not so long ago the industry regarded itself as remarkably mature with its Hang Badge pilot-rating system. But Hang Badges are no longer good enough. They're kid stuff.

The Pilot Proficiency Ratings, implying a sort of FAA seal of approval, are both awesome and necessary, and one way of bringing hang gliders into conformity with airplanes—which, some think, they almost are!

ROYAL RECOGNITION

As hang gliding's safety record has improved, so has its image in the outside world. Chris Price says, "I think the sport's coming along just fine. And I think that the public is accepting it. The Forest Service is accepting it. It's becoming a legitimate, reasonable pastime for people who want to do it."

Gil Dodgen, editor of *Hang Gliding* magazine, and Tracy Knauss, publisher of the monthly newspaper *Glider Rider*, have both brought a sense of hang gliding's new professionalism to their readers. Partly because of them, and partly because advertisers and story writers have chosen to show hang gliders increasingly on television, hang gliding has become a household word. No longer do people call it "hand" gliding. No longer do they stare uncomprehendingly when the subject comes up, or roll their eyes and say, "But isn't that *dangerous?*" Risks, as in scuba diving or skiing, are assumed, but are no longer paramount in everyone's mind.

Increasingly, cities, counties, the National Park System have given first, grudging acceptance of, and finally, active support to flyers. Jan Case says, "The National Park Service built a beautiful observation deck at Fort Funston, California, for spectators. Now, one thousand to two thousand people per day visit on summer weekends." She adds, "Rich Romero, the forest ranger at Glacier Point, Yosemite, can be contacted for flying there. He is the professional hang gliding ranger."[59]

The contrast with an earlier time is laughable.

A few years ago, the few pilots who dared fly in Yosemite made a point of folding their kites the minute they landed and fading into the forest. They knew the rangers would be stalking them like game. At that time Yosemite wanted nothing to do with hang gliding.

In 1979 hang gliding had its first intercollegiate meet in Massachusetts, with twelve participating schools, and the second American Cup meet, which introduced the concept of an international meet with team championships. Of this meet, Tracy Knauss says, "The British team beat the Americans at their own game, and Michael Jones wrote an editorial called, 'The Grand Illusion.' Here we thought we were the prima nation in hang gliding. All of a sudden the British come over here and beat us because they were *organized.*

"After the victory the British were presented the Cup of Wales by Prince Charles, as the highest award for sports aviation in Great Britain." Tracy Knauss's voice grows solemn. "Here it was—official recognition, royal recognition, by one of the most conservative elements in the entire world."

"AFTER A GOOD FLIGHT SHE RADIATES BEAUTY"

From Donnita Holland Kilbourne to the present. It's a long way.

An enormous jump. For months, perhaps a year, Donnita Kilbourne stood alone, the only woman flying hang gliders. Gradually, girls began trying the sport, but rarely successfully. Their injury rate was high, higher than the men's.

The Women's Competition group in the Southern California Regionals. Flyers (top row, left to right) Teri Mynahan, Elaine Chandler, Nadine Malcolm; (bottom) Teri Hughes, Lynn Miller, Cyndee Moore, Page Pfeiffer. (© Bettina Gray)

Early teachers like Bob Wills, Chris Price, and Chris Wills soon became wary of trying to teach girls. "They break too easily," the three complained. In exasperation, Chris Price exploded one day, "I'm *never* going to teach a girl again. Unless *she* wants to do it. No more girls egged on by guys. It just never works. They never succeed, and I'm just wasting my time."

But women—ever patient—*did* succeed, though it took longer. The highly motivated girls learned to fly, and gradually some of them caught up with the men. Carol Price, now Chris Price's wife, was the first person in history to fly off lofty El Capitan in Yosemite.

Women began entering hang gliding meets, and though they rarely won, some are now doing well.

Women today are not only flying in great numbers, they have also formed teams of professionals who travel about the world, fly in competitions, and expect no special favors from men. They carry their own gliders, climb the same hills, take the same risks.

Liz Sharp. (James H. Sharp)

In an early eighties issue of *Hang Gliding* magazine, Carol Price interviewed three of her fellow women pilots, Page Pfeiffer, Liz Sharp, and Katie Miller. Their views on themselves and their chosen sport reveal both a determination to be on an equal footing with men and a realistic appraisal of the special difficulties women face.

When asked whether hang gliding is harder for girls to learn, Liz Sharp said she thought it was, "Mostly because of the physical problem. From the very beginning most of the fellows can manhandle the glider and make it do what they want with sheer muscle power. The girls just don't have that muscle power."

Katie said, "I agree. It's definitely harder for a girl to learn. For one thing, the glider's harder to ground handle and I think a girl usually has a harder time figuring out how to let the wind help her."

But Page, who holds three women's world records, and once biked up the steep Ortega Mountains every night for a whole summer to get in shape for ski racing (she won the nationals), feels that a good conditioning program

Page Pfeiffer. (Carol Boenish Price)

helps. She is willing to do pushups and pull-ups on a bar, run, and ride her bike. Most girls would shy away from such rigorous preparation. Still, Page sees the women's physical inferiority ending in the air. "Maybe a woman would have more trouble ground handling the glider, but remember, that's not flying. It's not hard to launch because once you're running, the sail fills with air and the glider is not heavy. Once you're flying it makes no difference whether the pilot is male or female."

Liz says, "Girls can gain strength by carrying their own gliders back up the hill every time. Sometimes you think you don't really need much strength at all to fly, but after you've been in the air for a couple of hours there will be times when you wish you had more strength."

Page: "You can't generalize about women. . . . There are weak guys and strong girls. You have to realize that some women are in great shape, and hang gliding is not hard for them at all."

Katie: "More than being physically harder, I think it's psychologically harder for girls to learn. The hardest thing for a girl is to get the nerve to run as hard as she can and not know if the wind is going to lift her up or if she's going to plow into the ground. Guys play tackle football and are used to falling on the ground."

Katie Miller. (Carol Boenish Price)

When asked if women will be serious competitors, Liz answered, "Definitely. I think that with enough experience they can be. Most of the really competitive guys·have been flying five or six years. In a few years the girls will have that much experience. . . ."

Liz: "At this point girls aren't as good pilots as men . . . but in a few years I think that will change."

Page: "The only reason there aren't more women in the sport is that it's so dirty. That's the part I don't like about it. You're out in the hot sun, sweating in the dirt. I think that most women want to look nice, and you just don't when you're hang gliding. The dirt and the sweat—the circumstances, not the flying itself—are what scares girls away. Have you ever noticed that there's never a place to go to the bathroom when you're flying? You always have to go in the bushes . . . very unladylike."

Liz: "However, what Cyndee Moore said in her article is so true. She said something to the effect that a woman doesn't have to go to a beauty parlor after a good flight. She just radiates beauty."

Page: "But until they fly, they don't know that. They just see all the dirt." She adds, "One thing about competition, though, is that if women had their own separate category, I think it would entice them to compete. In ninety-nine percent of other sports, women are in a different category than men. But then there's the problem that there are too few women to put in a separate group."

When asked what they thought about competition and tournaments, all three women agreed that the main point of flying was fun; that when competitions got too serious or ugly, the fun of flying was lost.

Page described what it was like to fly distance. She says, "I've flown over fifty miles twice. Getting really high is a great experience. It was so beautiful and exciting: crossing canyons, going forever, the scenery keeps changing. I kept getting farther and farther away from takeoff, from familiar territory. It's sure a bummer getting back, though!

"Cross-country is much more challenging and grueling than anything I'd done before. You go through all these changes in temperature. The valley below is very hot. But when you're at eighteen thousand feet, it's very cold, so that even though I had on a down jacket, ski pants, and ski gloves, my hands got frozen. One time I lost a lot of altitude after takeoff, and until I gained altitude I was sweating in my down clothes. It drains you! Then I got up to sixteen thousand feet on the same flight and I was freezing. Then when I finally landed, it was really hot all over again. I was exhausted. I ripped those clothes off down to my bathing suit. And then I waited an incredible length of time to be picked up. I landed around three o'clock in the afternoon and was not picked up until nine o'clock in the evening. And there I was in the desert with no shade but my hang glider and it was one hundred degrees!"

The three were asked what hang gliding meant to them. Liz called it "a freedom I've never known before, an independence that I've always wanted to have and still don't have yet—but hang gliding is giving me a means to work toward it."

Camera mount on kite shows Liz Sharp flying over Telluride. (LeRoy Grannis)

Cyndee Moore places second, Grouse Mountain, 1980. (© Bettina Gray)

Katie: "Hang gliding is my livelihood. It's very important to me. [She and her husband own one of the largest hang gliding schools in the United States.] Also, flying is about the only time I have to myself. It's peaceful and relaxing. I get uptight when I haven't flown for a couple of weeks."

Page: "To me, hang gliding is just another sport. It's fun and it's the best kind of flying. You're not cooped up in a cockpit; you're really out there."

Liz seemed to echo Chris Price's earlier assessment that dedication is perhaps the deciding factor for women flyers. "A woman starting out in hang gliding should go as far off on her own as possible to learn. It's very important for a woman, especially, to make this decision and do it on her own. It might mean ten minutes carrying the glider up for a ten-second flight down. But in those ten minutes she's learning an awful lot about ground handling the glider. And when a girl has become a competent flyer, all under her own desire and work, she'll feel an accomplishment she may never have felt before and be well on her way to becoming the master of her own destiny."[60]

FROM BUTTERFLIES TO HORNETS

With his usual grin and a slight air of apology, Bill Bennett brought the first engine to hang gliding. The flyer wore it on his back—a noisy, inefficient thing that seemed to do more toward polluting the atmosphere and creating a racket than adding much to the sport.

In California, hang glider pilots quickly rejected Bill's Power Packs. They weren't needed with so many hills around, and anyway, most flyers found them a kind of antithesis to what they went flying for—to escape into the silent upper regions away from noise and gas fumes.

The Mad, Magical, Many-Sided World of Hang Gliding 123

Three species of craft in 1980 Perris powered hang-gliding contest. (Ken de Russy)

After a while Bennett quietly withdrew his Power Packs, deciding to let others buck the world's resistance. Besides, motor development was costly.

Now power is back, and it's here to stay. Mockingly, flyers in hilly areas call powered hang gliders a rediscovery of the airplane, but Tracy Knauss rejects this viewpoint. He calls engines "one of the really big assets to the sport." He says, "There are many ways to look at power. We don't see it as re-creating the airplane. We see it as another means of getting *up*. Most of this country is flat land. Power is an offshoot of hang gliding. It's going to be a tremendously big market.

"You still have the purists in there; but you have to *drive* a car to the top of the hill . . . right? Why not fly to the top of the hill?

"Back in 1977 we started that special section in *Glider Rider* called 'Motor Glider.' In 1977 Trip Mellinger (a long-time, well-known flyer) flew his powered hang glider from the mainland of southern California to Catalina Island, about twenty-six miles. In August 1979 a coast-to-coast powered hang glider flight was one of the big stories. In fact, the growth of the powered ultralight movement was one of the big stories of the year.

"For a long time there's been a big controversy between the purists and the power people. It finally came to a head in February 1980. The leaders of the ultralight movement—meaning powered hang gliders—agreed to merge with the Experimental Aircraft Association."

Knauss chided the USHGA lightly for being slow to recognize the importance of powered hang gliders. "USHGA realized too late the far-reaching implications of power . . . and they've always been against it."

Eventually the USHGA amended its bylaws to include powered craft, but by then powered craft had voted to leave hang gliding.

The Experimental Aircraft Association held advantages for ultralights that the USHGA couldn't offer. As experimental craft, they enjoyed the benefits of their association's lobby in Washington. Knauss says, "There were indications of possible restrictive state legislation. We didn't want to come up with fifty different sets of state laws preventing powered ultralights from flying. So now, having joined EAA, it's possible there will be *no* restrictive state legislation."

Tracy Knauss may be right. The ultralights may have solved their problems within the United States.

But in July 1980 a powered hang glider landed in Canada, en route to an attempted flight across the Atlantic. The hoped-for destination was Greenland. The Canadians shot the project down like a pheasant from the skies. Peering at the fragile little craft, they concluded it in no wise resembled an airplane. It wasn't sturdy enough, fast enough, protected enough. Right then, the Canadians decided that no li'l ol' hang glider was going to take off from

Canadian soil and wander off across the ocean. Moreover, they wouldn't even allow it to fly over the desolate areas of Canada.

On its first big flight out of the nest, powered hang gliding got its wings clipped.

ON THE BACK OF AN ENVELOPE!

The news media went wild. The feat was acclaimed almost like Lindbergh's solo flight across the Atlantic. It had been thought impossible. Now somebody had done it: flown across the English Channel under his own power—by pedaling! As incredible as the task seems, the circumstances, which should have doomed the flight to failure, are even more incredible. But man prevailed over circumstance and the flight of the Gossamer Albatross became history.

Paul MacCready, the creator of the project, has always been intensely interested in everything aeronautical. In the early days of hang gliding MacCready was often on the slopes, just "hanging around." Jack Lambie's first meet found Paul quietly enjoying the spectacle, amused by the madcap flights, but skeptical—even after flying Taras Kiceniuk's Batso—that the Rogallos would ever amount to genuine flying machines. (It was MacCready who, a few years earlier, stretched out his arms, ran down the hill, and said to Richard Miller, "I went farther and stayed up longer *without* the Rogallo, Richard.")

Today, MacCready still finds aviation so exciting "that I wonder that anyone works in anything else."

With him it has always been thus. He earned a pilot's license at sixteen,

Dr. Paul MacCready, the designer of the Gossamer Albatross. (James Collinson/Black Star)

and was the nation's soaring champion in 1948, 1949, and 1953; at Cal Tech, where he earned a Ph.D. in aeronautics, his colleagues remember best the model airplanes he was forever sailing down the halls.

Paul MacCready, his wife and three sons fly hang gliders. The hang gliding world considers Dr. MacCready one of its own, and his incredible achievements with man-powered crafts are triumphs that seem more closely related to hang gliding than anything else.

Yet the craft aren't hang gliders; but they're not quite airplanes either, nor soaring gliders, nor for that matter—*anything* you've ever seen fly.

But listen to Paul MacCready's story. He tells it best.

"The Gossamer Condor," Paul MacCready begins, "is the one where all the real development and research took place. This whole project, in the middle of 1976, was for us the most singular event. At that time none of us who subsequently got involved had any inkling that we would become ensnared in such a happening.

"Suddenly we were embarked on a once-in-a-thousand-lifetimes sort of program. We just had a great time doing it, and it turns out that many other people have found the project fascinating. It's received much more interest and appreciation and honors than any of us had envisioned or that really seems appropriate.

"The most creative part of this project was not the technical aspect at all. It was the putting up of aviation's largest prizes by British industrialist Henry Kremer. Once he put up the prizes, it was inevitable that somebody was going to win sometime. Nobody was forcing him to put up the money. It was an unselfish, creative act, and it resurrected this old goal of mankind to fly on his own, under his own power.

"The first Kremer prize, fifty thousand pounds, was won by the Gossamer Condor in 1977 for the first sustained, controlled, human-powered flight. That's the human-powered flight analogue to the Wright brothers' flight in 1903.

"The next large aviation milestone—viewed as even greater than the Wright brothers' achievement over in Europe—was Bolario's flight across the English Channel in 1909. Henry Kremer's next prize was one hundred thousand pounds for the human-powered analogue to that flight. That's what the Gossamer Albatross did this past summer [1979].

"The next major milestone in aviation, viewed alike on both sides of the Atlantic, certainly, was Lindbergh's flight across the Atlantic."

MacCready spoke of his motivations for attempting the first flight—that he owed money and had promised to guarantee the debt of a relative. "We thought that perhaps one could win the prize quickly and economically." In addition, he spoke of a background that involved working with a variety of very lightweight model airplanes that flew well at slow speeds. One of his early models was, he said, "In many ways analagous to the big model that we finally made of the Gossamer Condor. Structurally, it's the same; it turns out that the stability and control of the Condor and Albatross were more analagous to that model than to an ordinary model or hang glider or a regular airplane.

"After some thinking, working on hang glider instruction techniques, doing calculations on how big things should be, our calculations said we should make the plane with at least a seventy-foot wingspan. Then it would be low enough in power so we could fly it.

"So we made a ninety-six-foot wingspan so there'd be a margin . . . we wouldn't need to have everything perfect. There could be a little extra weight, a little extra drag, and still you'd get by."

The first model, with its ninety-six-foot wings, was supported with piano wires. "The plane could fly at about seven miles an hour. It *could* take off with the pilot pedaling pretty hard, but usually you just shove it into the air, you walk along with the pilot—he's pedaling—you listen for the sound of the Mylar, and then you talk to the pilot.

"The first flight-testing was really pretty easy. If something went wrong you just grabbed the plane so it wouldn't get hurt; or if it *did* get hurt, it was very quick to repair. If it landed hard, kind of sliding sideways so the main vertical tube broke, you could tape on a broom handle with duct tape and be flying in about five minutes . . . literally. And then you'd fix it up a little better at night.

"It was not a very efficient plane in any way; it didn't have good stability and control, and the structure was poor, and it was so bad in all these respects that it made all the problems very obvious and truly was a better starting point than if we had had a better first plane that somewhat obscured those problems.

"This is what the competition was doing at the same time: A dozen groups around the world had for seventeen and a half years been working on planes that actually flew under the power of the pilot. But not for very long distances. And the planes could not turn. And worst of all, when they crashed, which would be quite often, they were just horrors to fix . . . maybe two thousand man-hours to repair a broken wing, something like this. It was pretty discouraging to groups that were doing them.

"It subsequently dawned on me that one of the greatest talents I had for the project was complete lack of experience in aircraft-structure design. Very seriously, that gave me an advantage. I could just start from scratch and do whatever seemed logical. Every one of those other groups had excellent credentials in aircraft structures—what they built *looked* like an airplane—and was not a very good answer for this kind of pioneering project. I can assure you I'd rather fly in a Boeing 747 designed by these people than something that *I* would come up with.

"We went through a lot of design changes, computer analyses, aerodynamics, the latest things, also some very crude model tests in water. One of the dominant factors was the apparent mass of air you had to accelerate—much larger than the mass of the airplane.

"We didn't quite know how to proceed. There were a lot of questions and no clear clues, but we changed quickly to the next generation of the Gossamer Condor: smaller wing tips, a little faster speed of the plane by covering the pilot and the fuselage part so that he would have less drag. The plane was getting up to nine and ten miles an hour instead of seven and eight. This plane worked very well, or rather well, right from the start. It took a five-minute flight, the longest flight ever made by a man-powered airplane. We thought we'd even try the Kremer prize flight, though we knew we weren't ready for it. But it would be a chance to get some of the logistics worked out.

"The plane wasn't turning well, but we thought we'd give it a try and did this. [He shows a picture of a crash.] Which is the sort of thing we went through a half a dozen times on the project. It looks like the plane is destroyed. Of course it's flying so slowly, and we always kept it low—never more than about fifteen feet. Nobody gets hurt on these things except for their dignity.

"The plane could be fixed in about twenty-four hours—we always took about a week to do it. We made a lot of changes in it, repaired it. And the things that broke at various times, we made them stronger. Some parts that were *not* broken in a long time, obviously they were overweight and overstrength.

"To make a long story short, a lot of development began falling in shape, and finally—on August 23, 1977—the Kremer prize flight. By this time the plane had gotten pretty tidy and was not taking too much power.

"Bryan Allen was able to get it around the Kremer course, and about five minutes after that we got over the final hurdle; when I say *we*, of course Bryan was doing the pumping. But what he said the moment he went over that T bar at the end was just instinctively, 'We did it!' And it's a good example of the team aspect of the whole program.

"After the Kremer prize flight, we could relax and have fun with the plane, and everybody got a chance to fly it, and all the relatives of everybody. My wife, Judy, took a try at it. It's a simple thing to do, you don't need to be a pilot or an athlete, and you still make a flight of a half minute or a minute, whatever you can do safely to save the airplane and protect its delicate wheels. The assistants would push you into the air, rather than have you take off yourself, and then you'd continue on, on your own, and it always worked safely. Every time the person landed, he or she always had a big grin on his face and wanted to do it again.

"A ten-year-old boy flies it, a sixty-year-old woman, and everything in between. About twenty-five different people flew it. It was a lot of fun.

Gossamer Albatross on a trial run. (*Hang Gliding* magazine)

"The plane then went to the National Air and Space Museum, where it's the biggest airplane in Washington. It's in wonderful company—the 1903 Wright brothers' plane, the Spirit of St. Louis. Nobody in the project had ever dreamt that this Gossamer Condor, this very crude, seventy-pound plane, was going to end up a permanent exhibit in the National Air and Space Museum.

"The negative side of this honor, of course, was that we no longer had an airplane to fly.

"I worked out one night what changes one could make in a new plane that we could quickly put together that would make an even better plane. It turned out that if you made the plane more carefully, better structure so that the wing surface could be smooth, cut the wing chord a bit, the plane would be so efficient that Bryan, instead of being able to fly about ten minutes in good weather, could fly for five hours, and ordinary nonathletes could perhaps fly it five or ten minutes. It seemed like it would be a lot of fun to do, but we were sort of lazy until we heard that Mr. Kremer announced a one-hundred-thousand-pound prize for flying across the English Channel!

"I'm sure he thought it was going to take another eighteen years to accomplish. But we already had the design, right on the back of this envelope! We really thought if the day was quiet, we could probably fly across to France, and then we're debating . . . should we bring it back on a boat, or just fly it back?

"So the Albatross program zoomed into high gear. But now all focus was on structures because there was no need to do any more probing on stability and control.

"We used carbon-filament tubing for the spar instead of aluminum; it's much stronger, much lighter. And the black parts on the ribs are also carbon, expanded polystyrene for the ribs. We used Kevlar string for bracing, expanded polystyrene foam for the leading edge, and Mylar, again, as the covering. But now a specialized kind which, when it's heat-treated, shrinks or tightens more one way than the other. The airfoil shape was a little better. A twenty-four-foot wing panel weighed six and a half pounds!

"The plane worked perfectly right off the bat; we knew it would, it was just a straight copy of the Gossamer Condor, a little bit cleaned up. Thirty-seven and one-quarter flying horsepower.

"If the flight for the one hundred thousand pounds had been for a twenty-two-mile flight right here at Schafter airport, we could have done it in the summer of 1978. But unfortunately the prize was for flight across a rather dangerous piece of water halfway around the world. It was going to take a lot of effort to do the project. Especially because this plane could *not* be taken apart. We had to do a lot of reworking on the wings and fuselage to make it so it could come apart to be put in the trailer. So we sought a sponsor, and somewhat to our surprise, we were able to get the DuPont Company. And talking about creative acts . . . they really were very farsighted and had some corporate guts to put their reputation on the line on such a peculiar project. We're still not sure quite how it all got arranged. But there is a book coming out on the Gossamer Condor and Gossamer Albatross program, written by Dr. Morton Grosser, and he's probing into every bit of background. I'm really looking forward to reading the book and finding out why . . ." MacCready's voice trailed away, and he grinned.

"The only thing they asked us to do in the whole program is put their little logos on the side. In every other way we did the project our way. They said you absolutely have to do it safely, but that's the way we were going to do it anyhow.

"We tested and tested that plane down in Terminal Island, trying to get it to break. I think we got it to break about four times, and were delighted to have it happen—to break here where it's safe rather than halfway across the English Channel.

"By this time Bryan Allen, the pilot, was so experienced in accidents that you can see . . . [he pointed to a picture] you can see his leg out of the airplane with his weight completely out before it hit . . . after a wire pulled out due to a defective fitting in the wings. . . . And so the spar broke. It was quickly fixed. We had to fix the fuselage, too; Bryan came out this side. The door was on the other side.

Bryan Allen. (*Hang Gliding* magazine)

"A lot of development went on. The plane was not flying as well as it had a year before because we added weight with all these accidents. And little bits of drag were added.

"But we finally cleaned it up. We put on a new propeller. We were then flying out of Harker Dry Lake, and Bryan did a one-hour-and-nine-minute flight in very calm conditions. He said he could have flown another three hours.

"We knew we were ready to go to England, so we packed up that plane and two backup planes.

"In England, the RAF graciously gave us a hangar and let us operate out of their air base at Manston, in the southeast part of England.

"We did a lot of training, practicing; really worked the engine hard, day after day. The exercise physiologist, Dr. Mastropaolo, forced Bryan to do a lot of the training in very uncomfortable conditions—no ventilation; hot, humid —because that's the way it was going to be on the flight across the Channel, as the plane didn't have very good cooling.

"The weather was bad day after day after day. Finally we got a weather forecast saying one chance out of six tomorrow would be good enough, and we figured we'd take it. Those odds were better than any we'd had before, and we felt there was no chance of the flight working successfully the first time. There are just so many unknowns that you'd stumble up against.

"So we used our first plane, which we considered expendable because it was not all that efficient; the main backup plane was much better—much better cooling, much less power required to fly it.

"So we used this one and we knew that Bryan—from all the tests we had done with him—could only fly about two hours if the weather held.

"To give him the maximum chance, we only gave him water for two hours because that kept him from having too much weight in the plane. And we only put in batteries for the instruments for two hours.

"The weather forecast was pretty pessimistic, and as things transpired the weather forecast was right. The weather wasn't good enough to make a flight.

"And we were right in our calculations. Bryan was essentially all through in two hours. But somehow he continued on. He had given up, and used up all the normal stamina he had. The flight should have stopped then, but he found the mental stamina—the guts—to continue. I think he thought that if he didn't do it that day he'd have to do it all again." A pause. Laughter.

"We had an abortive takeoff when it went off this little runway because the wheels are a little bit crooked, and they hit the only large hole in all that concrete area. One of the front wheels was knocked off and the plane just stopped. Fortunately, nothing broke except the wheel. Taras Kiceniuk [who had helped actively on both projects] and some others rushed back and made the change.

"The eyes of the world were truly on the project. Film crews were over from Japan and stayed for four weeks. *National Geographic* had two guys for three months. American network TV, TV from Europe, and so on. . . . Some of them were beginning to make snide remarks.

"It's always darkest just before the dawn. And now the Gossamer Albatross soars over the ocean for the first time."

The movie about the Gossamer Albatross, *Gossamer Albatross: Flight of Imagination*, tells the rest of the story. The little plane leaves England, followed by its entourage of boats; for more than an hour the flight is uneventful. Bryan Allen lets the plane descend to take advantage of the reduced air drag near the water. He says, "Faint shouts of people in boats drift up. Inside, I hear nothing but my own breathing."[61] The small propeller at the rear of the craft turns at a lazy pace, the boats—many just rubber rafts—move along slowly. Cameras are directed upward, focused on the plane.

"As I continue cycling, heat builds in the cockpit from exertion. Now the sun has broken out of the mist, and the cocoon gets hotter."[62]

He pedals ceaselessly. The ocean roughens, small wavelets forming on the surface. A light wind comes up, but it does not affect him.

"Still pedaling," he says. "It's getting harder to maintain height."[63] Someone below asks him his speed and altitude, but when he tries to reply, they show no sign of hearing. Bryan speaks again, but still no response. He realizes his transmitter has malfunctioned, though he can still hear incoming voices.

The waves grow. "The Albatross yaws. I pedal harder just to stay level."[64]

Now the chase boats are rising and falling on the three-foot swells. "I must pedal harder. . . . I'm expending every ounce of energy just to stay

Pedaling's easy at first. (© Don Monroe, 1979)

Sun makes the cockpit steam up.
(© Don Monroe, 1980)

134 **The Mad, Magical, Many-Sided World of Hang Gliding**

Albatross sinks lower. (© Don Monroe, 1979)

above the waves."[65] He cannot let the waves touch the plane or the mission will be disqualified.

"I stare fixedly ahead," he reports. "Sweat stings my eyes, fogs my glasses. My churning legs feel leaden. Gasping, I sink lower."[66]

Below, the men become alarmed. Someone yells at him, warning of his dropping altitude. "Two feet!" Then, louder, "One foot!"

"My vision begins to fade. I taste blood in the back of my throat—signs of complete exhaustion. The wind turbulence is too much. I cannot go on."[67]

At just under two hours, the expected happens. With France nowhere in sight, all is going according to plan. Though he cannot talk to the trailing boats, the boats don't need to be told. Bryan makes a motion with his hand, the prearranged signal to abort, and the first trial run ends at the predicted moment.

The boats close in, ready to attach a towline to the Albatross with its failing "engine" and tow it to shore like a kite. The towline is guided by a fishing pole held by someone in a boat, but in order to allow room for the hookup, the plane must be pedaled upward to fifteen feet above the water; otherwise, the plane will be lost.

Bryan picks up his pedaling; ". . . gritting my teeth, I pump with my last surge of strength."[68] The craft rises, and then something strange happens.

As the man with the fishing pole tries to hook into the plane, the plane dodges out of the way. Again, an attempt is made and fails; the fisherman can't hook his prey because the prey is avoiding him.

Unable to speak to his pursuers, Allen maneuvers quickly to stay out of reach; one touch from anyone will disqualify the attempt. Finally he is seen through his semitransparent cockpit waving the boats off.

The men in the boats are perplexed, but accept Allen's sudden refusal to abort, learning only later that he has found easier air at the higher altitude.

"Now I maintain progress," he says, "with less effort."[69]

The craft resumes its slow trip toward France. But shortly afterward, the instruments die on schedule and the pilot runs out of water. "I reach for more water, only to suck dry air."[70] Henceforth, the "engine" will operate without "fuel."

The headwind increases. What nobody knows is that the man in the cockpit is suffering leg cramps, first in one leg, then the other. He pedals with the noncramping leg, then switches as the cramps switch. Finally, both legs have cramps. Dehydration is taking its toll.

The plane makes its way toward France, minute by teasing minute. The boats follow, the men in them resolved to feel no disappointment when the mission comes to its inevitable halt. Nobody expects that Bryan will force this second-choice craft all the way.

He says, "I am still pedaling. Against all hope."[71]

The suspense grows. Through it all, the funny-looking Albatross just keeps wending its way. On, on, on.

Suddenly the French coastline appears faintly in the distance. Bryan Allen sees it, and will doubtless pedal until his muscles burst. Yet he is already a half hour beyond the end of his endurance, and the landfall is indistinct—and twenty minutes away.

To make matters worse, the craft is fighting an increasing headwind, which consumes seventy-five percent of its flight speed. Bryan needs the wind-speed indicator and altimeter to find the easiest route. Above the ocean, altitude is impossible to gauge. The men in the boats relay approximate altitude.

Twenty more minutes?

The pedals turn; the legs push on. The hands grip the bar, the head is bent in concentration. Inside the cockpit moisture is everywhere except where it is needed. Around him, below him, the boats move tentatively forward.

The propeller turns in its unhurried way, as idly as though none of it matters, as though its turning is dependent on the whim of the breeze.

The shoreline comes closer. A crowd waits on the beach. But the turbulence close to shore is impossible, and a wind comes off the cliffs, forcing the Albatross to veer toward the right, where rocks await a crash-landing. There is still danger that the fragile craft will be blown down short, into the grasping waves. Bryan says, "She creaks and groans. They are the sounds this same plane made before it broke apart during tests in California. I fight to hold her toward the beach."[72]

Lingering off the rocks, the Albatross hesitates, battered by the wind. "I narrow my eyes and pedal harder."[73]

Its moment of helpless dangling passes, and the Albatross sets course again. "One final wrench of my muscles and I coast."[74]

When the plane crosses the sand and gently descends on France, the Cal Tech audience watching the movie—a sophisticated assemblage of scientists, Ph.D.'s, and scholars—breaks into a thunderous ovation. The cheers and clapping drown out the narration. The soundtrack is lost as Allen, too tired to do more than stare at the crowd, emerges from the plane. Hands grasp at him, a lady hands him flowers.

The audience continues cheering, as though Bryan Allen is there. For all of them he has done the impossible. Right before their eyes!

And so Paul MacCready and the enthusiasts who worked with him—and Bryan Allen—collected their second Kremer prize. DuPont's faith in the project was vindicated.

Since then Dr. MacCready has been swept out of his quiet AeroVironment offices into an unfamiliar arena of talk shows, speeches, and command performances. He is called on so often to speak that he wryly refers to "my new life in show biz."

Looking back, why did anyone doubt it would work?

All Bryan Allen had to do was pedal an airplane for two hours and forty-nine minutes!

IS THE FUTURE BEHIND US?

Even Paine Webber can't accurately predict what's ahead: If they could, their brokers would buy all the right stocks and retire. Yet the hang gliding community banks its future on modest extensions of the recent past, seeing only small refinements to the craft. Tracy Knauss says, "It seems to me that coming down in the eighties there will be no big breakthroughs . . . mostly what I would call cosmetic or convenience modifications in hang gliders. That's what we're seeing now. Moyes, [Steve Moyes, pilot and designer] and a lot of other designers are saying we won't have more quantum breakthroughs like we've had."

Flyer-instructor Rich Grigsby says, "I think you'll see far greater use of exotic materials such as carbon fiber, fiberglass used for tubing, and different sail materials rather than Dacron. Also, the advance of what MacCready used to call the controlled collapsibles like the Fledgling. They are rigid; they will have aerodynamic controls but fold up as conveniently as any flex wing or Rogallo.

"I think last year everybody saw that the Fledgling was certainly superior to any flex wing. And in order to achieve that level of performance and that speed, we're going to have to go to rigid airfoils. I don't think you're going to be able to do it with the flexible airfoil. So, in years to come—and it may take five years—I think you'll see a greater number of rigid wings flying."

When asked if he thought the Rogallo was on the way out, Grigsby replied, "No. Because it still is a very simple type aircraft that has very forgiving characteristics. It's uncomplicated. It will be offered at a lower price than the rigid wings. In instruction and intermediate flying, you're going to see flex wings will always be around.

"But as far as high-performance flying goes, I would think in five years you're going to see maybe fifty percent flex and fifty percent rigid. Now the rigid are probably about seven to ten percent—maybe even less than that."

Though they are sometimes deplored, aerobatics wait on the outer fringes of the sport and—like Lorelei, who sits on a rock in the Rhine luring sailors to destruction—beckon with an almost irresistible appeal.

"I know I shouldn't, but I want to," seems to be a common attitude toward aerobatics. Instructor Ken de Russy says, "I think anything that has improved the level of safety is most noteworthy. Paradoxically, radical aerobatics, such as ninety- to one-hundred-eighty-degree wingovers, are probably the most exciting thing I've ever seen in hang gliding."[75]

And Don Partridge, who flies in the Owens Valley and runs hang gliding's most advanced meet, says, "Loops . . . that's another direction I think hang gliding will be going. I think we'll see specifically designed aerobatic hang gliders capable of doing loops and things without endangering yourself to the point you may be doing now."

Most pilots are waiting until those specially designed hang gliders come along. Almost all believe it will happen eventually. And some can hardly wait.

Don Partridge, fresh from his own Owens Valley meet, speaks of future soaring capabilities. "I think we're going to become more and more like sailplanes. You see this in the machinery now. It's getting aerodynamically cleaner. Faster. I think that's what we're going to have to have, and I think faster gliders will make flying a lot safer. You see, we fly in situations where we'll be in the air for five to six hours, and land a hundred miles away where you can run into entirely different weather conditions.

"We fly around thunderstorms that cause squall lines, and the winds can

Rich Grigsby, his wife, Sheree, and Strider, their dog. (© Bettina Gray)

Eric Raymond, USHGA 1979 champion. (© Bettina Gray)

More streamlining every year—Crestline USHGA League, 1979–80. (© Bettina Gray)

be severe. I think, for safety's sake, we need a faster glider that can penetrate strong winds, should we get into something like that.

"Of course," he says with a little laugh, "the faster gliders win races, too. And they're going to get more streamlined. Even the pilots will be more streamlined.

"It takes a long time now to set up a new glider with all the equipment . . . CB radios and everything we've put on it. I think you're going to see a lot of polishing of the equipment to the point where gliders set up faster, and the equipment's modularly attached to the glider inside the double surface."

John Harris, flyer and owner of a large hang gliding school, adds, "I think the sport has made great strides technically and organizationally in the last several years. I expect to see the technical side slow down and be refined while organization and marketing catches up with technology.

"In other words, I think we have the flying machines to make flight possible inexpensively to many more people than are now involved in hang gliding. All we need to do is organize a little more and then present the sport to people in the right light. This is happening now, but will happen more in the next several years."[76]

Is it safe, then, to suggest that the great moments, the exciting leaps forward, the real drama in hang gliding all lie behind us?

Perhaps.

When airplanes first broke the sound barrier, no doubt men reasoned that aviation had gone as far as it could go. Flying had apparently reached the farthest extension of the dream—just before men landed on the moon!

THE LEADING EDGE

In a deep valley between two mountain ranges lies a corridor which may come to be the ultimate testing ground of both hang gliders and their pilots. The Owens Valley, a mostly empty piece of land stretched between the Sierras and the White Mountains in central California, already inspires awe, evokes a kind of reverence among hang glider pilots. A French flyer remarked in July 1980, "There are two types of hang glider pilots now . . . those that have flown the Owens Valley and those that haven't."

Chris Price, on his return from the Owens Valley Classic, said, "I hadn't flown there for four years because it was just too far out of hand. The conditions seemed too extreme for hang gliders. But this last trip up there I was pretty cautious . . . and it didn't seem so extreme; it seemed exciting."

Even Don Partridge, who grew up in the Owens Valley,. a Bishop boy all his life, says, "There were a few years there when I actually had quite a desire to move to the southern California area."

For years—until 1977, perhaps—the Owens Valley, with its strong thermals and high winds, seemed a foolhardy place for hang gliders.

And then George Worthington came to the Owens. A former Navy fighter pilot who turned to sailplanes after the Navy, the sixty-year-old flyer brought sailplane expertise to the rowdy winds and soon showed Don Partridge that his home ground might be better than southern California after all. Partridge admits that "Before George came I was dubious myself whether or not flying in the valley in the afternoon was a sane thing to do."

Gradually, Partridge and a handful of others learned to cope with the fast-rising bodies of air which, heated by an afternoon sun, swirled off the western face of the White Mountains and rose to towering heights, sometimes as great as twenty thousand feet!

Don's first hang glider was a Chandelle Standard, the kite equivalent of an early mass-produced Chevy. It did what it was supposed to do and no more —carried him on short trips from hilltop to landing, "those big sled rides."

But as Don progressed to higher-performing gliders, and people like George Worthington began poking around in the turbulence, it occurred to him that the best flying in the world might be at home. "After a while," he says,

Don Partridge. (© Bettina Gray)

"I could fly back and forth between a couple small thermals. Then we were flying in stronger and stronger conditions. We started doing it more and more and the turbulence . . . at least we learned techniques that could handle it.

"Eventually," he says, "I flew over fifty sites up here. Probably forty of 'em I flew first."

The Owens Valley Classic, a worldwide hang gliding competition held for the third time in 1980, drew flyers from twelve countries and gave the impression that out of it would emerge the world's most skilled cross-country pilots.

Here, launching from Gunter Peak in the White Mountains, pilots were attempting tasks that would probably be impossible at most flying sites. Where else could flyers pick and choose among thermals, bypassing those that seemed puny and sniffing out like hound dogs the thermal that would swirl upward at fifteen hundred feet a minute!

The ten-mile road to the top of Gunter launch is tortuous, steep, boulder-strewn, and full of surprise potholes. Los Angeles *Times* writer Earl Gustkey reports, "It requires a four-wheel-drive vehicle. And securely anchor the fillings in your teeth! One thing's certain—the people who leave Gunter Peak on hang gliders are taking the easiest route down!"[77]

Partridge's tasks are peculiarly suited to his terrain and its winds. There was what he calls, "a simple open-distance task. That was ninety-four miles, and Rich Pfeiffer took it." . . . [Rich Pfeiffer was the prior year's champion.]

"Then we had dog-leg distance, where we flew to Boundary Peak [each

Searching for thermals in the Owens Valley. (© Bettina Gray)

contestant photographed the peak to prove he was there] and then flew open distance to the east, which went to Tonopah, and Larry Tudor got that at ninety-nine miles.

Then we had goal and return, to Boundary Peak and back. We had some elapsed-time tasks. The very last day we ran a modified task, where we'd fly twelve miles to White Mountain Peak, then turn around and fly back to launch; and land at Zack's ranch, which was another sixteen miles out; making that about a forty-two-mile run, against the clock."

While Partridge may not find the level of flying exhibited at his Classic astonishing, Chris Price does. With excitement in his voice he says, "I think they had about sixty flights over eighty miles! One day somebody went ninety-four, the next day somebody went one hundred four, and the day after that somebody went eighty-four, winning the different days. They were having a lot of six-hour flights on one of those days, which is just . . ."; he pauses, taking a deep breath, "*Nobody* ever stays up six hours unless he has to. It's pretty amazing. And Rob Kells [manufacturer-pilot] set an unofficial altitude gain—he went down to about seven thousand feet and got up to twenty-two thousand feet from there. If he'd had a barograph on it would have been an official world record.

"A lot of people got up to nineteen thousand. Kells just hung around and went up into the clouds, you know, up there where the airliners are."

When asked whether he thought it was the ships or the pilots—or both, Price answered, "After the SST [a third-generation glider—1975] . . . you could do most anything those guys were doing in an SST. The ships *have* gotten better. In fact, there was a guy there flying an XC [a 1977 glider], to give you an idea. I think there was more than one XC in the meet. But I think it's more that the pilots are just getting better and better.

"As a whole, the ships have made small improvements, but there haven't been any large jumps, significant jumps. It's just been more . . . well, they're easier to fly for longer periods of time. They do have better performance and broader speed range, but the raw performance isn't that much better, to allow flights like this. I think it's mainly the pilots who've gotten better and better and better."

He pauses, thinking. "Of course, more better pilots accelerate the whole evolution of pilot skill, push it even further along. It feeds on itself."

Until the Owens Valley meet, there had never been a competition in which pilots routinely carried oxygen. The whole range of gear, in fact, was unlike anything in the past. Partridge says, "We had some pilots go well above twenty thousand feet this year. Freezing level averages around fourteen thousand to sixteen thousand feet. They all wore snowmobile suits and heavy gloves with liners. Oxygen masks covered their faces. It's like scuba diving, in a way, in that you know you're getting high up here when you get cold. Actually, if you're below twelve thousand feet you're dropping kind of low."

The CB radios were another phenomenon. Long used by meet officials at launch and landing, they were seldom carried by pilots, even as late as 1978. CB radios have changed the whole thermaling experience. Don Partridge is excited about what they've brought to the sport. "We started using CBs in '77–'78. In the first Classic there were quite a few of them used, and then by '79–'80, we saw a lot of them. I haven't quite required them yet, though I recommend them when I set my tasks, such that CB radios would be used to verify your line crossings.

"They were really interesting this year. You could follow the gaggles of pilots. See, what we get up there in flying is, say, twenty, thirty pilots taking off fairly close to each other, and they all get in the same thermal. So you have this fantastic gaggle that stacks up to sixteen thousand feet. And then they all break, and they fly down the range, and a few of them fall out. A few of them get ahead, but generally the gaggle stays together, sometimes for fifty, sixty miles. So you'll find a dozen people at seventeen thousand feet over the Nevada desert in the same gaggle.

"That contributes largely to our ability to fly great distances. In other words, you have seven different gliders going in different directions, and if one of them gets a thermal, the others are still close enough to get into it. You have seven chances of getting thermals instead of just one, if you were by yourself.

"The CB radios really contribute to that, too, because everybody can

From outer space? High altitude hang glider pilot. (Bill Bennett)

tell each other—you can hear it; it's just great to listen. They'll say, 'Oh, it's five hundred over here, you better come on over here,' or 'It's sink here, don't go here.'

"What *I* do is, I take off after everyone's off the hill and try to chase them down the range. I can tell how close I am by . . . the CB's only good for about ten or fifteen miles . . . so I can tell where the gaggles are, roughly, just by listening to their CB radios. I can sometimes pick up a gaggle that is a couple gaggles ahead of me, and I can tell where everybody's at.

"There were some fighter jets went under us one day when we were all about sixty miles out, and you could just hear everybody on their CBs, 'Look at that fighter!' "

Both Don Partridge and Chris Price are aware of subtle personal qualities that make today's hang glider pilot unique. Don Partridge says, "I think what we're seeing now in hang gliding are pilots that have gone beyond simple cognitive thinking in their awareness of thermals. There are people now who actually have so much confidence in their ability to find thermals that in a race situation, they don't take every thermal. They fly till they get to a certain elevation where they *know* a thermal is going to be, then they take that one. Pilots now don't fool around. They won't turn in anything less than five hundred feet per minute up. It just wastes their time.

"You think about your strategy, you think about where the other pilots are, how you're going to catch them, and you just move through this thermal atmosphere intuitively."

Chris Price uses different words, but there is a similarity in the message. "It takes a huge imagination and very little skill, actually, once you get to a certain skill level. Your ability to think clearly, especially in meets like the White Mountains, is much more important than your skill available to handle the glider in turbulence. Even glider performance becomes not that significant.

"It just so happens, of course, that the better pilots want the better ships, so you do have the better pilots flying better equipment.

"But Rich Grigsby, for instance, had just gotten a brand-new glider, and it glided well but he could not thermal worth a darn. It was being outclimbed significantly day after day in thermals. Yet he ended up coming in second, because once he got to the top of the thermal he would take the smarter path and go on to win."

Price compared various kinds of flying. "You've got to be able to think clearly in the air, five minutes, ten minutes ahead of time, up to an hour ahead of time. But in skydiving, you can't think ahead because the dive will be over. The thinking is done on the ground. Flying a jet fighter at speeds near the speed of sound over terrain and through canyons is very exciting, and you have to react very quickly. But to fly a hang glider in a place like the Owens Valley or in Elsinore, you have to keep thinking ahead. You've got to keep trying to imagine what the air looks like when you can't see it, and you have to imagine what the consequences are of each action you make.

"Imagination. There's the ability to work puzzles, and then there's imagination. I think that imagination and brains are the most important things it takes to become a pilot. That's what made Bob Wills so good. He had a very good imagination. He could imagine what was going to happen all the time. Also, he was able to concentrate. In fact, that had more to do with it than anything else.

"Most of the time, in hang gliding, you're so far up that your imagination doesn't really dwell on the negative, because if you make a mistake, it just means you have to get out of it. It doesn't mean you're going to hit a wall or something, like race-car driving. Usually you're going to have time to work it out.

"In hang gliding, if you imagine what's going to go wrong if you do this, then no matter what you do, it will be wrong. But there are degrees of wrongness, and so you end up imagining which is the least degree of wrongness. That takes concentration and imagination, and of course brains, just to figure out what to do once you've imagined all these things.

"One thing about being a successful hang glider pilot which I've learned in the last year is that if you look at hang gliding as an analytical problem and try to define all the parameters and come up with answers from formulas, you may or may not succeed. But I think that the human brain is able to look at all the possibilities and arrive at an answer through intuition and experience. You don't have to analytically figure it out. You just do it by feel. You go over there and sure enough you go up, and you're really not too sure why. The more you try to figure it out, the less you understand. It's kind of like Zen Buddhism, where the more you try to describe what it is to be enlightened, the more impossible it is.

"I find myself taking off, and with my experience, I don't try to concentrate on any *one* thing. I try to take in *everything* that's out there, and I find that the brain makes its own calculations.

"Hang gliding gives you this unbelievable opportunity to function on the intuitive level, where other sports don't. A pilot is a pilot no matter *what* he's flying. But in hang gliding, you get back to basics—back to the *essence* of flying. I think that the best pilots that ever have been, or ever will be, are hang glider pilots.

THE ULTIMATE FREEDOM

It was Coles Phinizy, writing in *Sports Illustrated*, who first described the kind of flying to which today's pilots aspire. The year was 1973, and then only a handful of men in the world had the rare gift he eulogized. Phinizy wrote "In so short a time at the game, Bob Wills seems to have won a mystical advantage. Like Paul Elvstrom, the great Danish sailor, he seems now to own a special part of the wind that not even he can see and no one else can find. In drafts where others sink, he gets an easy ride. Where rivals only glide, he finds air that lifts him above his takeoff point. In 30-mile-an-hour winds that discourage others, he casts himself off a hill competently, boldly holding the nose of his craft down in the blast until the trailing edge is grumbling in disbelief. On a fair day 3,000 feet up the mountains west of Lake Elsinore, half a dozen Rogallo men look for lift and find little. The best of them gets a 15-minute flight before landing in a farm field. Two of them, misjudging, come down short on brushy hillsides. Launching from the same spot, Bob Wills in two sweeping searches across the mountain face finds the lift. For half an hour he rides 200 feet above his takeoff point. Finally bored with it, he breaks out of the rising air and heads for the valley floor."[78]

Ask any advanced hang glider pilot what he considers the supreme experience and he will probably answer "Soaring." He will mean having the skill to find the hidden lift and stay up in it, circling in the effortless fashion of birds. Everyone has seen them: the flocks of white seabirds, turning, endlessly moving upward like scraps of paper caught in a swirling eddy. As they change direction in their ceaseless circling the sun turns their wings silver, then white, then shadowy gray. They move without motion, steadily upward, until the thermal gives out. Then, when they can hardly be seen, they take the altitude they've gained and set off cross-country.

This is the goal of hang-glider pilots: to set out cross-country, their knowledge of the wind and their machine so keen that only the birds can do it better . . . without engines, managing what pilots have heretofore done only *with* engines or after being towed to altitude.

Soaring is the ultimate "smarts"—the ultimate chess game of the skies. It is outthinking the winds, gravity, human limitations, sometimes flying by a sort of intuition. It is power and control and domination. To succeed is elevating, for who can but laud the intelligent conquest of gravity?

Book Two

The Education of
A Hang Glider Pilot

by Chris A. Wills, M.D.

THE TOUGH PART'S IN THE HEAD

Hang gliding—unlike most other types of flying—is technically simple, but *like* other forms of aviation is intellectually demanding, perhaps more demanding than most others. The control of the glider is a skill that can be acquired, at least in gross form, in a short period of time; however, the knowledge that is required to fly hang gliders safely in difficult conditions is something that requires hundreds of hours. The ultimate hang gliding experience, thermal soaring, may finally involve the development of an intuitive sixth sense.

Unlike conventional aircraft, the Rogallo hang glider pilot's body forms part of the aerodynamic unit, and it is used to control the glider's flight. Gradually, body and glider blend into a single machine, and the pilot loses conscious awareness of their separateness. By the time the pilot has learned to fly his hang glider with birdlike freedom, he not only knows intellectually all about his craft

149

Pilot and craft form a whole aerodynamic unit. Mike Meier at Monarch Bay, near Newport Beach in southern California. (Steve Pearson)

and the air in which he maneuvers, he has also acquired some of the sensory awareness of the creatures he imitates. His skill becomes instinctive behavior.

THE ALL-PURPOSE CONTROL BAR

The actual control movements of the hang glider are accomplished simply by moving one's weight through the use of the control bar:

Pulling your weight forward causes the nose of the glider to come down and the hang glider to accelerate or dive.

Pushing your weight back from the control bar makes the nose of the glider come up, which first causes the hang glider to slow down, and soon to stall.

By pulling your weight laterally to the right, the wing tilts to the right, and by pulling your weight left, the wing tilts left, causing either a right or left turn, respectively.

It's hard to believe, when watching a skilled hang glider pilot executing a series of extremely complicated maneuvers, that his whole control is based on these four simple actions. Gaining the knowledge that turns these four elemental control movements into a safe and exhilarating flight is the challenge of all new hang glider pilots.

In the early days of hang gliding it was common for one instructor to take a group of thirty or even more students to a hill and teach them all "how to fly" in a single day. Although this was good for promoting hang gliding at the time, and was even adequate for teaching new students to skim one to two feet off the ground down a small hill, the practice has no place in hang gliding today.

Nowadays hang glider pilots regularly fly off mountains thousands of feet high, or cross-country hundreds of miles; so it's important to have a solid understanding of the *airframe structure, safety equipment, basic aerodynamics,* and *meteorology.* A knowledge of these elements is essential for modern hang gliding pilots.

THE LEADING-EDGE BONE IS CONNECTED TO THE CROSSBAR BONE

The airframe of a Rogallo hang glider is built with special grades of aluminum tubing, whose main function is to support the Dacron sail that forms the airfoil. The Rogallo-type hang glider has an airframe that consists of five basic parts, the most obvious part being the tubing running along the front edge of each wing. This is called the *leading-edge tube.* The sail material usually wraps around the leading edge and is held in position by it.

The *crossbar* is the tube that connects the leading edges with the third part of the airframe, the *keel.* The term crossbar suggests what it does: It crosses the airframe and intersects the keel from edge to edge to form the letter *A;*

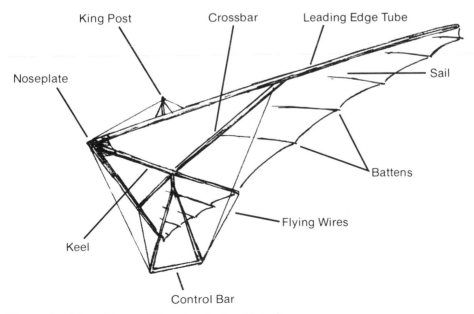

The parts of the airframe. (Drawing by Joe Linton)

whereas the keel runs from the nose of the glider to the center point of the rear, above the pilot, in a direction that parallels the hang glider's flight.

Usually, the fourth and fifth parts of the Rogallo frame, the *king post* and *control bar*, are connected to the airframe at the intersection of crossbar and keel. The king post rises vertically from the keel and acts as a compression strut, supporting the glider under negative loads (negative loads are forces working downward on top of the glider), which can be expected to occur when the glider is resting on the ground with nose down into the wind or (rarely and accidentally) when it is flying upside down.

The control bar is a triangular-shaped tubing, usually made of three different pieces of aluminum, which acts to support the glider under positive loads, such as during normal flight. It is also used by the pilot to exert his control movements.

LIGAMENTS OF STEEL

The real strength of the airframe is in the thin but incredibly strong stainless-steel cables or wires that support all the loads by, in effect, tying the tubes together. Cables prevent the tubes from flexing beyond their breaking point.

The *positive* or *flying wires*, of which there are usually six, run from the bases of the control bar to various parts of the airframe, and support the glider while in normal flight. The *top* or *negative wires*, usually four of them, run from the top of the king post to corresponding points on the airframe, and act to support the glider under negative loads, or inverted flight. The third set of structural wires, the *wing wires* or *leading edge wires*, help support the leading edges in either negative or positive loads. (Many hang glider designs do not have wing wires or may have other wires for structural or aerodynamic reasons.)

A DACRON MAGIC CARPET

The most easily recognized portion of the hang glider is the sail. Constructed of many panels of Dacron sailcloth, it is the same material used on small sailboats. The Dacron is sewn together in panels to create a shape which, when stretched on the airframe, will provide an optimal airfoil for flight.

Although to the untrained observer the sail appears to be the flimsiest and least substantial portion of the hang glider, it is its strongest single component—many times stronger than the other parts of a hang glider in flight.

In addition, the sail is often supported by *battens*, placed like ribs in various positions, which act to maintain a given shape or stability to the airfoil, or reduce drag. Often battens are specially designed to produce an airfoil in flight or are preformed to effect an airfoil even in the static (non-flying) condition.

The exact shape of a sail has to be precise, and many hours of calculations and computer time can result in adjustments in the sail of as little as one quarter of an inch to an inch. Yet even such minimal changes can produce substantial differences in performance or handling characteristics of the hang glider.

THE "HANG" PART OF HANG GLIDING

In many of the early hang gliders the pilot actually did hang on to the glider, thus giving hang gliding its early name. Modern hang gliders no longer require such physical effort. Today the pilot either wears a special *supine harness* or a *prone harness*, which is securely fastened to the glider, allowing the pilot to be suspended from near the point where the keel, crossbar, control bar, and king post meet.

Harnesses are usually made of woven Dacron cloth, foam-padded for comfort, with supports of nylon aircraft webbing, similar to seat-belt webbing. They're designed to allow the pilot hours of uninterrupted, fatigue-free flight. The pilot is comfortable and relaxed, yet able to move his weight in any direction for control.

Many harnesses allow the pilot to change from a seated position to a lying, or prone, position, or even to a standing position while in flight, thus minimizing the fatigue the pilot would experience from too long a time in one posture.

In recent years harnesses have been adapted to carry a parachute in case of emergency. With the new hang glider-harness combinations now in use, it is possible to fly a hang glider through steep maneuvers with only a minimal amount of control-bar pressure.

PROTECTING NUMBER ONE

Safety equipment is a major issue with most pilots today. The end of "low and slow" flying a few years ago also saw the last of a kind of what-the-hell attitude concerning personal safety. In the beginning seventies nobody used a helmet; today no one flies without one. A helmet isn't a guarantee of perfect safety, but it can help, and hang gliding helmets have become standard equipment.

Most helmets are specially designed for hang gliding, allowing the pilot to hear and feel the wind speed as much as possible. They are worn at all times when flying.

For flights over two hundred feet, pilots now carry parachutes as well, since they have saved numerous lives on occasions when flyers collided or flew in conditions strong enough to inflict structural damage to the hang glider. Parachutes designed for today's hang gliders are usually attached both to the pilot's harness and the hang glider itself. In the event of an accident requiring its use, the pilot deploys the chute, allowing both glider and pilot to come down beneath the canopy.

Parachute, helmet, prone harness, gloves—today's gear. (© Bettina Gray)

During the early learning period it is helpful as well to use knee pads, elbow pads, and even wheels on the control bar to help cushion the pilot in the event of a poor landing.

THE "SHIFTING SANDS" AIRFOIL

It used to be a common misconception that a hang glider pilot strapped himself into his flimsy contraption, walked to the edge of a sheer cliff, closed his eyes, and leaped off, to be tossed about at the mercy of the winds.

This could not be further from the truth.

A hang glider, like any other type of aircraft, is dependent upon creating lift in order to fly, and is a complex, highly refined *airfoil.*

The one notable difference between a hang glider and other types of fixed-wing aircraft is that in the Rogallo hang glider the airfoil isn't rigid. In fact, it is designed to *change* its configuration under different control inputs. This is what allows a hang glider to be controlled precisely, through pilot weight shift alone, yet still achieve high performance.

Moreover, like other aircraft, a hang glider is dependent upon its forward speed through the air to create lift and make control possible. Just as a conventional plane must accelerate down a runway before it can reach flying speed and lift off the ground, so too a hang glider pilot must run down a hill or into the wind to create enough airspeed to achieve flight. Once in the air, the airplane, sailplane, and hang glider are all doing the same thing: They're using their forward speed to create lift.

A powered airplane's forward speed is created by the engine turning a propeller, and thus it's able to maintain forward speed even though it may be climbing at a steep angle. The hang glider and sailplane, on the other hand, are both restricted in that they must always be gliding *downward* with respect to the air around them in order to maintain speed and lift. With a hang glider and sailplane, only if the air around them is rising faster than they are gliding down through it can they actually gain altitude. This can be compared to a bicycle with no pedals, which must constantly be going downhill in order to maintain its forward speed. Thus, only if the whole hill were rising faster than the bicycle was gliding down its slope would the bicycle actually be rising in altitude; yet it would always be going *down* in relation to the hill.

The goal of the sailplane or hang glider pilot is to find areas where a body of air is rising upward faster than the craft is sinking downward through it. By staying in such areas to gain altitude, the hang glider pilot achieves more time and distance in the air.

THE AXES TRIPLETS: PITCH, ROLL, AND YAW

The movements of the hang glider, like the movements of all aircraft, are described in terms of three different axes of rotation. The first is known as the *pitch axis*, and is the motion of the nose up and down as the aircraft dives or climbs. The pitch axis is usually described by drawing an imaginary line between the tips of the wings and noting how the aircraft rotates up or down on that line.

The next axis of rotation is the *roll axis*, and describes motions an aircraft makes by lifting one wing up or down. By drawing an imaginary line from front to rear through the center of the aircraft, and picturing the aircraft pivoting on that line, one can understand the roll axis.

The final axis of rotation is known as the *yaw axis*, and describes motions

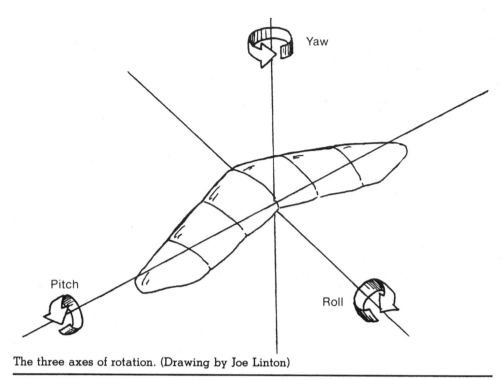

Yaw

Pitch

Roll

The three axes of rotation. (Drawing by Joe Linton)

that would occur about an imaginary line drawn through the center of the air-craft from top to bottom. For example, if a pilot were to hold up a hang glider by the control bar and another person were to pull the nose of the glider from side to side, the glider would be rotating about the pilot, and the motion would be occurring on the yaw axis.

SPEAKING THE LANGUAGE

There are many terms used in design and by pilots describing the flight char-acteristics of hang gliders, and it is important for the new pilot to understand them. The first is *glide angle*. This term actually defines the angle the glider's path makes with the horizontal line in flight, but is practically described by the vertical and horizontal components of that path. Thus gliders are described as having a glide angle of five to one, or ten to one, or twenty to one. If a glider has a ten-to-one glide angle, it means that the glider will move forward ten feet for every foot of altitude that it drops. To describe it further, if a hang glider pilot in a glider with a ten-to-one glide angle took off from a one-mile-high mountain, in calm air, he would expect to glide ten miles before he reached the ground. Similarly, a pilot with a craft with a lesser glide angle, perhaps five to one, would travel only five miles departing from the same location.

GLIDE ANGLE

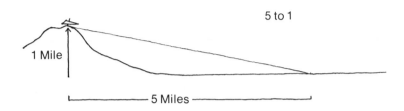

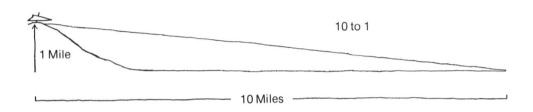

The glide angle. (Drawing by Joe Linton)

The glide angle of various hang gliders and the glide angle of a particular hang glider differ with the speed the hang glider flies. The glide angle given for a hang glider is usually the maximum glide it can achieve at *any* speed. Thus the best glide angle of two *different* hang gliders may occur at two entirely different speeds.

Sailplanes customarily have much greater glide angles than hang gliders. Many sailplanes achieve glide angles of forty to one at speeds near a hundred miles per hour. Most hang gliders, on the other hand, have glide angles of ten to one at speeds of twenty-five miles per hour. Thus the sailplane's glide angle is four times greater than the hang glider's, but its speed is also four times greater. Consequently, if both took off from the same mile-high mountain at the same time, both would land at the same time. The difference is, the sailplane would land forty miles away and the hang glider would land ten miles away!

Another term related to the performance of hang gliders is *minimum sink rate*, or *sink rate*, or even *minimum sink*. This is defined as the slowest possible rate that the glider descends vertically. Sink rate is usually given in terms of feet per minute. For hang gliders, this figure varies between approximately a hundred and fifty feet per minute to as much as five hundred feet per minute.

Sink rate, like glide angle, does not specify the glider's flying speed. However, by knowing any *two* of the three variables—glide angle, sink rate,

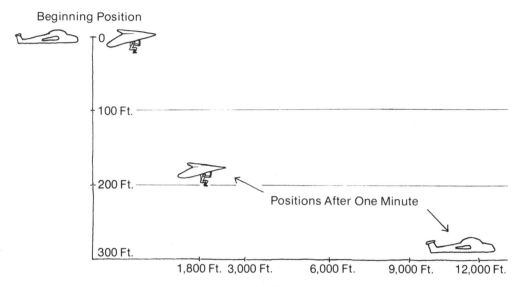

HANG GLIDER
Glide Angle 10:1
at Sink Rate 180 ft/min
20.5 mph

SAIL PLANE
Glide Angle 40:1
at Sink Rate 300 ft/min
136.4 mph

Beginning Position

0

100 Ft.

200 Ft.

Positions After One Minute

300 Ft.

1,800 Ft. 3,000 Ft.   6,000 Ft.   9,000 Ft.   12,000 Ft.

Speed, glide angle, and sink rate relationship. (Drawing by Joe Linton)

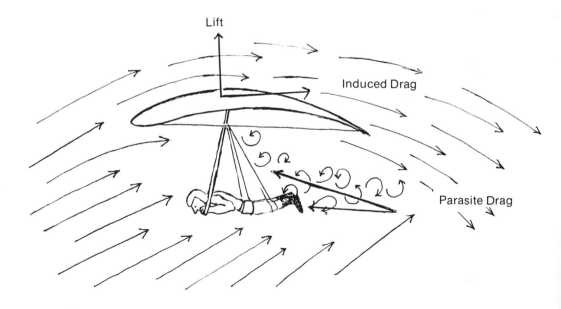

Lift

Induced Drag

Parasite Drag

Drag, induced and parasitic. (Drawing by Joe Linton)

or flying speed—it is easy to calculate the third, since mathematically the three are interrelated.

To illustrate in the case of the sailplane and hang glider taking off from the same mile-high mountain: The sink rate of the two are exactly the same, since both took off at the same altitude at the same time and both descended one mile of altitude to land at the same time. Since the vertical distance they descended was the same, and the time it took them to descend that distance was also the same, then the sink rate of the two was identical. Because the flying speed of the sailplane was four times greater than that of the hang glider, and their sink rate was the same, the sailplane had a four-times-greater glide angle.

Like its glide angle, the sink rate of a hang glider will vary with its speed, and the minimum sink of one hang glider may occur at an entirely different speed from the minimum sink of another.

A particular hang glider may have a very good glide angle and a very poor minimum sink rate, while another hang glider might have a very good minimum sink rate and poor glide angle. Which hang glider a pilot chooses depends on the type of flying he plans. A glider with good sink rate is ideal for large ridge-lift conditions, while a glider with excellent glide angle is best for cross-country flying for distance. Obviously, the ideal hang glider is one that has both a superior glide angle and an excellent minimum sink rate.

Another important term for hang glider pilots is *lift*. This is defined as the amount of upward force generated by the wing as it moves through the air. The lift of a particular wing also varies with its speed.

Drag is defined as the force generated by an object moving through the air which acts to slow that object's motion. The amount of drag produced is divided into two components: The first is the drag produced by a wing in creating lift, and is called *induced drag*. The second component is the drag produced by accessory parts of the aircraft, and is called *parasite drag*. Accessory parts to a hang glider would include such items as the pilot's body, the cables, and parts of the airframe. The pilot's body is, in fact, a considerable source of parasite drag, and a reduction in this drag was the reason for the development of the prone flying harness, which produced a streamlining of the pilot's body as it moved through the wind.

Drag, like lift, is proportional to the speed of the aircraft. By dividing the lift generated by the drag generated, one is able to determine L/D, a figure equivalent to the glide angle.

Lift, as we have noted, is the upward force created by an airfoil moving through the air; it is usually perceived by the casual observer as a mysterious force somehow created by a curved wing. Confusion over the *cause* of lift is often created by grade-school science books in an attempt to simplify what is already simple and needs no further simplification.

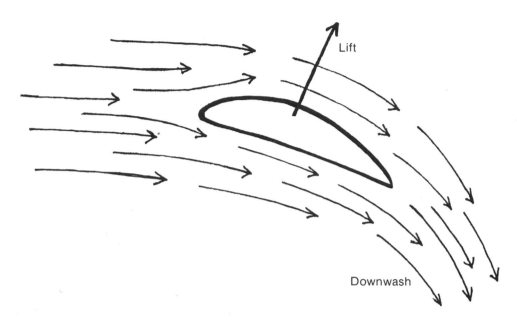

Lift

Downwash

Lift and downwash. (Drawing by Joe Linton)

The function of an airfoil, or wing, is to take a mass of air and move it downward. As the wing tries to force air down, the air resists and consequently forces the wing upward by the same amount. If the weight of the air which the wing moves downward is greater than the weight of the total aircraft, then the wing (and consequently the aircraft) will move upward by the amount of the weight differential.

The function of the curved-wing airfoil is to take the air that was happily bouncing about in one place and move it smoothly downward without creating turbulence, which would be seen as drag. This air, moved downward by the wing, is known as *downwash*. Since every action has an equal and opposite reaction, the action of downwash induces an opposite reaction which lifts the wing.

When one realizes that each cubic yard of air at sea level weighs two pounds, and that a hang glider is moving through hundreds of yards of air every second, it is easy to see that the force required to move this air is substantial; the reactive force, which is lift, is also substantial.

STALLS: THE NO-NOS

The stall is an important and potentially dangerous situation for *all* aircraft. The hang glider is no exception.

A stall creates turbulence. (Drawing by Joe Linton)

A stall occurs when the wing of the glider strikes the air at such an angle that the air can no longer flow smoothly around the airfoil. Instead of separating the air cleanly, the wing causes turbulent swirls to form on its top surface. In this situation, the wing stops producing lift. The disastrous result is an aircraft that has stopped flying and begun to fall, nose first. The falling continues until enough speed is regained for lift to be regained and flying resumed.

The stall is usually the result of insufficient airspeed, and it may occur gently and slowly or quite abruptly, depending on the particular design of the glider or airplane. Hang gliders, for the most part, have a rather mild, gentle stall, which will usually alert the pilot before he has lost too much altitude. If he knows enough to bring his weight forward and thereby increase his speed and lift, a substantial loss of altitude can be averted.

At low altitudes the stall is particularly hazardous, since the glider may not be high enough to regain flying speed before striking the ground. As low altitudes are a common situation for hang gliders, the stall lurks perpetually as *a real danger*, and its threat to novices cannot be overemphasized.

ANGLE OF ATTACK: A QUESTION OF ATTITUDE

Angle of attack is one of those slippery concepts, difficult to describe, and yet fundamental to an understanding of basic aerodynamics.

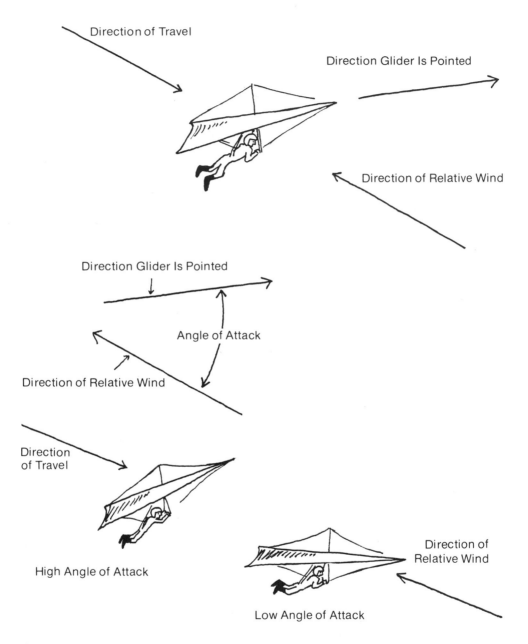

Angle of attack. (Drawing by Joe Linton)

First, angle of attack has nothing to do with the hang glider and its relationship, or angle (tilt), relative to the horizon. It is concerned only with the hang glider and its angle to the *wind*, and it relates only to the hang glider's angle to the *relative wind* (the wind created by the hang glider's motion through it).

Whichever direction a craft is moving—whether straight up, straight down, straight sideways, or any angled direction—the wind that is coming directly at the craft, head-on, is the relative wind. If a hang glider were to "pancake," with no forward motion at all, the relative wind would be coming straight up from below, and the hang glider would have a ninety-degree angle of attack. (Of course it wouldn't be flying, it would be falling.) Now, if instead of pancaking, the nose of the glider were pointed straight down in a screaming vertical dive, the relative wind would still be coming straight up to meet it head-on, and the glider would be thought of as having a zero angle of attack relative to the straight-on wind. These are two extremes, of course, and neither describes a flying hang glider, since one is pancaking, and the other diving. But one angle of attack is ninety degrees, the other zero.

Between these extremes, a hang glider normally moves both horizontally and vertically at the same time, creating a relative wind which comes at the hang glider from the direction of the hang glider's progress through air. The angle that the hang glider's wing makes with its own relative wind is its angle of attack.

A high angle of attack is one in which the front of the wing is high and the rear low, with respect to the relative wind hitting the wing.

Zero angle of attack means the wing is traveling parallel to the flight path of the glider and the relative wind. The wing in this situation can be thought of as slicing cleanly through the air.

Any given airfoil will have varying amounts of lift and drag at varying angles of attack. As one slowly increases the angle of attack there will be a certain angle at which the air can no longer flow smoothly over the upper surface of the wing. At this point the wing quickly produces decreasing amounts of lift and increasing amounts of drag, which results in a stall.

Since different parts of the wing fly at different angles of attack, they stall at different times. If a glider's whole wing stalls at nearly the same time, because it is all flying at nearly the same angle of attack, the stall characteristics of the glider will be severe, with the pilot discovering that one minute the glider is flying and the next, falling.

On the other hand, if the glider's wing is designed so that different portions of the wing are flying at different angles of attack, and consequently stall at different times, the stall characteristics of the glider are mild; the pilot can, in fact, fly the glider with much of the wing stalled, even though his glide angle will be greatly decreased.

It would seem ideal, therefore, to build a wing that has a wide range of angles of attack throughout the wing so the glider will have mild stall characteristics.

The problem with this lies in the fact that since the maximum performance of an airfoil occurs at a given angle of attack, in a glider with a wide range of angles of attack, only a certain portion of the wing will be flying at maximum efficiency at any given time; therefore the glider will have poorer performance than a glider with the whole wing flying well at a particular angle of attack.

The problem for the designer is to create a wing with good performance characteristics and also good stall characteristics. In the end it involves a compromise between the two goals.

THE DECEPTIVE DOWNWIND

Flying downwind, or *with* the wind at low altitudes, is particularly dangerous because wind speed is added to the hang glider's flying speed, adding noticeable ground speed. This situation may cause the pilot to misjudge the airspeed of his hang glider and inadvertently stall. Flying downwind at low altitudes should be avoided if possible. When unavoidable, the pilot must be alert to his airspeed in order to maintain it.

A RIVER OF AIR

Meteorology, or the study of weather, is important to all pilots. Micrometeorology—the study of weather in small, localized areas around hills or valleys—is of especial importance to hang glider pilots, since hang gliders so often fly low and near hills and valleys.

Although casual observers of hang gliding assume that the craft has to have wind in order to fly, such is not the case. A hang glider *creates its own wind*—the relative wind—by moving forward through the air. At the same time it is subject to winds external to itself, and the hang glider pilot must understand the nature and behavior of these winds as they relate to mountains, trees, valleys, and other obstacles. With such understanding, the wind can be used to gain altitude, while areas of predictable turbulence can be avoided.

Since air and water behave much the same when moving past obstacles, the best way to understand wind is to think of it as a river of water flowing over the terrain.

Just as a river flowing around a boulder is first separated by the boulder and then swirls and bubbles behind it, so the wind splits around an obstacle and boils turbulently on the lee side.

The air behind *all* stationary obstacles—such as buildings, trees, parked

Obstacles produce turbulence. (Drawing by Joe Linton)

Flying in the Rocky Mountains at Telluride, Colorado, is nearly always turbulent.
(© Bettina Gray)

cars, and even parked hang gliders—will be turbulent, in fact extremely turbulent in strong winds, and a hazard to flying hang gliders. Expectably, the air behind airplanes, helicopters, sailplanes, and even birds and other hang gliders will also be turbulent, but the degree of turbulence will be proportional to the size, shape, speed, and weight of the moving object.

How far behind any object the turbulence extends depends on a variety of factors. Most important are the speed of the wind moving past the object, and the object's size. Thus it's possible for turbulence to exist for many miles behind a ridge of ten- to fifteen-thousand-foot mountains and be negligible behind a small bird.

RIDGE LIFT: A PERPETUAL HIGH

Of particular importance to hang glider pilots is the behavior of wind near mountains and hills. As the wind begins to hit the slope of the hill, it accelerates upward and is forced to rise on the windward side. For some distance in front of the hill it creates an area of rapidly rising air, which is used by the hang glider pilot to maintain or gain altitude. This area of rising air is called *ridge lift*.

At the crest of the hill or mountain the wind reaches its maximum velocity, which may be several times greater than the velocity of the wind in other locations. At this point the wind fans out, some of it continuing to rise straight up, and some sweeping horizontally across the cliff top. It is the horizontal compo-

Reggie Jones flies in the ridge lift above cliffs at Torrey Pines, California. (© Bettina Gray)

Away from the cliffs, Tom Peghiny will lose the lift and be forced to land. (© Bettina Gray)

nent that the pilot uses to assist his takeoff, since by running into the wind he doesn't have to move nearly as fast to attain airspeed as he would if there were no wind.

Some distance from the edge of the cliff the wind boils downward in a violently turbulent swirl known as a *rotor*. A pilot accidentally getting into the rotor can find himself slammed into the ground with unbelievable force. A narrow cliff may not have enough rotor-free space for a landing back on top. Before attempting any cliff-top landing, pilots must find the *location* and *extent* of the natural rotors.

It's important for the hang glider pilot to assess his terrain before flying to determine ahead of time where he can expect to find areas of lift and where there'll be turbulence. Flying in the proper areas can assure both a safer and longer flight.

LIKE A MOVING SIDEWALK

Once a hang glider is aloft and flying over terrain free of obstacles that would create turbulence, the wind has no effect at all on the flying characteristics of the hang glider. In fact, if the pilot were blindfolded, he would not be able to tell whether he was flying into the wind, downwind, or crosswind, since the hang glider would always be flying into the relative wind created by its own forward speed.

The only observable effect of flying *against* the prevailing wind would be the hang glider's traveling over the ground with less speed than if it were flying *with* the wind. The situation would be analogous to a pedestrian walking on a moving sidewalk of the type seen at major airports. If he were walking on the moving sidewalk in the direction it was traveling, he'd be moving much faster than those walking next to him who weren't on the sidewalk. Obversely, by walking on the sidewalk in the opposite direction, he'd appear to others to be moving slowly, or possibly even going backward, yet he'd still be moving forward on the sidewalk at the same speed.

It is only quite close to the ground that a hang glider is affected by wind blowing over smooth, even terrain. As wind travels across a smooth surface, the wind nearer the surface moves at a slower speed than it does at higher altitudes. This situation is known as *wind gradient* and can be a problem when the pilot is near the ground in a landing or takeoff pattern.

As the pilot approaches his landing in a moderate wind, presuming he is flying *into* the wind, his groundspeed will be reduced by the amount of that wind. As he continues to glide downward, the wind velocity abruptly decreases, and the hang glider picks up ground speed. Since the pilot is often watching the ground at low altitudes near landing or takeoff, he interprets his increase in ground speed as an actual increase in his own airspeed, and may slow down the glider's airspeed to keep his ground speed constant. So, unless the pilot is aware of the effects of wind gradient, he can find himself stalled at low altitudes when he thought he was maintaining adequate airspeed.

HOT AIR A-RISIN'

If wind were the only factor a hang glider pilot had to consider, flying would be easy but would soon become boring.

Because the earth's surface is not completely flat, or the same temperature, or the same color, there exist areas which are hotter or cooler than others. This is fortunate for the soaring and hang glider pilots since differences in temperature create *thermals.*

Thermals are the lift used for most long-distance, cross-country flights. A thermal is created when an area of the earth's surface, for one reason or another, gets hotter than the surrounding area. The air directly *above* this surface becomes heated more than the air in adjacent areas. Because hot air is lighter than cold air, the warmed air begins to rise. The rising air, or thermal, may be a small, localized body of air a couple of feet across, or it can be an incredibly powerful, fast-moving mass of air hundreds of yards across and rising thousands of feet in altitude.

The types of terrain that create thermals are diverse, and the art of predicting and finding thermals is often what separates the championship pilot from the pilot who gets last place in hang gliding competitions. A black parking lot next to a lake would be an ideal area for a thermal, since the asphalt surface would absorb the sun's heat and become hot, whereas the lake would remain quite cool. Therefore, the air above the parking lot would become much hotter than the air over the lake and would rise. As the air rose it would draw in air from the lake, which would also quickly be heated and rise itself. Thus, just above the parking lot there would be a steady column of rising air next to a rush of air flowing from the lake toward the asphalt.

The air adjacent to the column of air high over the parking lot would be drawn downward to replace the missing air over the lake. The end result would be a tremendous motion of air, with air over the parking lot rising and air over the lake sinking.

How high hot air rises depends on conditions in the atmosphere at the time. Since all rising air cools as it rises, and since air at higher altitudes is usually cooler than air at lower altitudes, the eventual altitude of the rising air will depend on whether the rising air cools faster than the air surrounding it.

Conditions in the atmosphere are termed either *stable* or *unstable* according to the behavior of these columns of rising air. If the column of air maintains itself hotter than the surrounding air, even though it cools as it rises, it will continue to rise and may in fact increase its velocity. Such a situation is called an unstable condition; it is highly desirable for cross-country hang gliding flights.

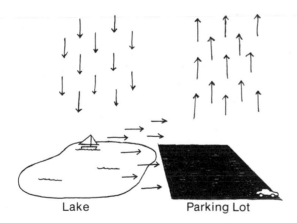

Lake   Parking Lot

Air rises over warm area (parking lot in example) and is drawn downward over cooler area (lake). (Drawing by Joe Linton)

THERMAL

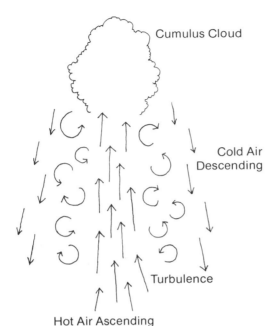

Cumulus Cloud

Cold Air
Descending

Turbulence

Hot Air Ascending

Portrait of a thermal. (Drawing by Joe Linton)

If the rising air quickly approaches the temperature of the surrounding air as it cools while rising, it will then stop rising when the temperatures have become similar. Conditions are then called stable. In such a situation, even extremely powerful thermals, rising quickly in the beginning, soon peter out and may limit a hang glider pilot's altitude gain to a fixed level.

Since there is usually some wind where a thermal is being generated, the thermal tends to move with the wind. So, rather than remaining a straight vertical column, the thermal goes off at an angle and drifts downwind. How far the thermal wanders depends on the initial strength of the thermal and the velocity of the wind. Often a thermal is physically marked by a big, fluffy white cloud—a cumulus cloud—an exciting sight to an experienced hang glider pilot.

When flying into and out of thermals, it's important to know that while the center of the thermal is rising rapidly, the air surrounding the core is *falling* just as rapidly, and between the rising and falling portions there is severe turbulence. The goal of the soaring pilot is to stay in the rising air and avoid the sinking air—which is why you so often see a group of hang gliders or sailplanes circling in a small, localized area. Even though the hang glider will sink through the air around it at two to three hundred feet a minute, if the center of the thermal is rising a thousand feet a minute, the pilot will enjoy a net gain of eight hundred feet of altitude a minute.

170 **The Education of a Hang Glider Pilot**

EVEN AIR CAN TURN UGLY

It is not enough to know about winds and thermals. The hang glider pilot must also be aware of *fronts*.

A front is an area where two different types of air or air masses come together or collide; fronts are responsible for most activity in bad weather.

As a large area of air sits over a particular portion of the earth's surface, it begins to take on the characteristics of the land below; thus air over tropical portions of the ocean becomes warm and moist, whereas air sitting over the arctic poles turns dry and cold. As these air masses move over the earth's surface, they change very slowly; when two entirely different air masses come together, an area of intense activity—a front—is created.

The behavior of a front may vary from an extremely large area of light lift or sink, to one of violent activity involving lightning, hail, rain, or even a tornado. Fronts are often associated with strong, unpredictable winds, which may change as much as ninety degrees within minutes.

Advice concerning violent fronts is simple: Avoid them.

THE COMPLACENCY SYNDROME

Once the new hang glider pilot understands something of the airframe structure, safety equipment, aerodynamics, and meteorology necessary for hang gliding, he is ready to be taken to a small, gentle hill for his first flight instruction.

While some instructors regularly use tandem hang gliders, most rely on slowly progressive solo flights for their instruction.

The new pilot is in for several surprises. Although hang gliding looks like it would feel terrifying, the first few flights convince the novice that it feels incredibly safe—even deceptively safe. There is no sensation of falling whatsoever; on the contrary, the pilot is apt to get the impression that nothing could possibly go wrong.

The good, solid, supportive feel of the hang glider is enough to make even those afraid of heights feel relaxed and secure in the air. In fact, it is not unusual for a new hang glider pilot with only three or four flights behind him to suddenly let go of the control bar and sit back and take in the sights, quite forgetting his responsibilities as a pilot. Many of the early accidents in the sport, and in fact much of its early reputation as an extremely dangerous activity, were attributable to this euphoric feeling of confidence that a hang glider gives.

A good rule to remember is, If you think hang gliding is dangerous, it can be perfectly safe; whereas if you think hang gliding is perfectly safe, it can be extremely dangerous.

Another of the early surprises for the new pilot is the duration of his first flight. As one watches beginners learning to fly, it is obvious that their first flights are incredibly short, lasting mere seconds. Yet to the new pilot, the flight seems to go on for hours.

THE ACTION'S IN THE HIPS

The actual flying instruction begins at the base of a small, gentle training hill— or better yet, at the ultimate in "forgiving" sites: a sand dune. The first flight consists of merely running along the ground into the wind with the hang glider, just to get the feel of it. The purpose is to practice control.

The kite is maneuvered by the pilot's shifting his weight, much like skiing or surfing. Control can be thought of in two ways: either shifting your hips the way you want to go or pushing the control bar the opposite way. In either case, the response feels like a conventional airplane, except the controls are reversed.

Thus, to turn right, the hips are slid to the right by moving the control bar left.

To turn left, the hips move left while the control bar is pushed to the right.

To dive, the hips are pulled forward, bringing the control bar into the stomach, and to climb and stall, the hips are pushed back, moving the control bar away from the stomach.

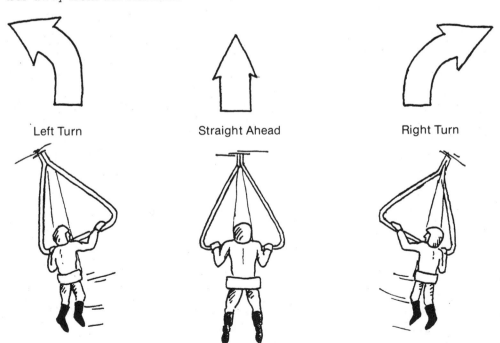

Left Turn   Straight Ahead   Right Turn

Pilot shifts body weight into the turn and pushes the control bar away from the turn. (Drawing by Joe Linton)

172 **The Education of a Hang Glider Pilot**

The neutral flying position is found with the hips centered in the control bar, and the bar about five inches from the stomach. This is where the kite will fly perfectly straight and level, neither turning, diving, nor stalling.

Most modern hang gliders are designed so that if the control bar is released completely, the kite will assume a neutral flying position. This fact can be used by the beginner to test whether he is diving or stalling. He should relax on the control bar and let the kite determine its best glide angle.

HOLDING THE BIRD DOWN

Once the pilot masters running and maneuvering with all his gear in place, the actual flight can begin.

The wind should be between five and fifteen miles an hour, with the ideal being ten miles an hour and blowing straight up the hill.

The pilot begins by carrying the glider up the hill to a location about fifty feet from where he intends to land. Although this sounds easy, it is often the hardest part of learning to fly a hang glider. Since the glider is designed to fly, and because of the slight breeze, from the moment the nose of the glider is lifted off the ground, the thing wants to take off. It can quickly become unmanageable.

Wind

Carrying the glider uphill. (Drawing by Joe Linton)

Therefore the pilot should walk with his back to the wind, holding the glider by the control bar with the nose pointed into the wind. When the nose of the glider is kept neutral into the wind, it neither tries to lift up nor push down.

If wind is a real problem, the instructor will help by walking up the hill with the student, holding the nose of the glider neutral.

Once the kite is set down, proper ground-handling is essential. Even on the ground, the nose of the hang glider must always be pointed into the wind, since wind hitting the glider from the side or rear tends to flip it over or make it take off. The glider rests on the control bar and nose, always pointed *down*. In such a posture, the wind helps keep the glider in place.

The eager novice may now want to attach his harness to the hang glider— a mistake. "Hooking in" is the last step, and the last part of preflighting the glider. Trying to ground-handle the hang glider while attached to it can result in both glider and pilot being blown over—with damage to either or both. Hooking in is the last thing a pilot does before departure, and *unhooking* the first thing he does on landing. No experienced pilot wants to be attached—on the ground —to a machine as wind-susceptible as a hang glider.

Trying to hang on to or grab a loose hang glider blowing around in the wind is also a mistake. Pilots are warned to let it go.

Wind

The glider rests on ground, pointed into the wind. (Drawing by Joe Linton)

174 **The Education of a Hang Glider Pilot**

Glider at Mere, England, blows straight up in wind. British Nationals, 1977.
(© Bettina Gray)

Chances are the hang glider won't be damaged. A hang glider by itself is light and seldom exerts enough force, unassisted, to damage the airframe. However, as soon as somebody attempts to grab it, the kite tries to lift the person off with it, and the forces involved suddenly become large, which may spell damage to both kite and rider.

If it's possible to swing the nose of the glider into the wind without much effort, OK. Otherwise, the glider should be left to blow over, and once upside down can be turned nose down to the wind. If the wind is really strong, the upended glider might have to be disassembled to get its nose right.

Preflighting a hang glider is very much like preflighting a conventional airplane. All parts are visually inspected, with particular attention to the areas of stress. The pilot looks over and feels each tube, feels the cable for frays, inspects the sail, checks the cable attachments. Then, and only then, he attaches his harness. As surprising as it may seem, a large number of pilots have actually forgotten this last step.

Failure to hook in looms as a frequent, preventable, and incredibly sad cause of pilot injury. Many a lapsing pilot has run off a large mountain or precipice, only to notice—too late—that he wasn't attached to the glider and would last only as long as the strength in his arms.

UP, UP, AND AWAY

Once the pilot is securely hooked into the glider, he picks it up, lifting it all the way so that the seat or harness straps are tight and tugging at his body.

If there is a reasonable breeze, this may involve no effort, since the glider wants to fly and will be tugging at the pilot. If there is no wind this can be quite tiring, and the pilot should spend as little time as possible holding the glider

Chris Price demonstrates the all-out run necessary for launch. (© Bettina Gray)

in this position. While at the ready, the control bar is always held in the neutral flying position.

When the instructor has indicated the wings are level and the glider pointed into the wind, the student verifies the wind by looking at the strip of Dacron, called the tell tale, which is tied to the flying wires in front and acts as a wind indicator.

Now, as fast as he can go, the novice begins running down the hill. He tries to accelerate the glider by leaning into the harness and seat ropes, rather than by pushing on the control bar. If the hang glider appears to be breaking his forward speed, he leans into the harness even farther, and perhaps pulls in on the control bar slightly.

The student's goal at this point should be to run the glider all the way down the hill, without ever lifting off the ground: Thus, at all times, the pilot should maintain his balance.

It is paradoxical that only by trying to keep the hang glider on the ground will the pilot have a good takeoff, and only by trying to keep the hang glider in the air will he have a good landing.

As the student runs down the hill and builds speed, he will sense his strides becoming longer and longer until, almost unnoticed, his feet are no longer on the ground. Often a good beginner will keep running even after he is well into the air, an event that an instructor likes to see.

On the first flight there is virtually no time for maneuvers, and the takeoff should blend imperceptibly with the beginning of the landing. The pilot's goal should be to keep the glider pointed into the wind and traveling down the slope, and the control bar in the neutral flying position.

As the pilot's feet come down to within approximately one foot of the ground, he should begin easing out the control bar, pushing his weight to the rear just enough to keep his shoes one foot off the ground.

If he notices his feet climbing more than a foot off the ground, he should ease the control bar back in; and if his feet come still closer to the ground, even though he pushed out, he should push out a little more and a little faster.

With the glider traveling down the slope and the slope leveling off, the pilot will have to push out farther and farther to keep his shoes one foot off the ground.

The more he pushes out, the slower the glider will fly, as it bleeds off airspeed. Finally, just before it all comes to a complete stop (if, in a wind, the glider *does* come to a complete stop), the wing will stop flying, or stall, and set the pilot gently on his feet.

At this point the student should carefully set the glider on the ground, nose down into the wind, and unhook his harness before dancing around wildly and screaming with delight.

Student stays low, follows straight path. Instructor offers continual guidance. (Ken de Russy)

First-flight elation. (Ken de Russy)

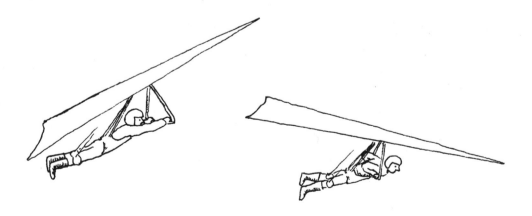

Control-bar attitudes for stall and dive. (Drawing by Joe Linton)

After a successful first flight, the experienced instructor will insist on several more well-executed takeoffs and landings before allowing the beginner to attempt any in-flight maneuvers.

WHO MOVED THE BULL'S-EYE?

The next step in flight training is to allow the pilot to start slightly farther up the hill for additional flight time and some very shallow ten- to fifteen-degree S turns.

At no time should the new pilot turn the glider more than twenty degrees away from a course directly into the wind, since wind speed subtracts from the pilot's airspeed, and the resulting slower ground speed can help lessen the effect of any mistakes the pilot might make.

As he proceeds higher up the hill, practicing maneuvers, the apprentice should constantly be aware of the dangers of the stall; all training flights are done at altitudes too low to recover from any kind of stall.

Once the student is skilled at making shallow turns across the path of the wind, he should try to curb his galloping overconfidence and remind himself his skills are still minimal; they include only takeoffs, landings, and minor in-flight corrections, and do not equip him for handling turbulence or any unusual conditions requiring judgment and experience.

After many more incident-free flights at low altitudes, the beginner is finally ready for the next big step—learning to set up an approach to a landing in a limited landing area.

With the instructor, the student should move to a larger hill with several hundred feet of altitude and a very large, unobstructed landing area. Though the instructor will doubtless choose the site, a caution applies to *all* new flying sites: The pilot must always learn his terrain. He should carefully note any hazards or obstacles, but particularly power lines or telephone lines which loom as insidious threats to hang gliders. For one thing, they're practically invisible, especially from above. For another, wrapping a hang glider around a high-voltage wire is a sure way of being electrocuted.

It seems odd that power lines can be such eyesores when viewed from the ground, yet virtually disappear when seen from above, but it's true. You might just as well try to spot a spider web as a power line from the top of a hill. The only clue is poles, and any pilot can conclude when he spots a pole that another lurks in the area. Having found a second pole, he can assume also that wires run from one to the other. Cleared strips of land are an additional clue that power lines are present.

Besides wires, a check should be made for any objects upwind of the intended landing area—such as buildings, trees, cars, or even other parked hang gliders—behind which there'll be turbulence that can mess up a landing. It's important as well to search out natural wind indicators—tall grass, areas of

Launch area needs to be checked for obstacles—rocks, trees, telephone poles (background); Mike Arambede, at the USHGA League Meet, February 1980, in New Moyes Mega, Crestline, California. (© Bettina Gray)

water, pliable trees, or reedy shrubs—which can give last-minute wind directions for landing. Without any of these, a small flag can be placed somewhere near the landing area.

A last area to double-check is the launch itself. Now that gliders often stretch to spans greater than thirty-five feet, the wing tips tend to be beyond the pilot's peripheral vision; by underestimating the width of the cleared launch area, many a pilot has caught his wing on nearby shrubs or trees during takeoff. Hooking the wing on something can spin the kite around just as it's getting airborne, with consequences ranging from embarrassing to disastrous.

Together, the student and his instructor mark out a limited landing area and formulate a plan for the novice to use up his altitude and land near a spot without overshooting or undershooting it. This involves calculating the wind direction in advance and planning the flight so that the pilot arrives about one hundred yards downwind from the landing area and about one hundred feet off the ground. The pilot can then fly toward the spot, making slow S turns to left and right, attempting to adjust the correct number and degree of turns so he'll arrive just short of the landing area several feet off the ground—and then proceed straight in for a normal landing on the target.

All this is difficult, since the pilot must correctly judge his altitude, the wind velocity, his airspeed, and his rate of descent as he decides how much to turn or how many turns to make.

Most pilots, on their first attempts, are positive they'll land right next to their bull's-eye. It is only after they've missed by several hundred yards that they realize how difficult the undertaking is.

Bob Wills pushes out to flare for landing. (Stephen McCarroll)

By this point in the pilot's training the intense, ecstatic thrill of flying, which he experienced in earlier flights, has given way to a more relaxed, intellectual satisfaction at being able to float quietly over the countryside in full control of his course and destination. The pilot realizes he can fine tune his glider's airspeed by the feel of the wind in his face and the sound it makes on his glider. He also begins to notice that the ease of control of the hang glider is proportional to his airspeed, so that while flying quickly only small efforts are required to effect substantial control movements. Conversely, at slow speeds even relatively large control actions result in only minor course corrections.

GOING IN CIRCLES

Once the beginning pilot has mastered landing in a limited landing area, it's time to start developing the skills necessary for soaring flight.

Until now, the student has been flying in conditions of relatively little lift, or at least in very smooth lift, and his main concerns were controlling the glider through a continuously descending flight path while maintaining control and setting up a landing. Now he is ready for several new experiences: launching from steeper sites—even cliffs—and flying in areas of strong lift. Mainly he must learn to make coordinated, continuous turns without increasing his rate of descent. Without turns, he can't stay up and soar, even in areas of very strong lift.

Cliff launchings are different from downhill launchings. The pilot must analyze the velocity and direction of the wind at both the cliff and the proposed

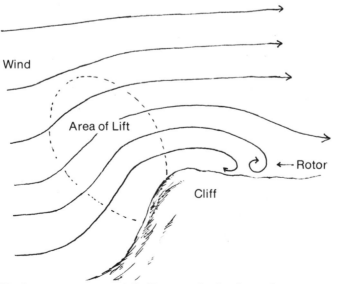

Wind patterns near a cliff. (Drawing by Joe Linton)

launch area, if it's back a bit from the edge. Some cliff launch areas have a tremendous vertical component to the wind immediately away from the cliff face, and this can cause problems for the unknowing pilot.

If the wind velocity at the cliff has a strong vertical component (a strong upward sweep), or if the horizontal component is strong, it's often necessary to have another pilot hold the glider down by grabbing the nose flying wires until the pilot has his glider at its optimum angle of attack and is ready for launch. This will insure the pilot's having sufficient airspeed when he leaves the ground, so he won't be blown backward into the hill.

The velocity of the wind at the takeoff spot should be carefully assessed, since it will determine the distance the pilot needs for launch and the course of the glider, once airborne. The greater the wind velocity at the takeoff area, the less distance the pilot will need to develop his forward speed and, consequently, his lift. If there is *no* wind, the pilot may need a substantial running distance to attain flying speed.

A word of caution: Downwind launches are extremely difficult and may be impossible if the wind velocity is significant or the launch area fairly level. Under no circumstances should a beginner attempt a downwind takeoff. There are very few reasons why an expert should attempt it.

A launch assist is necessary at cliff's edge. (Ken de Russy)

The prototype maneuver for soaring is the 360-degree turn, which, as the name implies, merely involves flying in a circle. Although the three-sixty turn looks simple to the observer or beginner, it is probably one of the most difficult skills the new pilot will acquire and can result in the loss of startling— or even fatal—amounts of altitude.

The term *coordinated turn* came about when pilots first realized they had to coordinate the surprising and unexpected glider responses to their control inputs at different attitudes.

The phenomenon can be explained: A Rogallo wing does not coordinate a turn by itself. It has a tendency to drop the nose or slip into a turn. The steeper the bank, and the longer the Rogallo is held in the turn, the more the wing will slip and the faster altitude will be lost.

In the beginning this is why it is important to have what seems like an excess of altitude for learning three-sixtys—at least a thousand feet. The thousand feet is drummed into beginners relentlessly by safety-minded instructors who understand the importance of having plenty of room for error plus enough altitude to set up for a safe landing approach.

A three-sixty is coordinated by the pilot's shifting his weight to the rear *after* the kite is banked in response to his lateral weight shift. The steeper the initial bank, the more it is necessary for the pilot to shift his weight back. Once in a tight banking turn, the pilot will soon realize the control actions have reversed: The fore-and-aft motions on the control bar that used to control the airspeed of the glider now control the amount of turn, and the lateral control actions that normally control the amount of turn now control the airspeed.

Before this understanding comes, many a new pilot attempting his first three-sixty gets midway through the turn, realizes with alarm he is losing altitude fast, and tries to hasten the turn along by shifting his weight into it. In shocked surprise, he finds the kite slipping quicker and losing altitude faster, with the potential for a straight-down spiral. Only by understanding the apparent control reversal and by initiating the turn with sufficient altitude—away from obstacles —is it possible to master this basic soaring maneuver.

One of the difficulties in learning to do three-sixtys is the ever-present possibility of stalling by shifting one's weight back too soon or too far. The exact degree and moment of weight shift can't be defined for every pilot in advance: It is something he must be alert to and work out for himself through experience.

During three-sixtys the wind affects the glider's ground course—which will probably be different than the hang glider's course through the air. While the pilot will travel in a circular path through the air, the air itself is moving relative to the ground. Thus the pilot's circular path is constantly being blown downwind, and his actual ground path will depend on the wind speed and the glider's flying speed. For this reason it's important that the pilot be well away from any hill or obstacles downwind, particularly since his visibility as he banks is greatly reduced. He may suddenly find he's drifted farther downwind than he ever anticipated and the mountain is looking him straight in the face.

If the pilot suspects he may be blowing off course, he should correct by leveling his wings and holding the glider straight for a suitable period of time when traveling *into* the wind, and by maintaining a tight bank and turn when flying *downwind.*

Certain hang glider designs add a third complication to three-sixtys: These gliders, once the bank is initiated, tend to either hold that amount of bank or, in some cases, to increase the bank. The pilot who has one of these gliders must compensate by initiating the bank normally, then centering his body on the bar—or even away from the turn—once the bank is in progress.

The steps of a good soaring three-sixty turn are:

1. Increase the airspeed slightly to insure a good bank response, since all control responses improve with higher air speeds.

2. Bank the kite with a straight lateral movement.

3. Begin pushing the bar out after achieving the desired amount of bank, while slowly trimming the pilot's weight toward center until the proper airspeed and nose attitude are achieved.

Gusty winds, thermals, bumps, and turbulence all require continuous trimming of the glider in order to maintain proper airspeed and nose attitude. In some gliders it is helpful to yaw the glider into the turn while initiating bank.

The three-sixty is terminated by returning the pilot's weight forward and to the center, or in some gliders even toward the uphill wing to a normal, level glide position.

As the pilot perfects his coordinated turns, he will notice that while in a tight turn his weight seems to increase if the turn is well coordinated; technically, he is experiencing more g force. One g is defined as the acceleration produced by gravity and felt by the pilot as his weight. For example, if a pilot is maintaining a sixty-degree bank in a coordinated turn, he will be experiencing almost two g's of force, and thus he will feel as though he weighs twice his normal weight. Lifting his arms will be twice as hard, and keeping his head up will be twice as difficult. The sensation is much the same as one feels when traveling tight turns on a roller coaster.

The pilot may now feel he's ready for anything, that his glider can be flown in any posture and is safe for all kinds of aerobatics. But there are cautions: The Hang Glider Manufacturer's Association recommends that a hang glider not be flown at attitudes exceeding thirty degrees up or down in pitch, and sixty degrees in either direction in roll. Since all normal and necessary maneuvers for both soaring and cross-country flying can be done well within these limitations, they are good guidelines for all hang glider pilots.

Although hang gliders have been repeatedly looped successfully, and are regularly put through accelerated tail-sliding hammerhead stalls as part of the manufacturer's testing procedures, no hang glider today is certified for aerobatics. Any pilot attempting high-g or aerobatic maneuvers must be aware of the fact that he is operating outside the design limitations for hang gliders.

The third and final phase of flying still lies ahead. The pilot can expect thrills and a great exhilaration at being able to explore fully the three dimensions of flight.

SCRAMBLE UP A THERMAL

Now that he's mastered the technique of the coordinated three-sixty, the pilot is no longer a beginner. He has the skills to gain altitude . . . and *soar!* But first he must learn the Rules of the Ridge.

Almost any place that's soarable is apt to have somebody—or several somebodies—soaring there, and rules have been worked out for everyone's safety: For ridge soaring, where gliders travel back and forth in a limited airspace in front of a ridge, the right-of-way rules are as follows:

1. The low glider always has right-of-way over the high glider.

2. The glider closer to the hill, or ridge, always has right-of-way over the glider farther from the hill or ridge.

3. Gliders at the same altitude and approaching each other from opposite directions down the ridge always pass to the right.

4. If a glider is overtaking another glider at the same altitude, traveling in the same direction, the overtaking glider must give way to the glider being passed.

5. If none of the above applies, the glider to the right always has right-of-way over the glider to the left.

6. If there is ever any doubt about who has right-of-way, always give way to the other pilot and assume he doesn't know the rules. Once safely on the ground you can argue who had right-of-way and who should go back and reread the rules.

With thermal soaring, there are some differences. Pilots don't have the presence of a nearby ridge to concern them—in fact, the airspace seems fairly limitless. Yet still they come together. The first man who finds a thermal and starts circling upward draws all the hang gliders in his area like magic, and everybody rushes over to hook into the lift.

A thermal filled with circling hang gliders needs rules, too:

1. Once a glider is established in a thermal and has started turning in one direction, all other gliders entering that thermal must turn in the same direction.

Who has the right-of-way? (© Bettina Gray)

2. If a glider is already circling in a thermal and another glider wishes to enter the thermal at the same altitude, the glider entering the thermal must give right-of-way to the glider already there.

3. The high glider must give way to the low glider, and if the low glider is climbing faster than the high glider, the high glider must let him pass. This is because the low glider, with the wing above him, can't see what's directly overhead.

4. The glider to the right always has right-of-way over the glider to the left.

5. As in ridge soaring, if there is any doubt about who has right-of-way, always give it to the other guy and argue the point later.

The ability to soar lift is a difficult, imprecise, and sometimes even a mystical art. It is often just a feel that the pilot can't describe in words. This feel is sometimes the only difference between a flight that lasts ten minutes and one that lasts four hours. Certain pilots, after hundreds of hours of flying time, seem almost able to "smell" or "hear" lift, and once airborne are able to home in on it without any reasonable explanation of how they do it. It is as though these pilots have a special sense that allows them to find lift and circle in the center of it. Soaring becomes an art more than a skill, and the only sure way to learn the art is with time spent in the air.

Terrain below holds key to thermal activity—Willi Muller flying a Moyes Maxi Mk. III at Mt. Buffalo, Victoria, Australia, January 1980. (Vincene Muller)

THE NEEDLE TRANCE

The art of soaring is aided by instruments, and the most important of these is the variometer. A variometer is a sensitive instrument that tells the pilot how much altitude he is gaining or losing. There are many different designs available, but all variometers act by measuring the change in atmospheric pressure that occurs with changes in altitude.

Variometers usually come with a gauge that reads in feet per minute, with the usual scale being from minus a thousand feet per minute to positive a thousand feet per minute. Some designs also incorporate an audio attachment that produces a tone which gets either higher or lower depending on how fast the pilot is going up or down—a tone that warbles on the up side.

Although it might seem to an observer that a pilot should know without instruments whether he's going up or down, such is not the case. Once a pilot is several thousand feet above the terrain, the feeling is one of being in space, since all visual clues to one's altitude above the ground are lost. It is possible to vary up or down hundreds of feet without noticing changes in the size of objects below; therefore, the pilot simply *can't judge* whether he's ascending or descending.

Take the pilot who's flying along and suddenly feels a bump *up*. One of three things could be happening. He might have been gliding down and suddenly hit lift that caused him to glide down less rapidly; he could have been gliding downward and hit lift that caused him to start flying level; or he could have been flying level and hit lift that made him suddenly start climbing. The feeling in all three instances would be the same, yet the actions he'd take would be different, depending on what his variometer had been telling him.

In the first case, since he was already flying in sink and gliding downward, the pilot would want to be flying quickly to get through the sink and, depending on his rate of descent after he hit the bump, would still prefer to keep his speed up until he hit an area of lift.

In the second instance, finding himself changed from downward to level, he'd want to slow up considerably in order to cover the maximum amount of ground without losing altitude; in the third case, with enough lift to make him rise, the pilot would slow up and begin to circle, using his variometer to modify his turns. If the variometer indicated he was going up more rapidly, the pilot would tend to straighten out his turn to move toward the center of the lift; whereas if the variometer indicated a slowing rate of ascent, he'd tighten up his turn to get back to the lift he was apparently leaving.

In this way, the experienced pilot becomes glued to his variometer, and after a period of time almost forgets he's in the air. The feeling is one of total concentration, as though trying to play some kind of computer game against the variometer. The pilot finds himself studying the silly little needle intently, and trying—by manipulating the wind in his face and the pressure on the controls—to make the needle go up, only up. He can be locked into this total concentration for ten, fifteen minutes at a time, and when he snaps out and remembers that he is indeed high above the earth, floating in space, can look down at the terrain and find it totally unfamiliar, as though he'd drifted into a foreign land. It's true, he's probably traveled several miles since he last looked at the terrain.

The feeling is one of incredible power. He has been playing a game with nature and he's won. He can reckon up his gains and find he's netted thousands of feet of altitude and several miles of distance. There's no feeling of supremacy quite like it!

Book Three

The Hang Glider Pilot's Baedeker

HANG GLIDING CHAMPIONS

This list includes most of the important self-launched United States meets that are still active, or were active for a long period of time. It also includes a few non-U.S. meets. But, because of sketchy reporting in our hang gliding sources, or our own inability to find data, some champions may have been most regretfully omitted.

In many cases, results of these meets through the first ten positions would have provided additional interesting information, as many of our major champions appeared over and over in the longer lists, reflective of various incredible accomplishments. A whole book could be written on hang gliding's champions.

Modern hang gliding's very first meet was Jack Lambie's first Lilienthal Meet on May 23, 1971 (reported in detail on pages 33–40). Results: Mark Lambie, prize for longest self-launched flight—thirteen seconds. Richard Miller: longest distance—seventy-five yards.

United States National Hang Gliding Championships—various sites

1973:
1. Chris Wills
2. Bob Wills
3. Mike Larsen

1974:
1. Bob Wills
2. Chris Wills
3. Chris Price

Fixed Wing
1. Jack Schroeder
2. Dave Cronk
3. Ron Richards

1975:
Overall
1. Dave Muehl
2. Steven Coan
3. Chris Wills

Open Class
1. Chris Price
2. Tom Peghiny
3. Sean Dever

Advanced Standard
1. Chris Wills
2. Doug Heath
3. Rob Reed

Standard Class
1. Dave Muehl
2. Steve Coan
3. John Seals

1976:
Standard Class
1. Robert Reed—
   Bennett 19/13
2. Dan Alban—
   Bobcat II
3. John McVey—
   Windlord III

Unlimited Class
1. Ken Koklenski—
   Fledgling
2. Tom Vayda—
   Fledgling
3. Scott Price—
   Quicksilver

Open Class
1. Keith Nichols—
   Albatross
2. Bruce Waugh—
   Albatross
3. Zane Wadley—
   Dragonfly

1977:
Class I (Standard)
1. Robert Reed—
   Cirrus
2. Dave Braddock—
   Stingray
3. Tom Goodman—
   Cirrus

Class II (Flex-Wing Open)
1. Henry Braddock—
   Moyes
2. Jim Braddock—
   Moyes Maxi
3. Jeffrey James—
   Phoenix 8

Class III (Rigid)
1. Brad White—
   Mitchell Wing
2. John Coyne—
   Fledgling B
3. Tom Vayda—
   Fledgling A

1978:
1. Dennis Pagan—Sirocco II
2. Tim Cocker—Phoenix 8
   Steve Moyes—Moyes Maxi
3. Sterling Stoll—10-Meter

1979:
1. Eric Raymond—Fledgling
2. Tom Wilson—Fledgling
3. Tom Vayda—Fledgling

1980:
1. Tom Haddon—UP Comet
2. Rich Pfeiffer—UP Comet
3. Bob Deffenbaugh—UP Comet

Masters—Grandfather Mountain, North Carolina

1976:
1. Mike Arrambide—Cumulus 5B
2. Charlie Baughman—SST

        3. Ed Cesar—Dragonfly
           Robbie Hendricks—Moyes Stinger
           Doug Lawton—Moyes Stinger

1977:   1. Tom Peghiny—Phoenix 8
        2. Chris Perkins—Phoenix 8
        3. Mike Arrambide—Cumulus 10

1978:   1. Dave Rodriguez—Moyes Maxi MK III
        2. Rich Grigsby—Phoenix 12 Prototype
        3. Sean Dever—Moyes MK III

1979:   1. Steve Moyes—Moyes
        2. Mike Arrambide—Moyes
        3. Jeff Scott—Lazor

1980:   1. Steve Moyes—Moyes Mega
        2. Peter Brown—Moyes Mega
        3. Rich Grigsby—UP Comet

The American Cup—Chattanooga, Tennessee

1978:   Team   Individual
        1. British   1. Graham Slater—Great Britain
        2. U.S.A.   2. Dennis Pagan—U.S.A.
        3. Canada   3. Dave Chernoff—Canada

1979:   Team
        1. British
        2. U.S.A.
        3. Canada

1980:   Team
        1. U.S.A.
        2. British
        3. France

Grouse Mountain—Vancouver, British Columbia

1978:   1. Steve Moyes—Moyes Maxi
        2. John Ogden—Moyes Maxi
        3. John Duthie—Lancer 4

1979:   1. John Davis—Moyes Maxi
        2. Glenn Hockett—10 Meter
        3. Larry Croome—MJ6

1980:   1. Rob Kells—Wills Wing
        2. Mike Meier—Wills Wing
        3. Joe Greblo—Moyes

Owens Valley Cross-Country Classic—Owens Valley, California

1978:   1. Joe Greblo—10 Meter
        2. S. Stoll—10 Meter
        3. L. Tudor—Spyder

1979:   Classic
    1. Rich Pfeiffer—
       Mosquito
    2. Keith Nichols—
       Floater
    3. Jeff Scott—
       Lazor

Open
1. George Worthington—
   Seagull 10 Meter
2. Tom Wilson—
   Fledgling
3. Dudley Mead—
   Fledgling

1980:   Classic
    1. Rich Pfeiffer—
       Comet
    2. Rich Grigsby—
       Comet
    3. Jeff Burnett—
       Sensor

Open
1. Eric Raymond—
   Self-built Voyager
2. Rex Miller—
   Fledgling
3. David Leadford—
   Mega

Alpine Kite-Flying Championships—Kossen, Austria

1975:   1. Dave Cronk, U.S.A.
    2. Werner Tscherne, Switzerland
    3. Roy Haggard, U.S.A.

First Annual F.A.I. Hang Gliding Championships—Kossen, Austria

1976:   Class I, Standard
    1. C. Steinbach, Austria
    2. J. Steinbach, Austria
    3. R. Duncan, Australia

Class II, Open
1. T. Delore, New Zealand
2. D. Kupchanko, Canada
3. S. Moyes, Australia

Class III, Rigid
1. K. Battle, Australia
2. S. Price, U.S.A.
3. O. Hofstetter, Switzerland

Second Annual F.A.I. Hang Gliding Championships—South Africa
(Cancelled—lack of participants)

Third Annual F.A.I. World Open/European Championships—Kossen, Austria

1978:   Class I
    1. Pirker, Austria
    2. Christandl, Austria
    3. Mercorelli, France

Class II
1. Thevenot, France
2. England, Great Britain
3. Glanville, France

Class III
1. Olschewsky, Germany
2. Evans, Great Britain
3. Loferer, Austria

F.A.I. World Championships—Grenoble, France

1979:   Class I
    1. Josef Guggenmos, Germany
    2. Johnny Carr, Great Britain
    3. Gerard Thevenot. France

Class II
1. Rex Miller, U.S.A.
2. Wolfgang Hartl, Austria
3. Hans Olschewsky, Germany

Telluride—Rocky Mountains, Colorado

1974: 1. Lloyd Short
2. Dave Muehl
3. Mike Poquiano

1975: Winter Meet
1. John Dunham
2. Charley Boughman
3. Reggie Jones

World Invitational Championships
    Overall High Points: Roy Haggard

Open Class	Standard Class	Fixed Wing
1. Roy Haggard	1. Bob McCaffrey	1. Dave Cronk
2. Greg Mitchell	2. Rene C. Angelot	2. Steve Patmont
3. Mike Arrambide	3. Rob Reed	3. John Lasko

1976: Manufacturers' Invitational
1. Barry Gordon—Electra Flyer, Cirrus II
2. Burke Ewing—Wills Wing, SST-100B
3. Rob Reed—Delta Wing, Phoenix 6B

1977: Manufacturers' Invitational

Team	Individual
1. Wills Wing	1. Keith Nichols
2. J & L Enterprises	2. Joe Greblo
3. Seagull Aircraft	3. Jeffrey Burnett

1978: Manufacturers' Invitational

Team	Individual
1. Moyes Delta Gliders	1. Philip L. Ray—Highster Aircraft 164
2. Seagull Aircraft	2. Tom Haddon—Seagull, 10 Meter
3. Highster Aircraft	3. Larry Tudor—UP, Spyder

After 1978, Telluride became an informal fly-in.

Midwest Open—Frankfort, Michigan

1974: 1. Tom Peghiny
2. Chuck Baughman
3. Jack Schroeder

1975: 1. Burke Ewing
2. Mike Bray
3. James Braddock

1976: Open Class
1. Mike Arrambide
2. Dave Arrambide
3. Jim Bogema

Cochrane—Alberta, Canada

1974:   1. Dave Toop
          2. Bill Taylor
          3. Bill MacDougal

1978:   1. Terry Selzer—MJ5
          2. Emil Segeren—Muller Marauder
          3. George Laing—Muller Marauder

1980:   1. Howard Vandall
          2. Willi Muller
          3. Dwayne Barrett

Escape Country, California—various meets

1974:   Tuborg Beer Championships

Expert

1. Greg Mitchell
2. Curt Stahl
3. Bob Wills

Class A

1. Dave Muehl
2. Dave Arrambide
3. Taras Kiceniuk

1975:   World Hang Gliding Championships
          1. Greg Mitchell—Seagull IV
          2. Bob Wills—Swallowtail
          3. Rick Montanaro—Brock 82UP

1976:   Hang Ten World Championships
          1. Brian Porter—Easy Riser
          2. David Saffold—SST
          3. Trip Mellinger—Phoenix 6B

Thunder Bay—Ontario, Canada, various meets

1975:   Can-Am Hang Gliding Festival
          1. Charlie Baughman
          2. Bob Wills
          3. Reggie Jones

1976:   Molson's North American Hang Gliding Championships
          1. Ed Cesar
          2. Dave Arrambide
          3. David Bailey

1977:   Molson's North American Hang Gliding Championships
          1. Dean Kupchanko—Olympus
          2. John Grobel—SST
          3. Jim Braddock—Maxi Stinger

Southeastern Springtime Championships—Crystal Caverns, Tennessee

1975:   1. Jackie Hinson
          2. Mike Hendrix
          3. Don Nocito

1976: 1. Dick Stern
2. Bruce Short
3. John Burkhalter

Eastern Championships

1975: 1. Tom Peghiny
2. John Volk
3. Jeff Kemp

Northwest Regional Hang Gliding Championships—Wisconsin

1974: 1. Bob Wills
2. Burke Ewing
3. Jim Debauche

Grand Targhee—Alta, Wyoming

1974: 1. Mike Larson
2. Dave Cronk
3. Bryan Jensen

Moab World Invitational Meet—Utah

1978: 1. Malcolm Jones—Sirocco II
2. Gordon Pollok—Oly 160
3. Bif Huss—Fledgling II B

Labatt's World Snow-Kite Championships—British Columbia, Canada

1973: 1. Bob Wills

1974:	Overall	Soaring	Towing
	1. Harry Christie	1. Lee Wilson	1. Bob Wills
	2. Bob Wills	2. Willi Muller	2. Bill Joplin
	3. Dean Tanji	3. Harry Christie	3. John Ford

1975:	Fixed	Flexible
	1. Dave Cronk	1. Bob Wills
	2. Bill Johnson	2. Dean Tanji
	3. Jack Schroeder	3. Ed Cesar

1976: 1. Joe Greblo—Kestrel
2. Bill Johnson—Cumulus VB
3. Willi Muller—Unavailable

Canadian National Championships—Newson, British Columbia

1974:	Soaring	360's
	1. Neil Smith	1. Jim Buckley
	2. Dave Toop	2. Dave Toop
	3. Bill MacDougal	3. Deiter Baumgart

1975: 1. Tom Peghiny

British Hang Gliding Championships

1974: 1. Brian Wood

1975:	Overall	British
	1. Bob Wills	1. Brian Wood
	2. Chris Wills	

British League Championships

1978: 1. Brian Wood
2. Johnny Carr
3. Bob Calvert

Scottish Open

1979: 1. Bob Harrison—Chargus Cyclone
2. Jim McDougall—Wasp Gryphon III
3. Ron Freeman—Wills Wing XC

New Zealand Nationals

1978: 1. Bryan Hayhow
2. Rodney Milne
3. John Riley

Guatemalan Hang Gliding Championships

1979: 1. Haroldo Rodriguez—Wills Wing XC
2. Juan Jose Del Carmen—Wills Wing XC
3. Fernando Linares—Sirocco II

HANG GLIDING OFFICIAL WORLD RECORDS

Thirty-two official world records are available to hang glider pilots. By 1980, ten were established. All records are held by pilots in the United States. George Worthington holds seven world records, Page Pfeiffer two, and Alan Reeter one.

To prepare for a world record, write the USHGA and enclose a check or money order for five dollars for the Record Attempt Kit. Detailed information about setting a record can be found in *Hang Gliding* magazine, August 1980, page 33.

The following categories have been established by Federation Aeronautique Internationale (FAI) in hang gliding: distance, goal, out-and-return, and gain of height. In each of these categories there is a classification for flex wing, one for fixed wing, and one for multiplace (tandem). There is a further classification of general (men) or feminine. This is standard FAI practice. Women are not limited to the feminine category; they may submit claims in the general category if they so choose. Men, however, are restricted to the general classification.

This listing of official records as of December 1, 1980, does not contain unratified claims. Claims may be pending in any category.

New world record attempts must exceed minimum requirements. They are:

Distance	25 km (16.5 miles)
Goal	25 km
Out-and-Return	25 km
Height Gain	1,000 meters (3,281 feet)

Existing distance records must be exceeded by at least 2 kilometers (1.24 miles), altitude records by at least 3 percent.

Men — Flex Wing

SINGLE PLACE

7/22/78	Gain of Height George Worthington Seagull 10 Meter Cerro Gordo Peak, northeast of Keeler, California	USA	3,566 m	11,700 ft
7/25/80	Distance in a Straight Line George Worthington Moyes Mega Cerro Gordo, California	USA	178.89 km	111 mi
7/21/77	Straight Distance to a Goal George Worthington ASG-21 Albatross Sails Cerro Gordo Peak, California, to Benton Station, California	USA	153.61 km	95.45 mi
7/17/79	Out-and-Return Distance George Worthington Seagull 10 Meter Cerro Gordo Peak, California	USA	79.06 km	49.12 mi

MULTIPLACE

Gain of Height
No record established

Distance in a Straight Line
No record established

Straight Distance to a Goal
No record established

Out-and-Return Distance
No record established

Men — Fixed Wing

SINGLE PLACE

7/22/80	Gain of Height George Worthington Mitchell Wing Cerro Gordo Peak, California	USA	2,701.5 m	8,859 ft
7/23/80	Distance in a Straight Line George Worthington Mitchell Wing Cerro Gordo Peak, California	USA	168.3 km	104.58 mi
8/3/79	Straight Distance to a Goal George Worthington Mitchell Wing Gunter Canyon, California	USA	53.15 km	33.03 mi
7/23/77	Out-and-Return Distance George Worthington Mitchell Wing Gunter Canyon, California, to Benton Station, California, to Gunter Canyon, California	USA	76.38 km	47.46 mi

MULTIPLACE

Gain of Height
No record established

Distance in a Straight Line
No record established

Straight Distance to a Goal
No record established

Out-and-Return Distance
No record established

Feminine — Flex Wing

SINGLE PLACE

7/12/79	Gain of Height Page Pfeiffer UP Mosquito Gunter Canyon, Bishop, California	USA	3,291.84 m	10,799.97 ft

Distance in a Straight Line
No record established

Straight Distance to a Goal
No record established

| 7/12/79 | Out-and-Return Distance | USA | 37.18 km | 23.05 mi |

7/12/79   Out-and-Return Distance   USA   37.18 km   23.05 mi
Page Pfeiffer
UP Mosquito
Gunter Canyon, Bishop, California

MULTIPLACE

Gain of Height
No record established

Distance in a Straight Line
No record established

Straight Distance to a Goal
No record established

Out-and-Return Distance
No record established

Feminine—Fixed Wing

SINGLE PLACE

Gain of Height
No record established

Distance in a Straight Line
No record established

Straight Distance to a Goal
No record established

Out-and-Return Distance
No record established

MULTIPLACE

Gain of Height
No record established

Distance in a Straight Line
No record established

Straight Distance to a Goal
No record established

Out-and-Return Distance
No record established

BOOKS

Adleson, Joe, and Bill Williams. *Hang Flight: A Flight Manual For Beginner Intermediate Pilots*,
     3rd ed. Redlands, California: Eco-Nautics, 1974.
Becker, Beril. *Dreams & Realities of the Conquest of the Skies.* New York: Atheneum, 1967.

Carrier, Rick. *Fly: The Complete Book of Sky Sailing.* New York: McGraw-Hill, 1974.

Dedera, Don, photography by Stephen McCarroll. *Hang Gliding: The Flyingest Flying.* Flagstaff, Arizona: Northland Press, 1975.

Desfayes, Jean-Bernard. *Delta: The Hang Gliding Handbook.* Newfoundland, New Jersey: Haessner Publishing, Inc., 1975.

Dickens, Peter L. *Hang Gliding—The Natural High of Self-Launched Flight.* New York: Warren Books, 1977.

Doyle, Lorraine M. *Hang Gliding: Rapture of the Heights.* National City, California: Lion Press, 1974.

Duke, Neville, and Edward Lanchberry. *The Saga of Flight.* New York: John Day Co., 1961.

Dwiggins, Don. *Man-Powered Aircraft.* Blue Ridge Summit, Pennsylvania: TAB Books, 1979.

Emrich, Linn. *The Complete Book of Sky Sports.* London: Collier Books, 1970.

Finley, Rich, and Bob Skinner. *Guide to Basic Rogallo Flight.* San Diego: Flight Realities, 1974.

Halacy, D. S., Jr. *The Complete Book of Hang Gliding.* New York: Hawthorn Books, Inc., 1975.

Hirata, Minoru. *Hang Glider,* 1st ed. Tokyo: 1978. 2nd ed., Tokyo: 1979.

Hunn, David, and Martin Hunt. *Hang Gliding.* New York: Arco Publishing Co., Inc., 1977.

Karlev, Emil. *Delta Flying.* Sofia, Bulgaria: 1980.

Lilienthal, Otto. *Birdflight as the Basis of Aviation.* London: Longmans, Green and Co., 1911.

Markowski, Michael A. *Hang Glider's Bible.* Blue Ridge Summit, Pennsylvania: TAB Books, 1977.

Mendelson, Michael. *The Complete Outfitting & Source Book for Hang Gliding.* Sausalito, California: The Great Outdoors Trading Co., 1977.

Messenger, Ken, and Ronnie Pearson. *Birdmen: A Guide to Hang Gliding.* London: Corgi Books, 1978.

Mrazek, James E. *Hang Gliding & Soaring.* New York: St. Martin's Press, 1976.

Myhre, Bjorn Elton. *Hang Gliding.* Norway: 1979.

Olney, Ross R. *Hang Gliding.* New York: G. P. Putnam's Sons, 1974.

Pagen, Dennis. *Hang Gliding and Flying Conditions.* Published by Dennis Pagen, P.O. Box 601, State College, Pennsylvania 16801.

_____. *Hang Gliding and Flying Skills.* Published by Dennis Pagen, P.O. Box 601, State College, Pennsylvania 16801.

_____. *Hang Gliding for Advanced Pilots.* Published by Dennis Pagen, P.O. Box 601, State College, Pennsylvania 16801.

_____. *Powered Ultralights.* Published by Dennis Pagen, P.O. Box 601, State College, Pennsylvania 16801.

Paul, Eddie. *Skysurfing: A Guide to Hang Gliding.* New York: Sports Car Press, Ltd., 1975.

Poynter, Dan. *Hang Gliding: The Basic Handbook of Skysurfing,* rev. ed. North Quincy, Massachusetts: Daniel F. Poynter, 1976.

_____. *Manned Kiting: The Basic Handbook of Tow Launched Hang Gliding.* Santa Barbara, California: Daniel F. Poynter, 1974.

Radlauer, E., and R. S. Radlauer. *Racing on the Wind.* New York: Franklin Watts, Inc., 1974.

Rice, Herman. *True Flight,* rev. ed. San Jose, California: True Flight, 1974.

Richards, Norman. *The Complete Beginner's Guide to Soaring & Hang Gliding.* Garden City, New York: Doubleday & Co., 1976.

Schmitz, Dorothy Childers. *Hang Gliding.* Mankato, Minnesota: Crestwood House, 1978. (Children's literature.)

Severance, Don. *Reach for the Sky.* Sacramento: Jalmar Press, 1978.

Siposs, George. *Hang Gliding Handbook: Fly Like a Bird.* Blue Ridge Summit, Pennsylvania: TAB Books, 1975.

Worthington, George. *In Search of World Records.* San Diego: Hang Gliding Press, 1980.

HANG GLIDING PUBLICATIONS

Aerie
    55 Lyncroft Road
    New Rochelle, NY 10804
Glider Rider
    Editor: Buzz Chalmers
    Publisher: Tracy Knauss
    P.O. Box 6009
    3710 Calhoun Ave.
    Chattanooga, TN 37401
    (615) 867-4970
Hang Gliding (formerly
    Ground Skimmer)
    Editor: Gil Dodgen
    U.S. Hang Gliding Association
    P.O. Box 66306
    Los Angeles, CA 90066
Houston Hang Gliding Association
Newsletter
    1026 Dreyfus, No. 16
    Houston, TX 77030
Oregon Hang Gliding Association
Newsletter
    Box 5592
    Portland, OR 97228
The Ridge Rider
    New England Hang Gliding Association
    P.O. Box 395
    Newton Highlands, MA 02161

Skyline
    Official publication of
    Capital Hang Gliding Association
    Editor: Chip Wilson
    P.O. Box 64
    Annandale, VA 22003
Soaring Times
    Utah Hang Gliding Association
    898 South 900 East
    Salt Lake, UT 84102
Southland Flyer
    526 East Manchester Terrace
    Inglewood, CA 90301
The UFO Flier
    Publisher: UFO
    P.O. Box 81665
    San Diego, CA 92138
Whole Air Magazine (formerly
    Whole Air Catalog)
    Editor: Starr Tays
    Publisher: Dan Johnson, Idea Graphics
    P.O. Box 144
    Lookout Mountain, TN 37350
Winds Aloft
    P.O. Box 1781
    Bellevue, WA 98009

Non-U.S. Publications—Alphabetized by Country

Ladas Monthly Bulletin
    San Martin 359-5539 Las Heras
    Mondoza, Argentina
    Telephone: 257750
Skysailor (Journal of TAHGA)
    Sydney, Australia
Drachen Flieger magazine
    6064 Rum-Tirol, Weidenweg 5
    Steinbach/BRD
    Austria
The Kingpost
    1200 Hornby Street
    Vancouver, British Columbia
    Canada

The Flypaper
    Box 4063, Postal Station "C"
    Calgary, Alberta
    Canada
HGAC Newsletter
    Box 4063, Postal Station "C"
    Calgary, Alberta
    Canada
Dansk Dragesport
    Dansk Drageflyger Union
    Howitzvej 21
    2000 København F, Denmark

Vol Libre
   3, Rue Ampéré
   R94200 IVRY-Sur-Seine
   France
   Telephone: 672.74.60
Aufwind
   Postfach 1144D-7770
   Uberlingen, Germany
Wings
   Magazine of BHGA
   167a Cheddon Road
   Taunton, Somerset
   Great Britain
Irish Hang Gliding Journal
   Editor: Roy Hammond
   Publisher: IGHA
   40 Beaumont Crescent
   Cork, Ireland
L'Aquilone
   Bologna, Italy
Bungel Shunjū Number
   Tokyo, Japan
Kōdansha Sport
   Tokyo, Japan

Kōfusha Shuppan
   Tokyo, Japan
Fly Nytt
   NAK. Nedre Slottsgate 17
   Oslo 3, Norway
Hangog Slang
   Bodø, Norway
Kingpost
   B.E. Bjørketo
   Slyngun. 28
   Oslo 3, Norway
Norsk Hang Gliding
   Oslo, Norway
Hypoxia
   Rullharvsvgen 1B
   43140 Mølndal
   Sweden
Delta Info
   SHV Association Magazine
   Postfach 1019
   Solothurn 4502
   Switzerland

HANG GLIDING ASSOCIATIONS

ARGENTINA
Liga Argentina de Aerodeslizadores
Superlivianos (LADAS), San Martin,
359-5539 Las Heras, Mendoza, Argentina
Telephone: 257750

AUSTRALIA
The Australian Hang Gliding Association
(TAHGA), P.O. Box 4, Holme Building,
Sydney University N.S.W. 2006 Australia

AUSTRIA
Draghen Flieger Club, Innsbruck, c/o Gast-
haus "Engl," Innstrasse 22, A-6020,
Innsbruck, Austria

"Himmelhunde," c/o Markus Villinger,
Arzlerstrasse 118, A-6020 Innsbruck,
Austria. Telephone: 07743/5222/62434

BRAZIL
Associacão Brasileira de Voo Livre (ABVL),
c/o Patrick Bredel, Barao de Jaguaribe 323/3,
Ipanema, Rio de Janeiro, CEP 22421 Brazil

BULGARIA
Hang Gliding Club—Zmei—Sofia
N:11 Kursk St., Sofia, 1407, Bulgaria

BRITAIN
British Hang Gliding Association (BHGA),
167a Cheddon Rd., Taunton, Somerset,
Great Britain. Chris Corston, Secretary

CANADA
The Hang Gliding Association of Canada,
Box 4063, Postal Station "C," Calgary,
Alberta T2T 5M9, Canada

DENMARK
Danish Hang Gliding Association, Dansk
Drageflyver Union, Kongelig Dansk Aeroklub,
Københauns lufthaun, Post Box 68, DK 400,
Roskilde, Denmark. Telephone: 03-090811

FINLAND
Helsingin Ruppuliidäwät
Vuolukwende g B 21 00710
Helsinki, 71, Finland

FRANCE
Federation Francaise de Vol Libre,
29-P Rue de Severs, 75006, Paris, France

INDONESIA
Gantolle (Dragonfly) Hang Glider Club,
Bandung, Indonesia

ITALY
Federazione Italiana Volo Libero,
c/o Dr. Mario Prezioso, 69 VL., Grigoletti,
Pordenone, Italy

Federazione Italiana Volo Libero,
Via C. Varese, Vicenza, Italy

JAPAN
Japan Hangglider Flyers Federation 1-18-2,
Shinbashi Minato-Ku Nippon Kōkū Kyō Kai,
Japan

LUXEMBOURG
Delta Club de Luxembourg,
6A Rabatt/Echternach, Luxembourg

MEXICO
Club Vuelo Libre De Mexico A.C., Apartado
Postal 27-176, Mexico City 27DF, Mexico

NORTHERN IRELAND
Ulster Hang Gliding Club, 95 Killyleagh Rd.,
Killinchy, Co. Down, Northern Ireland
Telephone: Killinchy 541778
Ernie Patterson, Secretary

NORWAY
Hang Glides Seksponen ov Norsk Aero
Klubb, Boks, 9514 Egertorget, Oslo 1,
Norway. Telephone: (02) 415224

REPUBLIC OF IRELAND
Irish Hang Gliding Association, c/o Tom
Hudson, 60 Hillcrest Rd., Gleneageary,
Co. Dublin, Ireland

RUMANIA
"Delta Sport"—ARAD, Kiss Arpad—ARAD,
Dimitrov Str. Ho 39, 2900 Arad, Rumania

"Federatia Aeronautica Romano"
Vasile Conta Street Ho 16, Bucharest,
Rumania

SCOTLAND
Scottish Sailwing Association,
105 Clermiston Rd., Edinburgh, Scotland
Robin Laidlaw, Secretary

SOUTH AFRICA
Aero Club of South Africa, Hang Gliding
Section, P.O. Box 2312
Johannessburg, 2000, South Africa

SWITZERLAND
Association pour l'aviation autonome
(USHGA Foreign Chapter 12), Avenue de
Belmont 17, Montreaux 1820, Switzerland

Schweizerischer Hangeglieitverband,
Postfach 1019, Solothurn 4502, Switzerland

HANG GLIDING SCHOOLS AND DEALERS
USHGA CHAPTER CLUBS AND CERTIFIED SCHOOLS

The following list of schools, dealers, chapter clubs, and certified schools is reprinted from the most current lists published by the USHGA Membership and Development Committee. A number of changes have occurred since press time for this book that we were unable to include in the current edition. Separate amended maps and lists will be available to all members of the USHGA at periodic intervals.

HANG GLIDING SCHOOLS & DEALERS, USHGA CHAPTER CLUBS & CERTIFIED SCHOOLS

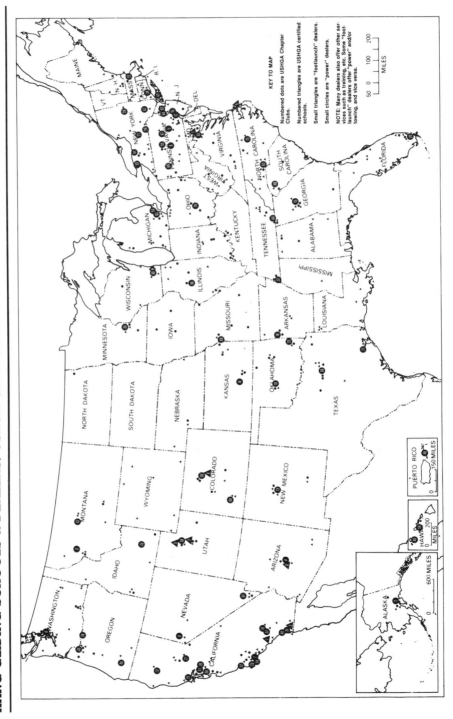

KEY TO MAP

Numbered dots are USHGA Chapter Clubs.

Numbered triangles are USHGA certified schools.

Small triangles are "footlaunch" dealers.

Small circles are "power" dealers.

NOTE: Many dealers also offer other services such as training, etc. Some "footlaunch" dealers offer "power" and/or towing, and vice versa.

HANG GLIDING SCHOOLS & DEALERS, USHGA CHAPTER CLUBS & CERTIFIED SCHOOLS (continued)

Please send all additions, deletions, and/or corrections to USHGA Membership and Development Committee, c/o Terri Turner, 5913 N.W. Creek View Dr., Kansas City, MO 64152, preferably on 3 x 5 index cards or post cards. DO NOT call or write USHGA office. A separate amended map will be available to all members and interested parties at a later date.

A SPECIAL THANKS TO THE FOLLOWING WHO MADE THIS MAP POSSIBLE:

C G S AVIATION
4252 Pearl Rd.
Cleveland, OH 44109

DELTA WING KITES & GLIDERS, INC.
P.O. Box 483
Van Nuys, CA 91408

GLIDERS & GADGETS, INC.
Liberty Landing Airport
5913 N.W. Creek View
Kansas City, MO 64512

LES KING
Sport Flight
9041 B Comprint Ct.
Gaithersburg, MD 20760

LEADING EDGE AIR FOILS, INC.
331 South 14th Street
Colorado Springs, CO 80904

MANTA PRODUCTS
1647 E. 15th Street
Oakland, CA 94606

MITCHELL WING
Mitchell Aircraft Corporation
1900 S. Newcomb
Porterville, CA 93257

SEAGULL AIRCRAFT
1160 Mark Avenue
Carpinteria, CA 93013

SEEDWINGS
1919 Castillo
Santa Barbara, CA 93101

SKY SPORTS INC.
P.O. Box 507
Ellington, CT 06029

ULTRALIGHT FLYING MACHINES
1960 Corwin Dr.
Santa Clara, CA 95051

ULTRALITE SOARING INC.
14095 N.W. 19th Ave.
Opa Locka, FL 33054

UNITED STATES HANG GLIDING ASSN.
P.O. Box 66306
Los Angeles, CA 90066

U.S. MOYES, INC.
11522 Red Arrow Highway
Bridgman, MI 49106

WILLS WING, INC.
1208-H East Walnut Street
Santa Ana, CA 92701

YARNALL TECHTONICS INC.
1891 Dublin Road
Penfield, NY 14526

USHGA CHAPTER CLUBS
(see map)

ALASKA

ALASKA SKY SAILORS (2)
Box 181
Palmer, AK 99645

ARIZONA

ARIZONA HANG GLIDING ASSN. (4)
4319 W. Larkspur
Glendale, AZ 85304

ARKANSAS

FORT SMITH HANG GLIDING ASSN. (18)
Rt. 2, Box 4788
Ft. Smith, AR 72903

CALIFORNIA

SOUTHLAND HANG GLIDING ASSN. (7)
2410 Lincoln Blvd.
Santa Monica, CA 90405

TORREY PINES HANG GLIDING ASSN. (46)
Box 833
Carlsbad, CA 92008

ULTRALIGHT FLYERS ORGANIZATION (31)
Box 81665
San Diego, CA 92138

SAN BERNARDINO HANG GLIDING ASSN. (16)
P.O. Box 1464
San Bernardino, CA 92401

RIVERSIDE HANG GLIDING ASSN. (57)
9448 Mission Blvd.
Riverside, CA 92509

TOPA TOPA FLYERS (54)
702 Cedar Pl.
Ventura, CA 93001

SANTA BARBARA HANG GLIDING ASSN (26)
Box 40114
Santa Barbara, CA 93103

SAN LUIS OBISPO SOARING ASSN. (52)
835 Mission
San Luis Obispo, CA 93401

MARIN COUNTY HANG GLIDING ASSN. (25)
20-A Pamaron
Ignacio, CA 94947

WINGS OF ROGALLO (66)
2681 Plaza Americas
San Jose, CA 95132

MOTHER LODE SKY RIDERS (39)
2025 Shaw Ave.
Modesto, CA 95354

NO. CALIF. HANG GLIDING ASSN. (27)
4216 Roseville Rd.
North Highlands, CA 95660

NORTHERN CALIF. SKY MASTERS (72)
P.O. Box 34
Igo, CA 96047

COLORADO

FELLOW FEATHERS OF DENVER (50)
Box 1775
Boulder, CO 80306

TELLURIDE AIR FORCE (64)
Box 38
Telluride, CO 81435

CONNECTICUT

CONNECTICUT HANG GLIDING ASSN. (34)
35 Harvest Ln.
Farmington, CT 06032

FLORIDA

FLORIDA FREE FLIGHT (20)
10250 SW 37th St.
Miami, FL 33165

GEORGIA

GEORGIA HANG GLIDING ASSN (15)
448 Rue Andeleys
Stone Mtn. GA 30083

HAWAII

KAUAI HANG GLIDING ASSN. (40)
Box 843
Koloa, HI 96756

HAWAIIAN HANG GLIDING ASSN (59)
Box 22232
Honolulu, HI 96822

IDAHO

SOUTHERN IDAHO HANG GLIDING ASSN. (70)
1261 City Creek Rd.
Pocatello, ID 83201

ILLINOIS

ILLINOIS VALLEY HANG GLIDERS (56)
5800 W. Hevermann Rd.
Peoria Hts., IL 61614

KANSAS

KANSAS FLINT HILL FLYERS (14)
2625 S. West #413
Wichita, KS 67217

MAINE

NEW ENGLAND HANG GLIDING ASSN. (22)
¼ Box 295
Newton Highlands, MA 02161

MICHIGAN

MICHIGAN HAWKS (53)
24851 Murray Dr.
Mt. Clemens, MI 48045

MICHIGAN ULTRALIGHT GLIDER ASSN. (63)
4622 Mandalay
Royal Oak, MI 48073

MINNESOTA

NORTHERN SKY GLIDERS ASSN. (35)
Box 364
Minneapolis, MN 55440

MISSOURI

KANSAS CITY HANG GLIDING ASSN. (49)
5913 N.W. Creek View Dr.
Kansas City, MO 64152

MONTANA

GREAT FALLS HANG GLIDING ASSN. (13)
c/o Deaconess Hospital
Great Falls, MT 59045

HANG GLIDING SCHOOLS & DEALERS, USHGA CHAPTER CLUBS & CERTIFIED SCHOOLS (continued)

MONTANA HANG GLIDER ASSN. (3)
2515½ No. Ave W.
Missoula, MT 59801

NEVADA

SOUTHERN NEVADA HANG GLIDING (61)
3150 S. Decatur Blvd.
Las Vegas, NV 89102

SIERRA SKYSURFERS (9)
1450 E. Second St.
Reno, NV 89501

NEW JERSEY

NORTH JERSEY HANG GLIDING CLUB (44)
33 Carlton Ave.
Washington, NJ 07882

NEW JERSEY HANG GLIDING ASSN. (62)
Box 334
Wharton, NJ 07885

NEW MEXICO

SANDIA SOARING ASSN. (73)
P.O. Box 8176
Albuquerque, NM 87108

NEW YORK

LONG ISLAND HANG GLIDING ASSN. (42)
Box 114
West Islip, NY 11795

CONDOR HANG GLIDING CLUB (21)
73 Hunting St.
Cortland, NY 13045

SOUTHERN TIER SKYSURFERS (29)
Box 592
Endicott, NY 13760

INTERNATIONAL SKY RIDERS (32)
1055 Sweeney St.
N. Tonawanda, NY 14120

GENESEE VALLEY HANG FLYERS (41)
283 Merchants, NY 14609

NORTH CAROLINA

ULTRALIGHT PILOT'S ASSN. (65)
908 Lexington Ave.
Charlotte, NC 28203

OHIO

OHIO FLYER'S HANG GLIDING CLUB (74)
P.O. Box 15380, SR 104
Ashville, OH 43103

OKLAHOMA

OKLAHOMA HANG GLIDING ASSN. (10)
Box 756
Bethanny, OK 73008

HEAVENER RUNSTONE HANG GLIDING ASSN. (23)
Box 361
Heavener, OK 74937

OREGON

MID-COLUMBIA GORGE GLIDERS (24)
402 E. 2nd St.
The Dalles, OR 97058

OREGON HANG GLIDING ASSN. (36)
Box 5592
Portland, OR 97228

ROGUE VALLEY HANG GLIDING ASSN. (45)
P.O. Box 621
Grants Pass, OR 97526

PENNSYLVANIA

DAEDALUS HANG GLIDING CLUB (69)
Box 308, Rd. #1
Cowansville, PA 16218

HYNER HANG GLIDER CLUB (55)
731 Appleview Ln.
Duncanville, PA 16635

NITTANY VALLEY HANG GLIDING (8)
1184 Onieda St.
State College, PA 16801

SUSQUEHANNA SKY SURFERS (67)
Rd. 3, Box 147
Cogan Station, PA 17728

WIND RIDERS HANG GLIDING CLUB (17)
1017 Spruce St.
Collingdale, PA 19023

DELAWARE VALLEY HANG GLIDERS (19)
631 Lincoln Ave #5
Morrisville, PA 19067

EASTERN PENN HANG GLIDERS (5)
Box 524
Reading, PA 19603

SOUTH CAROLINA

SOUTH CAROLINA HANG GLIDING ASSN. (68)
Rt. 7, So. Rockview Dr.
Greenville, SC 29609

TEXAS

LEAGUE OF ULTRALIGHT FLIGHT (38)
2200 C' S. Smith Barry Rd.
Arlington, TX 76013

HOUSTON HANG GLIDING ASSN. (71)
1026 Dreyfus #16
Houston, TX 77030

TENNESSEE

TENNESSEE TREE TOPPERS (60)
Box 329
Ooltewah, TN 37363

UTAH

UTAH HANG GLIDING ASSN. (58)
9th So. 9th East
Salt Lake City, UT 84105

VIRGINIA

CAPITAL HANG GLIDER ASSN. (33)
P.O. Box 64
Annandale, VA 22003

WASHINGTON

PACIFIC NORTHWEST HANG GLIDING ASSN. (6)
P.O. Box 1781
Bellevue, WA 98009

WISCONSIN

WISCONSIN ULTRA LIGHT PILOTS SOC (30)
1971 Cascade Dr.
Waukesha, WI 53186

SWITZERLAND

ASSOCIATION POUR L'AVIATION (12)
AV. Belmont 17/1820
Montreux. Switz.

VIRGIN ISLANDS

VIRGIN ISLAND HANG GLIDING ASSN. (48)
Box 10012
St. Thomas, VI 00801

SCHOOLS HOLDING USHGA CERTIFICATION (see map)

ELSINORE VALLEY HANG GLIDING CENTER (1)
31381 Riverside Dr.
Lake Elsinore, CA 92330

FREEDOM WING INC. (2)
9235 S. 255 W.
Sandy, UT 84070

FREE FLIGHT INC. (3)
7848 Convey Ct.
San Diego, CA 92111

GOLDEN SCHOOL OF HANG GLIDING (4)
572 Orchard St.
Golden, CO 80401

INFINITY FLIGHT SCHOOL (THE KITE SHOP) (5)
898 S. 900 E.
Salt Lake City, UT 84102

KITTY HAWK KITES (6)
Rt. 158
Nags Head, N. C. 27959

SPORT FLIGHT (7)
9041-B Comprint
Gaithersburg, MD 20760

U.S. HANG GLIDERS INC. (8)
10250 N. 19th Ave.
Phoenix, AZ 85021

*KEN McCOLLISTER
P.O. Box 81187
Fairbanks, AK 99706
(907) 479-3595

ARIZONA

*U.S. HANG GLIDERS
10250 N. 19th Ave.
Phoenix, AZ 85021
(602) 944-1655

DESERT HANG GLIDERS
4319 W. Larkspur
Glendale, AZ 85304

SCHOOLS AND DEALERS

*Indicates Dealers Known To Sell Power Equipment

ALABAMA

*4 SEASONS CYCLE CENTER
Make Pair/Hoke Graham
7428 N. First Street
Birmingham, AL 35206
(205) 833-0116

DENNIS ODEM
116 South Pine St.
Florence, AL 35630
(205) 767-0096

AUTODYNE CO. INC.
113 Beirne Ave
Huntsville, AL. 35801

*TENNESSEE VALLEY U.F.M.
2011 E. Tuliptree Dr.
Huntsville, AL 35803
(205) 811-3952

ALLIED SPORTS CO.
Yank Dean
1 Hummingbird Lane
Eufaula, AL 36027
(205) 687-6615

DEAN HOFFMAN
121 Samples Street
Auburn, AL 36830
(205) 821-4218

ALASKA

*MIKE JACOBER'S
605 W. 2nd Ave., Apt. A
Anchorage, AK 99501
(907) 349-2603

DWIGHT JACOBSON
PSL #2, Box 3078
Anchorage, AK 99506

SKY HIGH SPORTS
Michael Bayle/Tom Sandage
Star Rt. A. Box 491H
Anchorage, AK 99507
(007) 753-2423

KLEAN FUN KITES
P.O. Box 4-2990
Anchorage, AK 99509

SOUTHWEST AEROSPORTS. INC.
2215-18th Place
Yuma, AZ 85364

U.S. HANG GLIDERS, INC.
357 W. 24th Street
Yuma, AZ 85364
(602) 782-1518

GALEN WILLIAMS
7362 S. Westover
Tucson, AZ 85706
(602) 883-4027

CHARLIE LUTZ'S
962 Via Terrado
Tucson, AZ 85710

HIGH COUNTRY HANG GLIDERS
111½ S. O'Leary St.
Flagstaff, AZ 86001

*BERKELEY ENGINEERING
Berkeley Eastman
2051 Wallapi Dr.
Lake Havasu City, AZ 86403

ARKANSAS

BOAG CHUMBLEY
18 Ridge Road
Cabot, AR 72023
(501) 843-5735/375-3803

HOT AIR, INC.
Bill Munday
2701 Vancouver
Little Rock, AR 72204
(501) 227-8032

*EARTH & SKY
Big Creek
Mt. Judea, AR 72655
(501) 434-5550

ARKANSAS HANG GLIDING
Ted Grissom
Rt. 1. Box 109
Springdale, AR 72701
(501) 751-3049

HANG GLIDING SCHOOLS & DEALERS, USHGA CHAPTER CLUBS & CERTIFIED SCHOOLS (continued)

*AERIAL ACCESSORIES
Mark Stump
601 Wheeler Ave.
Ft. Smith, AR 72902

*WESTARK WINGS
Larry Edwards
3109 Grand
Ft. Smith, AR 72904
(501) 782-3456

CALIFORNIA

SCOTT DITTRICH'S
P.O. Box 301
Malibu, CA 90265

*DARK STAR ENTERPRISES
1516 Boivdoin St.
Pacific Palisades, CA 90272

CHE HOBBIES
10900 Eastwood Ave.
Inglewood, CA 90304

HANG GLIDERS OF CALIFORNIA
Greg DeWolf
2410 Lincoln Blvd.
Santa Monica, CA 90405
(213) 399-5315, 592-5754

MACE HANGFLIGHT
Larry Mace
1600 Oak Street
Santa Monica, CA 90405
(213) 392-7969

*THE HANG GLIDER SHOP
1351 E. Beach Blvd.
La Habra, CA 90631
(213) 943-1074

DENNIS HIBDON
1048 15th St.
San Pedro, CA 90731
(213) 548-5877/373-8402

*WINDHAVEN
12437 San Fernando
Sylmar, CA 91042
(213) 367-1819

DICK SNYDER
695 E. Villa #7
Pasadena, CA 91101

SUNBIRD ULTRALIGHT GLIDERS
12501 Gladstone Ave #A-4
Sylmar, CA 91342
(213) 361-8651

*SOUTHERN CALIFORNIA SCHOOL
OF HANG GLIDING
5219 Sepulveda Blvd.
Van Nuys, CA 91411
(213) 789-0836

BEST FLITE
7669 Grandby Ave.
Cucamonga, CA 91730

MIKE KENDALL
8940 Reeves Ct.
Rancho Cucamonga, CA 91730
(714) 987-0489

W.A. (PORK) ROECKER
2373 Manchester Ave.
Cardiff, CA 92007
(714) 436-5451

WINDWAYS FLYING MACHINE
1368 Max Street
Chula Vista, CA 92010

*PACIFIC ULTRALIGHTS
100 Stoney Knoll Rd.
El Cason, CA 92021

MARTIN PADILLA'S
634 Rosemont
La Jolla, CA 92037
(714) 488-2193

ULTIMATE HI
Lorin Ellsworth
Poway, CA 92064
(714) 748-1739/276-6092

MONTEREY PHOENIX
53 West Garzas Road
Carmel Valley, CA 93924
(408) 659-2966

*LEE GARDNER
3019 Kings Circle
Marina, CA 93933
(408) 384-3107

*PTERODACTYL
Jack McCormac
847 Airport Rd
Monterey, CA 93940
(408) 375-0328

*CHANDELLE OF
SAN FRANCISCO
Jan Case
198 Los Banos
Daly City, CA 94014
(415) 756-0650

SKY SAILERS SKY SCHOOL
Steve Groat
11844 Selo Drive
Sunnyvale, CA 94087
(408) 732-9616

SPECTRUM ELECTRONICS
Jack Street
65 Joost Street
San Francisco, CA 94131
(415) 333-4649

FREE-FLIGHT OF SAN DIEGO
Mitch Mitchell
7848 Convoy Court
San Diego, CA 92111
(714) 560-0888

*FLIGHT REALITIES INC.
1945 Adams Ave.
San Diego, CA 92116
(714) 298-1962

*LARRY FORQUERAN
Haig Construction
874 Beaumont, Suite D
Beaumont, CA 92256
(715) 363-6721

UPWARD-BOUND HANGLIDERS
P.O. Box 1175
Palm Desert, CA 92260
(714) 568-2250/363-6721

RON RUSSOW
69325 Nilda
Palm Springs, CA 92262
(714) 328-7287

ELSINORE VALLEY HANG
GLIDING CENTER
33403 Adelfa Street
Lake Elsinore, CA 92330
(714) 678-2050

CHRIS PRICE
32970 Lillian Road
Lake Elsinore, CA 92330
(714) 678-1984

PINECREST
Andrew L. Jackson
655 N. Pine
San Bernardino, CA 92407

RICH MATROS
452 E. Washington
Ramona, CA 92605
(714) 789-3103

GEORGE DYER
6221 Chapman
Garden Grove, CA 92645
(714) 894-6448

HANG FLIGHT SYSTEMS
Erik Fair
1208 N. Walnut
Santa Ana, CA 92701
(714) 542-7444/493-5039

MICHAEL ARRAMBIDE
139 Red Circle
Ventura, CA 92002
(805) 644-0034

THE HANG GLIDER SHOP
8887 N. Ventura Ave.
Ventura, CA 92011

BOB WALCK
1415 Kuehner
Simi Valley, CA 93063

*CHANNEL ISLAND
HANG GLIDING EMPORIUM
613 N. Milpas
Santa Barbara, CA 93103
(805) 965-3733

ROBERT MILLINGTON
1305 E. Yanonali
Santa Barbara, CA 93103

*PAUL BRAGG
3415 Miguelito Ct.
San Luis Obispo, CA 93401
(805) 541-2771

MARK CLEMENT
413 Sandercock St.
San Luis Obispo, CA 92401

*MIKE SMITH'S
5133 Olemeda
Atascadero, CA 93422
(805) 466-5155

JERRY ROBERTSON
1451 Refugio Road
Santa Ynez, CA 93460
(805) 688-4320

SIERRA SOARING SERVICE
Star Route 4, Box 3a
Bishop, CA 93514

STRIPLIN AIRCRAFT CORP.
45503 N. Sierra Hwy.
Lancaster, CA 93534
(805) 945-2522

FRESNO HANG GLIDERS
Dan Fleming/Den Flowers
627 E. Belmont
Fresno, CA 93701
(209) 264-8002/674-1310

MONARK SKY SAILS
1916 E. Home
Fresno, CA 93703
(209) 264-6880

*FLIGHT DESIGNS
Marty Alameda
P.O. Box 1503
Salinas, CA 93902
(408) 758-6896

SEAGULL SOARING
P.O. Box 5474
Carmel, CA 93921

*KILBOURNE SPORTS SPECIALTIES
Dave Kilbourne
701 Chimolus Drive
Palo Alto, CA 94306
(415) 493-9319

SUSPENDED ANIMATION
John Reisig
2151 Arnold Indust. Hwy. Sh. 5
Concord, CA 94520
(415) 798-9993

*MISSION SOARING CENTER
Pat Dennivan
43551 Mission Blvd
Freemont, CA 94538
(415) 656-6656

KENNETH B. HARK
2777 Willow Pass Road #2
Pittsberg, CA 94565
(415) 458-2237

JIM LANG
7796 Redbud Court
Pleasanton, CA 94566
(415) 462-5081

*STEVE PATMONT
7223 Dover Ln.
Dublin, CA 94566
(415) 829-3386/846-8549

*HANG GLIDERS WEST
1011 Lincoln Ave.
San Rafael, CA 94901
(415) 543-7664

*POWER FLIGHT ENGINEERING
P.O. Box 1226
Rohnert Park, CA 94928

HANG GLIDERS WEST
Banana
20 A Pameron
Ignacio, CA 94947
(415) 883-3494

AIR SUSPENSION
Jerry Kern
2901 O.O.F. Ave.
P.O. Box 155
Gilroy, CA 95020
(408) 842-9705

NOLAND HANG GLIDERS
Jerry Noland
1415 Pacific Ave.
Santa Cruz, CA 95060
(408) 432-4442

*PAJARO POWER GLIDER
191 Tarfton Rd.
Watsonville, CA 95076

ULTRAFLIGHT SYSTEMS
Tim Morley
P.O. Box 4763
Modesto, CA 95352
(209) 578-1978

BARNEY CURTICE
418 3rd Street
Eureka, CA 95501
(707) 442-6044/443-0288

*HANG GLIDING OF
NORTH CALIFORNIA
Jim Wyatt
1865 Zehnder
Arcata, CA 95521
822-6435

HAPPY HANGER
P.O. Box 2028
Santa Cruz, CA 95603
(408) 475-2526

DAN KELLY
5103 Fairoaks Blvd.
Carmichael, CA 95608
(916) 483-0556

DINGER WINGS
Dean Aldinger
4216 Roseville Road
North Highlands, CA 95660
(916) 489-4778

*SIERRA ULTRALIGHTS
Bob McIntyre
P.O. Box 6292
South Lake Tahoe, CA 95729
(916) 541-7009

CRAIG BECK
4435 Huckleberry Street
Cedar Flats, CA 95732
(916) 583-6136

SILVER WING
1187 E. 7th St.
Chico, CA 95926
(916) 342-1951

BRIAN ELHARDT
Rt. 2, Box 130
Durham, CA 95938
(916) 343-9743

*AL KENSTLER'S
4925 Eastside Rd
Redding, CA 96001
(916) 241-5419

COLORADO

*GOLDEN SKY SAILS, INC.
572 Orchars St
Golden, CO 80401
(303) 278-9566

*GOLDEN EAGLE GLIDERS
Sean Dever
501 Lookout Mt. Road
Golden, CO 80401
(303) 526-1300

*LEADING EDGE AIR FOILS, INC.
881 So. 14th St.
Colorado Springs, CO 80904
(303) 632-4959

*U.F.M. OF COLORADO
P.O. Box 4803
Aspen, CO 81611
(303) 925-3835

THE SOAR STORE
P.O. Box 241
Salida, CO 81201

*4 CORNERS SCHOOL OF HANG GLIDING
P.O. Box 38
Hesperus, CO 81326
(303) 533-7550

JACK CAREY
Box 192
Telluride, CO 81435
(303) 728-3688

SEAGULL AIRCRAFT/TELLURIDE AIR FORCE
P.O. Box 38
Ft. Walton Beach, CO 81435

*GET HIGH, INC.
Box 7115
Aspen, CO 81611
(303) 963-1504

CONNECTICUT

*TEK FLIGHT
Ben Davidson
Colebrook Stage
Winsted, CT 06098
(203) 379-1668

CONNECTICUT COSMIC PRODUCTIONS
14 Terp Road
East Hampton, CT 06424
(203) 267-8980/267-0676

CONNECTICUT HANG GLIDING CENTER
1816 Meriden-Waterbury Road
Milldale, CT 06467

TEK FLIGHT
Den Davidson/Jim Hugo
362 State St.
No. Haven, CT 06473
(203) 288-5430

SOUTHERN CONNECTICUT SCHOOL OF HANG GLIDING
11 Greenfield Ave.
Stratford, CT 06497

*BALAISE THOMPSON
12 Lindencrest Dr.
Danbury, CT 06810
(203) 792-5522

DISTRICT OF COLUMBIA

U.F.M. OF WASHINGTON
Fred Klein
3017 "M" Street N.W.
Washington, D.C. 20007
(202) 337-7120

FLORIDA

*POWER SYSTEMS
963 Village Dr.
Ormand Beach, FL 32074
(904) 672-6363

*U.F.M. OF FLORIDA
Mike Grossberg
2503 South 2nd St.
Jacksonville Beach, FL 32250
(904) 246-2568

*GULFPORT MICROLIGHT AVIATION
321 Hollywood Blvd. N.W.
Ft. Walton Beach, FL 32548
(904) 244-5347

MAP OF GAINESVILLE
1031 N.E. 20th Ave.
Gainesville, FL 32601
(904) 376-4367/496-2222

JACK HUTCHINSON
150 Highline Dr.
Longwood, FL 32750
(305) 831-4790/293-3104

ROLAND ALEXANDER
222 Weber Street
Orlando, FL 32803
(305) 425-6697

JIM WALSH
6904 Seminole
Orlando, FL 32809
(305) 859-3550/851-5988

JIM STAYLOR
409 Red Sail Way
Satellite Beach, FL 32937
(305) 777-1132

HOWARD ANDERSON
c/o H.H. Warehouse
1040 E. 26th St.
Hialeah, FL 33013

*JAIME MARULL
Heileah Gardens #2417
10000 NW 80th Ct.
Heileah, FL 33016
(305) 557-2356

*WINGS & SAILS OF MANDALAY MARINA
Don Noble
Rt. 1, Box 80
Key Largo, FL 33037
(305) 852-9183

CHUCK SMITH'S
15158 N.E. 6th Ave.
No. Miami, FL 33100
(305) 944-2337

FUTURE FLIGHT INC.
Gary Matthews
4211 Salzedo Ave
Coral Gables, FL 33146
(305) 446-0505/442-8000

*FRIGATE AIRCRAFT
6321 N.W. 37th Ave.
Miami, FL 33147
(305) 696-4449/696-4440

KITECO, INC.
Ralph Linero
P.O. Box 520892
Miami, FL 33152

KITE CO.
Richard Hensen
10250 S.W. 37th
Ft. Lauderdale, FL 33165
(305) 226-6951

JEFF JAMES
324 Claremont Lane
Palm Beach Shores, FL 33404
(305) 844-6144

*GOOSE HARBOR AVIATION
4645 Lakeworth Rd.
Lakeworth, FL 33463

*RICHARD CLENNEY/R.J. ALDERMAN
812 59th St. N.W.
Bradenton, FL 33505
(813) 792-6565

*JAY BRAWDER'S
207 3rd St. N.
Safety Harbor, FL 33572

*GULF AIR SPORTS
Bob Mahaffey
505 Barcelona Ave. #5
Venice, FL 33595
(813) 484-5141/485-5113

HOLIDAY AQUA SPORTS
Hal Elgin
6629 Emerson Ave. South
St. Petersburg, FL 33707
(813) 360-4035/345-3697

BOB EMERSON
Rt. 2, Box X403
Avon Park, FL 33825
(813) 453-7749

JOHNSON FLEX-WING KITE CO.
Richard Johnson
P.O. Box 91
Cypress Gardens, FL 33880
(813) 293-8255

LYNN NOVAKOWSKI
1213 Lake Buckeye Dr. W.
Cypress Gardens, FL 33880

GEORGIA

VAN & HANG GLIDER SHOP
760 So. Cobb Drive
Marietta, GA 30060
(404) 427-7782

SKY CRAFT
448 Rue Andeleys
Stone Mountain, GA 30083

*ROD GAY
434 Euclid Terr. NE
Atlanta, GA 30307
(404) 588-1897

SOUTHERN AIR TIME, INC.
Doug Lawton
590 No. Ave. N.W.
P.O. Box 93701 Martech Station
Atlanta, GA 30318
(404) 525-1818

*WHITT WINGS
P.O. Box 13207
Atlanta, GA 30324

FRANCIS "TUT" WOODRUFF
3537 Castlegate Dr. N.W.
Atlanta, GA 30327
(404) 233-3842

*SUN SOUTHEAST
3798 Valley Bluff N.E.
Atlanta, GA 30340

*ATLANTA HANG GLIDERS
Peachtree DeKalb Airport
No. 4 Aviation Way
Chamblee, GA 30341
(404) 458-4584

*AIR SPACE
Ray Schaal
Rt. 1, Box 625
Trenton, GA 30752
(404) 657-7170

*U.F.M. OF GEORGIA
Jerry Saye
108 Francis St.
Hihira, GA 31632

HAWAII

HAWAII SCHOOL OF HANG GLIDING
P.O. Box 460
Kailua, HI 96734
(808) 262-8616

*JEFF COTTER
84-736 A Lahaina St.
Waianae, HI 96792
(808) 695-8356

DA KITE SHOP
Ray Hook
P.O. Box 304
Waimanalo, HI 96795
(808) 259-5457

ALOHA HANG GLIDING CENTER
6308 Puakea Place
Hawaii Kai, HI 96825
(808) 377-9804

IDAHO

*BONNEVILLE AVIATION
Route 1
Inkom, ID 83245
(208) 775-3409

FRANK GILLETTE
Rt. 1
Burley, ID 83318
(208) 654-6381

CURRENT RECREATIONS
618 Stewart Ave.
Lewiston, ID 83501
(208) 746-0352, (509) 758-9282

SLICK ROCK FLYERS
1234 Ash
Caldwell, ID 83605

SLICK ROCK FLYERS
246 Caldwell Blvd
Nampa, ID 83651

*U.F.M. OF IDAHO
114 13th Ave. So.
Nampa, ID 83651

HANG GLIDER SHOP *CHUTES
3312 N. 36th
Boise, ID 83703
(208) 343-1141

*NOVA HANG GLIDERS
6910 Westfield Place
Boise, ID 83704
(208) 376-3082

RON SNIDER
2208 Cherry Lane
Boise, ID 83705
(208) 344-0584

ILLINOIS

BUNNER BROS. HANG GLIDING
1600 Carmel Blvd.
Zion, IL 60099

FREE SPIRIT
Andrew Harper
940 Western Ave.
Geneva, IL 60134
(312) 232-6822

DYNAMIC SPORTS
7 N 090 Medinah Road
Medinah, IL 60157
(312) 894-6622, 640-7605

*RUSSELL AVIATION
Joe Russell
Rt. 1 Box 166
Kankakee, IL 60901

*WOCKNER FLYING SERVICE
308 South 3rd St.
Watseka, IL 60970

LEON FARSTER
Rt. 3
Dixon, IL 61021
(815) 652-4589

ADVENTURE SPORTS
Rob Kessler
7784 Forest Hills Rd.
Rockford, IL 61111

ILLINOIS MOYES
Lou Anders
Box 167
Granville, IL 61326
(815) 339-2431

ILLINOIS VALLEY SCHOOL OF HANG GLIDING
Dave Anderson
210 W. Main
P.O. Box 100
Granville, IL 61326
(915) 339-2282

BOB MOSER'S
208 N. Meyers St.
Eureka, IL 61530

PRAIRIE FLYTE
2004 Karen Ct., Unit 1
Champain, IL 61820

*WING OVER THE WORLD
2729 Viewland
Alton, IL 62002
(618) 465-0550

HAROLD LEWIS
29 Islander Dr.
Brighton, IL 62012
(618) 372-8758

*SEAN AND FRANK O'NEIL
791 Livingston St.
Cartyle, IL 62231
(618) 594-2661

INDIANA

BAT-SAIL ENT.
Dean Batmon
6040 Sahway Ct.
Indianapolis, IN 46224
(317) 291-9079

INDIANA SUN
5377 W. 86th St.
Indianapolis, IN 46268

*AIRBORNE SALES IND.
Richard Sacher
6 Sylvan Ln.
Jeffersonville, IN 47130
(812) 288-6597

*U.F.M. OF INDIANA
Dennis Hastings
P.O. Box 962
Columbus, IN 47201
(812) 372-1670

*MARCO POLO ENTERPRISES
Mark Smith
1121 N. Locust Street
Mt. Vernon, IN 47620
(812) 838-6351, 838-6071

*U.F.M. OF SOUTHERN INDIANA
6933 Willow Rd.
Newburg, IN 47630
(812) 853-3140

IOWA

IOWA GLIDER, INC.
Dick Ford
1324 Grand
Des Moines, IA 50309
(515) 244-4464

*MOTORIZED GLIDERS OF IOWA
Dale Kgeilsen
Rt. 1
Clear Lake, IA 50428
(515) 357-5334

THE KITE SHOP
Pat Conrad
Box 150
Little Sioux, IA 51545
(712) 649-2952

*THE FOUR WINDS
Cary Colton
2708 Mt. Vernon Rd. S.W.
Cedar Rapids, IA 52403
(319) 365-6057, 363-0189

KANSAS

*AIRMASS
Old Hyway 10 and Mize Road
Desoto, KS 66018
(913) 441-2222

L.E.A.F.
Randy Hansen
1733 W. 24th St.
#32
Lawrence, KS 66044

*MONARCH FLYING MACHINES
10301 W. 77th #109
Shawnee Mission, KS 66214

GLIDERS & GADGETS, INC.
2527 Ohio
Topeka, KS 66605
(913) 266-7146, 357-4340

*GIRARD & JONES
1306 N. B St.
Wellington, KS 67152

*GARY OSORA'S
Suite 221
1900 W. Amidon
Wichita, KS 67203
(316) 832-0603

PRAIRIE SKIMMER HANG GLIDERS
2625 S. West #415
Wichita, KS 67217
(316) 942-0626

KENTUCKY

GREAT OUTDOORS
3824 Wilmington Ave.
Louisville, KY 40207
(502) 895-7353

DERBY CITY KITE SALES
Ron Oakley
Louisville, KY 40207
(502) 969-4836

*U.F.M. OF KENTUCKY
Mike Loehle
3001 Dale Ann Drikve
Louisville, KY 40220
(502) 458-6912

LOUISIANA

LEE MARTIN JR.
603 St. Charles St.
Thibodaux, LA 70301
(504) 446-0381

FOX MANUFACTURING
Al Fox
Rt. #1, Box 801
Gray, LA 70359

BRAD CASE
437 James Comeaux Rd.
Lafayette, LA 70501

DARYL ROYSTON
P.O. Box 634
Cullen, LA 71021

BUD WHEELER
P.O. Box 4351
2620 Centenary Room 202
Shreveport, LA 71104
(318) 221-0013

HIGH FEVER
Paul Mitchell
146 Moor Toad
Shreveport, LA 71106
(318) 686-6193

SPORTS SOUTH, INC.
Box 1367
Shreveport, LA 71164

MAINE

*ULTRALIGHT SPORTS
P.O. Box 401
Birchcroft Lane
Berwick, ME 03901
(207) 698-5729

KEVIN WEATHERBEE
RFD 1 Box 83
Dixmont, ME 04932
(207) 234-4921

MARYLAND

*HANG GLIDERS INTERNATIONAL
5603 McKinely St.
Bethesda, MD 20034
(301) 530-8612, 977-2680

*JAMES HARRIS SR.
4918 Powder Mill Rd.
Beltsville, MD 20705
(301) 937-3252

*SPORT FLIGHT
Les King
9041 B. Comprint Ct.
Gaithersburg, MD 20760
(301) 840-9284

WASHINGTON SCHOOL OF HANG GLIDING
1828 Metzerott Road, Suite A5
Adelphi, MD 20783

MOUNTAIN HIGH
8206 Savage Gilford Rd.
Savage, MD 20863

*SAM DAWSON
227 Owensville Rd.
West River, MD 20881
(301) 867-2008

*WHEEL POWER
203 Baltimore Pike
Bel Air, MD 21014

HOWARD BROWN
Rt. 3, Box 187
Love Pt.
Stevensville, MD 21666
(301) 645-6745

THE OTHER BROTHERS CO.
c/o Glenn Higgs
108 Welty Ave.
Emmitsburg, MD 21717
(301) 447-6386

MASSACHUSETTS

*ECO-FLIGHT
Bob Stewart & Paul Kjellia
North Valley Road
Amherst, MA 01002
(413) 253-5852

*CLOUD STREET
Chuck Laversa
69 Bryan Ave.
E. Hampton, MA 01027
(413) 527-9075

FREE FLIGHT SUPPLIES
Danar Gary Parker
16 Gaugh St.
East Hampton, MA 01026
(413) 527-4403, 584-3513

*ALBRIGHT ENTERPRISES INC.
84 Boxboro Rd.
Stow, MA 01175

BROOKS ELLISON
P.O. Box 282
Williamstown, MA 01267

MICHIGAN

AL D'EATH MARINA
Roger Death
555 Green Dr.
Harsens Island, MI 48028
(313) 748-9943

SOUTHEAST MICHIGAN HANG GLIDERS
24851 Murray
Mt. Clemens, MI 48045
(313) 791-0614

MIKE STIMAC
10547 Reeck Road
Allen Park, MI 48101
(313) 383-1232

TIM FLINN
619 Highland
Lincoln Park, MI 48146

MASTER HARNESS, INC.
2085 Ruffel
Lincoln Park, MI 48146

RON VALMOSSOI
1620 Pagel
Lincoln Park, MI 48146

*ECO FLIGHT
Brad Phillips - Joe Siesken
17390 Redman Rd.
Milan, MI 48160
(313) 529-8637

*NIXON PENOYAR
4281 Pepper
Ecorse, MI 48226

KITES IN FLITE
5502 E. McNichols
Detroit, MI 48212
(313) 891-4922, 372-3652

*GORDON'S GLIDERS
Gordon Parker
367 North Drive
Davison, MI 48423
(313) 653-2968

DAVE V/DOVICK
1011 Chester S.E.
Grand Rapids, MI 49506
(616) 458-6655

*AERO FLOAT FLIGHTS
Gary Ballard
350 Morningside Dr.
Battle Creek, MI 49015
(616) 965-6455

*MID-WEST SCHOOL OF HANG GLIDING
11522 Red Arrow Highway
Bridgman, MI 49106

*U.F.M. OF S.E. MICHIGAN
12675 Lime Creek Road
Morenci, MI 49256
(517) 458-6896

DELTA WING OF MICHIGAN
766 Leonard. N.E.
Grand Rapids, MI 49503
(616) 456-1942

*ACME TOOL & DIE
Lewis Griffith
P.O. Box 208
Acme, MI 49610

ECO FLIGHT HANG GLIDERS
Jim Nelson
826 Michigan Ave.
Benzonia, MI 49616
(616) 882-5070

*MICHIGAN MANTA
David Nelson
327 Main St.
Frankfort, MI 49635
(616) 352-9312

*GREAT LAKE SKY SAIL
Kim Hiller
Box 170 Port Oneida
Maplecity MI 49664
(616) 334-4865

MINNESOTA

*NORTHERN SUN
Bosir Popov
628 Larpenteur Ave.
St. Paul, MN 55113
(612) 489-8300

MINNESOTA GLIDER #516
Tom Haley
1505 Burnsville Crosstown
Burnsville, MN 55337
(612) 890-7265

BLACK HAWK AIRCRAFT
Jay Rydquist
4716 Colfax Ave. South
Minneapolis, MN 55409
(612) 825-0096

*CLOUD 9 SPORT AVIATION
Tracy Tillman
1902 Fourth Ave.
Mankato, MN 56001

MISSISSIPPI

SOUTH HANGER
Rt. 1 128A
Pelahatchie. MS 39145

HANG GLIDING SCHOOLS & DEALERS, USHGA CHAPTER CLUBS & CERTIFIED SCHOOLS (continued)

MISSOURI

MONARCH FLYING MACHINES
246 Winchester Mall
Winchester, MO 63011

*MONARCH FLYING MACHINES
Tim Emerson
No. 3 Marblehead Court
Brentwood, MO 63144
(314) 726-4620

*WILBER PADGENT
Star Route Box 28
Canton, MO 63435
(314) 767-5356

*FALCON HELICOPTERS
Bob Schlotzhauer
310 E. Walnut
Raymore, MO 64083
(816) 331-8200

AEROSPORT ULTRALIGHTS
Steve Daleo
3228 Anderson
Kansas City, MO 64123

*GLIDERS AND GADGETS, INC.
Dick Turner
5913 N.W. Creek View
Liberty Landing Airport
Kansas City, MO 64152
(816) 587-1326, 781-2250

*AERIAL ADVENTURE INC.
Steve Allen
P.O. Box 1084
Sedalia, MO 65301
(816) 826-7582

*ROAD & TRACK SALES INC.
Jerald Loveland
600 College
Springfield, MO 65806
(417) 869-3800

MONTANA

*BEARTOOTH HANG GLIDERS
Steve Baran
543 Yellowstone Ave.
Billings, MT 59104
(406) 248-4383, 656-5409

THE HANGER
3104 5th Ave. North
Great Falls, MT 59401
(406) 454-3379

JACK OLSON HANG GLIDING
421 Riverside Drive N.E.
Great Falls, MT 59401

GALLITIN HANG GLIDERS
Jeff Sims
1722 South Rouse
Bozeman, MT 59715
(406) 586-1421

THE HANGER
Rt. 2 Mullan Road
Missoula, MT 59801
(406) 542-2725

INTER-MOUNTAIN SKY SAILORS
154 Burlington Ave.
Missoula, MT 59801
(406) 543-6989, 543-8776

*STEVE HASTERLICK'S
1734 S. 8th W.
Missoula, MT 59806
(406) 543-8673

CROWN ENTERPRISES
578 Youngs Lane
Kalispell, MT 59901
(406) 755-5856

ACME FLYING CO
Box 1773
White Fish, MT 59937

NEBRASKA

DON PIERCE
11009 "R" Plaza #6
Omaha, NE 68137
(402) 339-3211

BILLY B. BEAMWAYS FLYING MACHINE
Sam Burchard
Box 561
Paxton, NE 69155

*SAM BURCHARS
P.O. Box 671
Sutherland, NE 69165

PRAIRIE SAILS
Rt. #2
Mitchell, NE 69357

NEVADA

SPORTS DESIGNS
4660 W. Charleston Blvd
Las Vegas, NV 89102
(702) 870-3554

*STARSHIP ENTERPRISES
Ed/Gary Underhill
2635 Sherwood Dr. #2
Las Vegas, NV 89109

GLIDE PATH, INC.
Phil Sherrett
820 Hemlock Circle
Las Vegas, NV 89128
(702) 878-6422

JOE DORY CHEVERON'S
1000 W. Main St.
Auston, NV 89310

SIERRA HANG GLIDER SCHOOL
P.O. Box 4557
Sataline, NV 89449

*CLOTHES ENCOUNTERS
Steve Lantz
761 North Wood Ave.
Incline Village, NV 89450

FREE AIR SPORTS
40 S. Wells
Reno, NV 89512
(702) 786-7329

NEW HAMPSHIRE

TERRY'S GLIDER SUPPLIES
Terry Sweeney
34 South Street
Milford, NH 03055
(603) 673-8450

*AGUILAR ODDSEY
P.O. Box 60
Wilton, NH 03086
(603) 654-6155

FLIGHT RESOURCES CO-OP
Al Copertino
Wilton, NH 03086

*U.F.M. OF NEW HAMPSHIRE
Main St. P.O. Box 263
Tilton, NH 03276
(603) 286-3311

MORNINGSIDE REC AREA
RFD 2
Claremont, NH 03743
(603) 542-9726, 542-5849

NEW JERSEY

APPALACHIAN HIGH
Joe La Mantia
96 Jacksonville Rd.
Towaco, NJ 07082

SKYBOUND GLIDERS
Andre Lucas
213 Grahm Terrace
Saddle Brook, NJ 07662
(201) 794-0414

*N.J. SCHOOL OF HANG GLIDING
Tom Saville
Rd. 1, P.O. Box 240 A
Oxford, NJ 07863
(201) 256-2873, 852-3287

BERNIE YAGED
564 Snyder, Box 36
Berkeley Heights, NJ 07922
(201) 464-0383

*JERSEY GLIDERS
Glenn Ferrarie
1528 W. Garden Rd.
Vineland, NJ 08360

NEW MEXICO

SKY HIGH
2340 Britt
Albuquerque, NM 87102

*NIEL BAKKUM'S
2303 El Nido Ct. NW
Albuquerque, NM 87104

BUFFALO SKYRIDERS INC.
1811 A Coal Pl. S.E.
Albuquerque, NM 87106
(505) 342-5314

*SKY HIGH INC.
3324 Alvarado N.E.
Albuquerque, NM 87110
(505) 883-0391

RIKER DAVIS
Box 2599
Ruidoso, NM 88245
(505) 257-2873

*DRY CANYON HANG GLIDERS
1017 Cuba Ave
Alamogordo, NM 88310
(505) 437-0980

NEW YORK

*ISLAND HANG GLIDERS
22 Morris Street
Staten Island, NY 10309
(212) 984-3125

FLIGHT SCHOOL
393 Rye Beach Avenue
Rye, NY 10580

WINDBORN ASSOCIATES
414 Harrison Street
Franklin Square, NY 11010
(516) 328-2124

*LONG ISLAND KITE DIST.
5 Bethpage Rd.
Hicksville, NY 11081
(516) 681-8738, 931-6996

HANG GLIDING ORGANIZATION OF NYC
Michael Gamble
142 6th Avenue
Brooklyn, NY 11217
(212) 783-5480

*WINGS FOR MAN
Greg Brasier
167 Sherry, P.O. Box 249
East Islip, NY 11730
(516) 581-3943

*AERIAL TECHNIQUES
T.J. Young
Rt. 209 South
Ellenville, NY 12428
(914) 647-3344

McCARRON AERONAUTICAL CORP.
Mike McCarron
17 Vicky Dr.
Saratoga Springs, NY 12866
(518) 587-1957

CROWN CITY KITES
Charles O. Murry
5229 Route 91
Truxton, NY 13158
(607) 842-6463, 842-6576

DAVE INGLEHART
160 Tenyck
Watertown, NY 13601
(315) 688-6404, 482-2275

DICK REYNOLDS
R.D. #1 Upper East Street
Oneonta, NY 13820
(607) 432-5418

DALE SHERMAN
15 Endicott Ave.
Johnson City, NY 13905

WESTERN N.Y. HANG GLIDING
6567 Powers Rd.
Orchard Park, NY 14127
(716) 662-4563, 662-1077

TOM WIRTH MARINE SPORTS
20 Glendale Terrace
Orchard Park, NY 14127
(716) 662-1968

*YARNALL TECHNONICS
1891 Dublin Rd.
Penfield, NY 14526
(716) 377-2854

ROCHESTER HANG GLIDERS, INC.
74 E. Park Rd.
Pittsford, NY 14534
(716) 381-0075

*QUAKERTOWN HANG GLIDING
Jeff Ingersoll
3635 Quakertown Rd.
Warsaw, NY 14569
(716) 786-5141

HAROLD F. MEESE
2604 Shadyside Dr.
Findley Lake, NY 14736
(716) 769-7624

SOUTHERN TIER HANG GLIDERS
Randall Sprague
P.O. Box 192
Portville, NY 14770
(716) 933-6637

MARTY DODGE
959 Oake St.
Elmira, NY 14901
(607) 732-1490

FLYING CASSETTA BROTHERS
614 Hart Street
Elmira, NY 14904
(607) 634-2802

NORTH CAROLINA

*U.F.M. OF KING
301 Kingstree Road
King, NC 27021
(919) 963-9064

MIKE SHELTON
Sides Mobil Court
W. Clemmonsville Rd.
Winston Salem, NC 27107

ROBERT TURNER
938 Gargrove St.
P.O. Box 962
Henderson, NC 27536
(919) 438-4654

PAY HAYES
5705 Claremore Drive
Durham, NC 27712
(919) 471-3798

MATT TABOR
P.O. Box 631
Kill Devil Hills, NC 27948
(919) 441-6877

*KITTY HAWK KITES
John Harris
Bypass 158
Nags Head. NC 27959
(919) 441-6247

FOOTHILLS HANG GLIDING
Route 8 Box 237 A
Shelby, NC 28150
(704) 434-2261

*SCOTT'S MARINE
Scott Lambert
908 Lexington Ave.
Charlotte, NC 28203
(704) 376-7348

FOOTHILLS HANG GLIDING
Ned Linds
1120 Scaleybark Road 207D
Charlotte, NC 28209
(704) 527-2860

CLIFF WHITNEY'S
6614 Candlewood Dr.
Charlotte, NC 28210

TOMMY FAIRCLOTH
8B Oakdale Apts
Fayetteville, NC 28304
(919) 424-4302

STEVE COAN
Cherry Tree Farms
Route 1 Box 291
Creston, NC 28615

GRANDFATHER MOUNTAIN
Highway 221, Entrance Bldg.
Linville, NC 28646
(704) 733-2800

KITTY HAWK KITES -
MORGANTON
Route #5
Morganton, NC 28655
(704) 584-3118

SOUTH MOUNTAIN AIR SPORTS
Rt. 10 Box 72
Morganton, NC 28655
(704) 433-7185, 667-0878

DAVED LEDFORD
328 New Leicester Highway
Asheville, NC 28806
(704) 253-1681

NORTH DAKOTA

*STEVE HANSON'S
3401 Gateway Dr.
Grand Forks, ND 58201

OHIO

DAVE BOYERS PRODUCTIONS
Dave Boyers
10350 Riverside Dr.
Powell, OH 43065
(614) 889-9653, 889-2983

*CENTRAL OHIO HANG GLIDING
Mike Hollingshead
Box 15380 St. Rt 104
Ashville, OH 43103
(614) 870-6053, 983-2307

*ULTRALIGHT FLYING MACHINES,
OF COLUMBUS
4131 Sexton Dr.
Columbus, OH 43228
(614) 274-3566

BOB LEE
215 Locust St.
Oak Harbor, OH 43449
(419) 691-4377, 536-0654

METALHAWK II
Edward MOrrison
501 Geneva
Toledo, OH 43609

WAYNE BERGMAN
1448 Rollins
Toledo, OH 43612
(419) 478-6032

*SANDY COLEMAN
Irondale, OH 43932
(216) 532-4852

TERRY FULLER
978 Center Rd.
Connecticut, OH 44030

*CHUCK'S GLIDER SUPPLIES
4252 Pearl Road
Cleveland, OH 44109
(216) 398-5272

CARLSON AIRCRAFT
Ernie Carlson
1346 Howell Rd.
E. Palestine, OH 44413

DAVE LOUPE
48400 Allegheny Tr.
Negley, OH 44441

*JOHN GREEN'S
125 Woodside St.
Hartville, OH 44632

*MIKE BOERSCHIG
73 Shady Lane
North Bend, OH 45052

MTN STATE HANG GLIDING
E.C. Brown
Route 3 Box 151
Chesapeake, OH 45619
(614) 867-8159

OKLAHOMA

OKLAHOMA MONARCH
Bob Weiss
6814 N.W. 52nd
Bethany, OK 73008
(405) 947-8701

eSTEPHEN E. CRUME
6605 N.W. 31st Terrace
Bethany, OK 73008
(405) 787-5638

*SKY ADVENTURES
4415 E. Reno
Oklahoma City, OK 73117

GENE BLEDSOES HANG GLIDER
SHOP
612 Hunter Hill
Oklahoma City, OK 73127
(405) 787-3125

TULSA HANG GLIDING SUPPLY
George Moore
721 North Forrest St.
Jenks, OK 74037
(918) 299-3219

MICHAEL HUFFMAN
1403 S. 135th East Ave.
Tulsa, OK 74108

*HESS BROS ULTRALIGHTS
221 Tapp Road
R.R. No. 6 Box 137
Ponca City, OK 74601

CAMERON SOARING SUPPLY
P.O. Box 282
Cameron, OK 74932
(918) 654-3250, 654-3219

JERRY FORBUGER
P.O. Box 385
Heavener, OK 74937
(918) 653-2112

*SKY UNLIMITED
Richard Kingrey
Star Route, Box 34
Heavener, OK 74937
(918) 853-2437, 653-2246

OREGON

*MARCELLIUS DODGE
1635 Hwy. 101 South
Tillamook, OR 97141
(503) 442-6722

PACIFIC GULL
Jim Boscole
524 S. W. 5th
Portland, OR 97204
(503) 625-7650, 226-2281

*SKI & SKI HANG GLIDERS
Craig Ashford
2604 N.E. 61st
Portland, OR 97213
(503) 281-1484

*DEAN CALDWELL
4524 S.W. Nael Rd.
Milwaukie, OR 97222
(503) 653-5103, 761-3200

OREGON SKY SPORTS
John Searce
5085 S.W. Laurelwood
Portland, OR 97225
(503) 292-4375

NORTHWEST H.G. SUPPLY
John Davis
10600 N.W. Laidlaw
Portland, OR 97229
(503) 292-2955

*KEN HOWE
544 Tierra Drive
Salem, OR 97301

P. & R. WINGS
1045 Aspen
Springfield, OR 97401
(503) 746-0987, 726-8280

SUPERFLY HANG-GLIDERS
Jeff Van Datta
853 N.E. 8th St.
Grants Pass, OR 97526
(503) 479-0826

PELICAN SKY SAILS
Box 500
Sprague River, OR 97639

PENNSYLVANIA

*AIRBORNE
Venice Road, RD 3
McDonald, PA 15057
(412) 926-2477

TRI-STATE HANG GLIDING SHOP
Ron Kisow
RD #1
Imperial, PA 15126
(412) 695-3833

BARNSTORMERS
David Lauter
327 Kenney Avenue
Pitcairn, PA 15140
(614) 537-2024

WESTERN PENNSYLVANIA HANG
GLIDING
Monty Edgar
131 Blair Dr.
Butler, PA 16001
(412) 283-8891

MISCHA BECK
Box 235
New Bedford, PA 16140

DONALD BLANK
R.D. 2 Box 94A
West Middlesex, PA 16159
(412) 528-2636

RIVERVIEW HANG GLIDING
Fred Booher
RD 1, Box 308
Cowansville, PA 16218

*KARL'S GLIDERS
Karl Kodrzycki
3230 W. 12th
Erie, PA 16505
(814) 883-9902

JOHN COCKETT
731 Apple View Ln.
Duncansville, PA 16635
(814) 942-1603, 696-1242

*SKY LIGHT FLIGHT
Dennis Hager
1184 Oneida St.
State College, PA 16801
(814) 235-1967, 237-9811

*K.H.R.C. SUPPLIES
RD 1
Hershey, PA 17033
(717) 244-8672, 534-2458

MIKE MARKOWSKI/
DENNY FRANKLYN
P.O. Box 4371-H
Harrisburg, PA 17111

BALD EAGLE HANG GLIDING
EQUIPMENT
146 N. Fourth St.
Hughesville, PA 17737
(717) 584-5275

THE HOLE IN THE SKY
Bb Mohr
5835 Main St. Box 221
Fogelsville, PA 18051
(215) 395-8492

*MYSTIC AIRCRAFT
Pat Hirst
148 So. 7th St.
Allentown, PA 18101
(215) 437-9955

DENNIS SITLER
Rd #3. Box 3176
Berwick, PA 18603

JOE MILLER
68-B E. Montgomery Ave.
Hatboro, PA 19040
(215) 672-3299

JOHN WILLIAMSON
465 Darby Paoli Rd.
Paoli, PA 19301
(215) 644-4729

*SWEET SKY
David Starbuck
109 Norwood Rd.
Downington, PA 19335
(215) 269-5109

CHAMP ENTERPRISES
322 N. High St.
Westchester, PA 19380

*FLIGHT SYSTEMS, INC.
Jim Hoser
2920 DeKalb Pike
Norristown, PA 19401
(215) 279-1076

SOUTH CAROLINA

*SKY RIDER
2432 Pleasant Ridge
Columbia, SC 29209
(803) 776-4106

KITTY HAWK KITES - GREENVILLE
2613 Poinsett Hwy.
Greenville, SC 29609

*HILLSIDE FLYING MACHINES
Ward Luben
Box 285
Pendleton, SC 29670
(803) 224-0050

SOUTH DAKOTA

ROBERT STREETER
P.O. Box 5
Pollock, SD 57648
(605) 889-2313

TENNESSEE

TENNESSEE WIREHOUSE
Box 1. Hwy. 27 Bypass So.
Dayton, TN 37321

*RANDY'S
Randy Wilson
130 N. Tennessee Ave.
Etowah, TN 37331

REBEL WINGS
Rt. #3. Box 329
Ooltewah, TN 37363
(615) 238-4887, 238-4267

CRYSTAL AIR SPORTS
Rte 4 Cummings Hwy.
Chattanooga, TN 37409
(615) 825-1995, 821-2546

*IN-FLIGHT
Rt. 1 Box 50
Blouville, TN 37617

TIM COCKER
Shields Station
Blain, TN 37709

*GERALD SIMPKINS
11604 Mt. View Drive
Concord, TN 37720

SCHOOL KIDS RECORDS
1727 Cumberland Ave.
Knoxville, TN 37916
(615) 637-6284

BRUCE D. HAWK
4823 Martin Mill Pike
Knoxville, TN 37920

JOHN WALKLING
10000 Hampshire Dr.
Knoxville, TN 37922
(615) 966-7138

*OLIVER GREGORY
982 Parkhaven Ln.
Memphis, TN 38111

*TRUE FLIGHT/AIR POWER INC.
Bert Alderson
3832 Guernsey
Memphis, TN 38122
(901) 324-8922

TEXAS

KITE ENTERPRISES
Dave Broyles
1402 Austin St.
Irving, TX 75061
(214) 438-1623

GERRY KIEFER
Shiloh Airport
P.O. Box 1923
Shiloh Road
Richardson, TX 75080
(214) 750-5853, 363-6085

*ROTEC
703 B. Big Stone Gap
Duncanville, TX 75116
(214) 296-2505

SO. CENTRAL SKI KITE & HANG GLIDING ENTERPRISES
8310 Southwestern Blvd.
Dallas, TX 75206

*ANDERSON'S ULTRALIGHT FLY-ING
504 E. 4th Street
Mt. Pleasant, TX 75455
(214) 572-7300

CALVIN MORGAN
Box 458
Queen City, TX 75577
(214) 796-6167

LONE STAR HANG GLIDERS
Stan Palmer
2200 "C" South Smithbarry Rd.
Arlington, TX 76013
(817) 469-9159

*HOELLER INC.
P.O. Box 116
Mineral Wells, TX 76067

*ARMADILLO AVIATION
703 N. Henderson
Ft. Worth, TX 76107
(817) 332-4668

BILL DAVIS
1407 Eagle St.
Houston, TX 77004

AMERICAN PRO KITES
16 A Woodlake Sq.
Houston, TX 77063

GULF COAST HANG GLIDERS
Jimmi Youngblood
2022 Derby Rd.
Houston, TX 77067
(713) 893-4967, 893-4939

*HOUSTON POWER GLIDERS
Gordon Cross
515 Harding
Baytown, TX 77520

ROCKY WHITMAN
555 Jones
Bridge City, TX 77611

MARK HEES
11654 Research
Austin, TX 78759

UTAH

*WASATCH WINGS
David Rodriguez
700 E. 12300 South
Draper, UT 84020
(801) 571-4044

*BRUCE YANCY'S
Rt. 1 Box 53B
Roosevelt, UT 84066
(801) 353-4510

FREEDOM WINGS, INC.
226 West 9240 South
Sandy, UT 84070
(801) 566-4991

*KITE SHOP AT NATURES WAY
898 So. 900 E.
Salt Lake City, UT 84102
(801) 359-7913

MARK S. COOK
1964 South 1700 E.
Salt Lake City, UT 84108
(801) 484-6933

*MIKE TINGY'S
3049 No. Apache Ln.
Provo, UT 84601
(801) 375-4000

VIRGINIA

SUPERMAN GLIDERS
W.L. Combs
P.O. Box 541
Dumfries, VA 22026
(703) 221-1759

CONDOR FLIGHT SYSTEMS, INC.
John C. Taugner
4105 Hunt Road
Fairfax, VA 22038
(703) 323-0797

NOVA HANG GLIDERS
Woody Jones
112 Oak St.
Vienna, VA 22180

*BLUE RIDGE POWER GLIDERS
William Dunwoody
Rt. 1, Box 120 A
Madison, VA 22727
(703) 948-4560

HERB POTTS
KHK-Richmond
Totopotomy Trail
Ashland, VA 23229
(804) 798-5729

ATLANTIC ULTRALIGHTS
P.O. Box 1179
Norfolk, VA 23501
(804) 583-5339

*U.F.M. OF TIDEWATER
402 Honberry Avenue
Portsmouth, VA 23702
(804) 397-6172

*CLOUDHOPPER
Pete Larson
5526 Twilight Rd. N.W.
P.O. Box 7646
Roanoke, VA 24019
(703) 345-7518, 563-1031

BLUE RIDGE MOUNTAINEERING CO.
Wayne Sayer
211 Draper Road
Blacksburg, VA 24060
(703) 552-9012

KITTY HAWK KITES-BLACKSBURG
420 N. Main St.
Blacksburg, VA 24060

*THE SKY IS THE LIMIT INC.
P.O. Box 56
Lynchburg, VA 24505

WASHINGTON

VERN ROUNDTREE
30003 112th S.E.
Auburn, WA 98002
(206) 833-3003, 852-5483

*U.F.M. OF WASHINGTON
39416 - 264th Ave. S.E.
Enumclaw, WA 98022
(206) 825-3782

AERIO SAILS
Steve Halester
800 Mercer
Seattle, WA 98109
(206) 624-7977

BIG BIRD WINGS
L.W. Fitzpatrick
1203 N.E. 82nd St.
Seattle, WA 98115
(206) 534-2436

ALEX DUNCAN'S
2601 Elliot Ave. #3200
Seattle, WA 98121

*ULTRALITE SPORTS OF AMERICA
14800 Westminster Way No.
Seattle, WA 98133
(206) 363-6364

SEATTLE SAILWINGS
George Madden
7130 California Ave. S.W. #101
Seattle, WA 98136
(206) 935-4539

*ULTRALIGHT SPORTS OF AMERICA
1242 N.E. 175th
Seattle, WA 98155

TERRY WITHAM
Box 1272 Highway 101 S.
Forks, WA 98331
(206) 374-5652

RECREATION NORTH WEST
Ken Fine
5429 South Island Drive
Sumner, WA 98390
(206) 863-2779

*AERIAL ADVENTURES INC.
Less Williams
9219 Madrone Circle West
Tacoma, WA 98467

*COLYAR ENGINEERING
Mike Colyar
1315 Dayton St.
Olympia, WA 98501

DAN THACKER
Rt. #6 Box 39
Yakima, WA 98906

*PARADISE AIR RANCH
Jack and Joy Rose
Sprangler, WA 99031

ALEXANDER'S GLIDERS
E. 3408 Jackson
Spokane, WA 99207

DAVE DORION'S
610 Sunrise Drive
Clarkston, WA 99207

INLAND EMPIRE S.G.
N. 6520 Normandie
Spokane, WA 99208
(509) 455-3770

DESERT SCHOOL OF FLIGHT
Dan Armstrong
518 W. Bonneville #3
Pasco, WA 99301

LANE HINERMAN
3065 S. Johnson #1
Kennewick, WA 99336

*DESERT SCHOOL OF FLIGHT
1425 Marshall
Richland, WA 99352

MIKE REINCKE
425 10th St.
Clarkston, WA 99403

WEST VIRGINIA

JOHN UPTON
Box 19
Leon, WV 25123

DONALD WALTER
2310½ E. Washington St. Apt. B
Charleston, WV 25311
(304) 342-2022, 768-9711

MOUNTAIN STATE HANG GLIDING
Mark Kenyon
1400 Cedarcrest Dr. Lot 126
Huntington, WV 25705
(304) 736-5968

FLAT TOP HANG GLIDERS
Rod Pendry
102 Randolph St.
Beckley, WV 25801

GREGORY LILLY
Box 144
Hinton, WV 25951
(304) 466-1219

*MOUNTAIN AIR
Kenny Cross
326 Central St.
Elkins, WV 26241
(304) 636-2900

*MOTORIZED HANG GLIDERS OF WEST VIRGINIA
P.O. Box 339
Craigsville, WV 26205

AERIE FLIGHT SCHOOL
Fred and Harold Wieneke
Star Rt. #1
Burlington, WV 26710
(304) 289-3403

WISCONSIN

SHEBOYGAN AQU FLYERS
Charles Mayers
721 S. 27th
Sheboygan, WI 53081
(414) 458-8635

*U.F.M. OF WISCONSIN
John Moody
P.O. Box 248
Kansasville, WI 53139
(414) 878-4380

ELASTIC FROG GLIDERS
Eric J. Wallner
18560 W. Evergreen Pl.
New Berlin, WI 53151

CASCADE SCHOOL OF HANG GLIDING
1971 Cascade Drive
Waukesha, WI 53186

*THIRD COAST SYSTEMS
Jay Leitschuh
Box 12400
Milwaukee, WI 53212
(414) 265-4648

COMPETITION SPORTS
Joe Kreuger
8620 W. Auer
Milwaukee, WI 53222
(414) 444-8181

TOW KITE & GLIDER EXCHANGE
Bob Grassle
2531 Cedar Piney Dr.
Janesville, WI 53545
(608) 756-2957

*JON BAUTSCH
203 No. 14th Ave.
Wausau, WI 54401
(715) 842-4013

RUSSELL BROWN
1525 King St.
LaCrosse, WI 54601
(608) 784-2110, 782-3545

*GLIDERS GALORE
Buck McMinn
Star St. Box 5995
Solon Springs, WI 54873
(715) 795-2618

LEE FISHER
2822 John Avenue
Superior, WI 54880
(715) 392-8794

WYOMING

BUFFALO SKY RIDERS
Steve Yestness
1919 Morrie Avenue
Cheyenne, WY 82001

CENTRAL WYOMING HANG GLIDING SCHOOL
Box 4206
Casper, WY 82604

BIG SKY HANG GLIDERS
Perry Austin
Box 1941
Gillette, WY 82715
(307) 686-2574

BIG HORN HANG GLIDERS
Neil Johnann
Box 312
Dayton, WY 82836
(307) 655-9742

HIGH PLAINS DRIFTERS
Mark McIntire
Box 106
Evanston, WY 82930

WESTWIND FLIGHT SCHOOL
1508 9th St. #12
Rock Springs, WY 82901

TETON SOARING CENTER
John Dresser
Ponderosa D-3
Jackson, WY 83001

KEN BIRD
Box 144
Kelly, WY 83011

HANG GLIDER MANUFACTURERS

Bill Bennett's Delta Wing Kites and Gliders, Inc.
1360 Saticoy Street, Van Nuys, CA 91402
Telephone: (213) 787-6600

Eipper Formance, Inc.
1070 Linda Vista Drive, San Marcos,
CA 92069. Telephone: (714) 744-1514

Electra Flyer
700 Comanche N.E., Albuquerque,
NM 87107. Telephone: (505) 344-3444

Flight Designs
P.O. Box 1503, Salinas, CA 93902
Telephone: (408) 758-6896

Highster Aircraft, Inc.
1508 6th Street, Berkeley, CA 94710
Telephone: (415) 527-1324

King Horizon Corp.
23230 Del Lago, Laguna Hills, CA 92653
Telephone: (714) 951-5001

Leading Edge Air Foils
331 South 14th Street, Colorado Springs,
CO 80904. Telephone: (303) 632-4959

Manta Products
1647 E. 15th Street, Oakland, CA 94606
Telephone: (415) 536-1500

Seagull Aircraft
1160 Mark Avenue, Carpinteria, CA 93013
Telephone: (805) 684-8331

Seedwings
1919 Castillo, Santa Barbara, CA 93101
Telephone: (805) 682-4250

Sunbird Gliders
12501 Gladstone Avenue, No. A-4, Sylmar,
CA 91342. Telephone: (213) 361-8651

Ultimate Hi
14328 Lolin Lane, Poway, CA 92064
Telephone: (714) 748-1739

Ultralite Products Up, Inc.
28011 Front Street, Temecula, CA 92390
Telephone: (714) 676-5652

U. S. Moyes, Inc.
11522 Red Arrow Highway
Bridgman, MI 49106

Waspair Corp.
1881 Enterprise Boulevard,
West Sacramento, CA 95611

Wills Wing, Inc.
1208-H E. Walnut, Santa Ana, CA 92701
Telephone: (714) 547-1344

ARGENTINA

Johan Byytebier
Mendoza, Argentina

Jorge Borria
Buenos Aires, Argentina

Jorge Cleva
Cordoba, Argentina

Guillermo Franceskin
Buenos Aires, Argentina

AUSTRALIA

Sky Trek Hang Glider Designs
81146 Oberon Street, Coogee, NSW, 2034
Australia

AUSTRIA

Steger
Scharnitz, Austria

Steinbach Delta
Kitzbühel, Austria

BRITAIN

Vulture-Lite
Sussex

Birdman Sports Limited
Marlborough, Wiltshire

Hiway Hang Gliders, Ltd.
Tredegar, Gwent.

Skyhook Sailwings Ltd.
Oldham, Lancashire

Chargus Gliding Co.
Gawcott, Buckingham

CANADA

Birdman Enterprises
8027 Argyl Road, Edmonton
Alberta, Canada

Sport Innovations
813 Shefford Street, Bronmont
Quebec, Canada

FRANCE

La Mouette
I. Rue De La Petite Fin
21121 Fontaine les Dijon, France
Telephone: 80/56-66-47

JAPAN

Falhawk
Tokyo, Japan

Bigbird
Tokyo, Japan

New Wings
Shizuoka, Japan

Homebuilt Mikawa
Shinshiro, Japan

SWITZERLAND

Hans Gygax
Switzerland

POWERED HANG GLIDING MANUFACTURERS

American Aerolights
700 Comanche, N.E., Albuquerque,
NM 87107. Telephone: (505) 344-6366

CGS Aviation, Inc.
4252 Pearl Road, Cleveland, OH 44109
Telephone: (216) 398-5272

Catto Aircraft
Box 1619, Cupertino, CA 95014

D.S.K. Aircraft Corp.
14547 Arminta Street, Van Nuys, CA 91402

Eipper Formance, Inc.
1070 Linda Vista Drive, San Marcos,
CA 92069. Telephone: (714) 744-1514

La Fayette Aviation Aircraft, Inc.
P.O. Box 10139, Orlando, FL 32809
Telephone: (305) 859-5551

Maxair Sports
P.O. Box 95, Glen Rock, PA 17327
Telephone: (717) 235-5512

Mitchell Aircraft Corp.
1900 S. Newcomb, Porterville, CA 93257

Power Systems, Inc.
39-B Coolidge Avenue, Ormond Beach,
FL 32074. Telephone: (904) 672-6363

Rotec Engineering
P.O. Box 124, Duncanville, TX 75116
Telephone: (214) 298-2505

Sky Sports, Inc.
394 Somers Road, Ellington, CT 06029
Telephone: (203) 872-7317

Ultraflight, Inc.
6 George Street, Port Colborne
Ontario, Canada L3K 3S1
Telephone: (416) 835-1933

Ultralite Soaring, Inc.
14095 N.W. 19th Avenue, Miami, FL 33054
Telephone: (305) 685-8265

Weedhopper of Utah, Inc.
Box 2253, 1148 Century Drive
Ogden, UT 84403

Wrong Brothers Aviation
1091 S.W. 1st Way, Deerfield Beach,
FL 33441. Telephone: (305) 427-3218

Yarnall Techtonics, Inc.
1891 Dublin Road, Penfield, NY 14526
Telephone: (716) 377-2854

THE FLYERS' FLYING SITES

This site information is provided mainly to let flyers know how widespread
and available hang gliding is throughout the world. However, pilots who live
near popular or exceptionally good flying sites are generally concerned that
others outside their area might come in and disregard the local customs and
rules for use of the land—in effect, spoiling its availability for everyone. Thus
our frequent admonition to check with local flyers. There is also the chance
that an unfamiliar site might present dangers known only to the locals.

The following information comes to us from flyers all over the world,
and we have used it nearly verbatim—with all the local color, sense of fun,
and whatever inadvertent inaccuracies might have crept into the reports.

Those sites marked with a footnote were graciously donated by *Whole
Air Magazine*.

We happily present The Flyers' Flying Sites.

ARIZONA

A-Mountain. Nearest city: Tucson. Directions: Close to downtown Tucson. Winds
and terrain: Southeast or south. Cactus. Skill
required: Hang 3. 500 feet vertical.

Helvetia. Nearest city: Tucson. Directions:
Ask local flyers. Winds and terrains: West to
northwest. Rocky. Skill required: Hang 4.
Special instructions: Good ridge soaring.
1,200 feet vertical.

Carr and Miller Canyons. Nearest city:
Sierra Vista (82 miles southeast of Tucson).
Directions: Ask local flyers. Winds and ter-
rain: Carr—north. Miller—northeast to east.
Skill required: Hang 4. Special instructions:
Carr and Miller are our best sites in south-
western Arizona. Flights of 20 miles are
common. 1,650 feet vertical.

ARKANSAS

Blanchard's Bluff. Terrain: 1,000 feet. Ask
local flyers for more information.

Magazine Mountain. Nearest city: Havana.
Directions: Ask local flyers. Terrain: 2,000
feet vertical; tree-covered. Winds: South.
Skill required: Hang 2 in smooth conditions.
Special instructions: Must join local club.

Petit Jean Mountain. Terrain: 800 feet. Ask
local flyers for more information.

Roger's Ridge. Nearest city: Little Rock.
Location: 15 miles northwest of Little Rock.
Terrain: Tree-covered slope facing southwest, two miles long, used as ramp launch;
landing in field at base of ridge. Skill required: Training.

CALIFORNIA

Crestline. Nearest city: Crestline/San Bernardino. Directions: 1/4 mile from Crestline off Playground Drive. Terrain: Mountain flying; launch fairly easy; vertical drop 3,000 feet; open-field landings. Wind: Ridge lift and thermals; winds start building from 10 to 11 A.M. and peak around 2 P.M. Skill required: Supervised intermediate and advanced. Special instructions: Very popular site—can be a lot of traffic, so you must know right-of-way rules. Controlled by local flyers with cooperation of Forest Service.

Ed Levin Park. Nearest city: Milpitas. Location: Foothills of Diablo Range east of Milpitas. Winds and terrain: South, west, soarable in pre- and post-frontal conditions; ridge lift and thermal activity; 1,700 feet ASL, launch from Monument Peak, landing large and flat, also 600- and 700-foot launches and 50-foot training hill. Skill required: Novice with supervisor and up. Special instructions: Must have USHGA card. Contact Mission Soaring Center, (415) 656-6656.

Elsinore/Edwards Canyon. Nearest city: Lake Elsinore. Directions: From top of the Ortega Highway take dirt fire road to launch site—ask locals. Winds and terrain: Often flyable only in the morning; around noon the winds switch. Flyable in Santa Ana conditions; 1,800-foot vertical drop, landings in fields below. Skill required: Intermediate to advanced, depending on conditions. Special instructions: Winds can become quite turbulent at times.

Fort Funston. Nearest city: Daly City. Directions: Adjacent to the Great Highway on the coast, just west of Daly City. Winds and terrain: 350-foot cliff facing southwest to west-northwest. Winds—Zero to over 25 mph. Skill required: Intermediate. Special instructions: Site is regulated and monitored by the local San Francisco club, Fellow Feathers. Contact Chandelle, San Francisco. (415) 756-0650.[79]

Guadalupe Dunes. Nearest city: Santa Maria. Directions: From Highway 101, take Main Street west to the beach; flying is at south end. Winds and terrain: Sand dunes up to 350 feet; ocean breezes, picking up in the afternoon. Skill required: All levels, depending on takeoff point and conditions. Special instructions: Need four-wheel or dune buggy to reach site.

La Cumbre. Nearest city: Santa Barbara. Directions: Go with local flyers. Winds and terrain: Winds vary considerably, need south or southwest to fly; rocky, mountainous terrain with manzanita brush. Skill required: Advanced—dangerous launch. Special instructions: Controlled by local flyers with support from Forest Service. You *must* go with locals. Call (805) 965-3733.

Mount Tamalpais. Nearest city: Stinson Beach. Directions: Off Coast Highway 1. Winds and terrain: 2,000 feet, overlooking the Pacific Ocean. Landing on beach north of town. Southwest to northwest. Skill required: Intermediate. Special instructions: Must contact Marin County Hang Gliding Association through Hang Gliders West, 20-A, Pameron, Ignacio, CA 94947, (415) 883-3494. Also sign in with park rangers at headquarters on top.[80]

Pine Flats. Nearest city: San Bernardino. Directions: Ask local pilots. Winds and terrain: Winds build from 10 to 11 A.M., peak about 2 P.M., ridge lift and thermals; vertical drop 2,500 feet, open-field landings. Skill required: Supervised intermediate and advanced. Special instructions: Can be crowded—know right-of-way rules.

Rincon Peak. Nearest cities: Santa Barbara and Ventura. Directions: Contact local flyers or call (805) 965-3733. Winds and terrain: Winds from the southwest, light coastal breezes, winds much higher if a storm front has passed through; 1,400-foot takeoff most popular, landing on beach. Skill required: Supervised novice, intermediate, and advanced. Special instructions: Contact local pilots, (805) 965-3733, for more information.

Sylmar. Location: Sylmar. Directions: East of I-5 off the Foothill Freeway. Winds and terrain: Flyable in south, southeast, and southwest winds; 1,500-foot vertical drop, mountain terrain, manzanita brush, landing field. Skill required: Intermediate and advanced, depending on conditions. Special instructions: Check with locals.

Torrey Pines. Nearest city: La Jolla. Directions: Take Genesee exit off I-5. Turn right, follow road to Torrey Glider Park. Winds and terrain: 300-foot vertical cliff overlooking beach. Winds 0 and up. Skill required: Intermediate and up depending on conditions. Special instructions: *Must* follow all posted regulations. Site is shared with RC (radio-controlled) gliders and sailplanes.

White Mountains and Gunter/Piute. Nearest city: Bishop. Directions: Contact Don Partridge at (714) 873-4434. Winds and terrain: Mornings generally calm, thermal activity picks up as day progresses, can be quite turbulent, especially during fall and spring; very rugged terrain, Gunter: 7,200 ASL, Piute: 9,000 ASL. Skill required: Advanced. Special instructions: Talk with local pilots about conditions and where to land.

CONNECTICUT

Avon Mountain. Location: Avon. Nearest city: Hartford. Directions: Contact Barton W. Blair, (203) 267-8980. Terrain: 6,500-foot cliff launch. Winds: Northwest. Skill required: Hang 2 through Hang 4. Special instructions: Must be a member of USHGA and Connecticut Hang Gliding Association. 1-1/2 mile ridge cross-country rides, over 20 miles, 7,800 feet above takeoff logged.

Brace Mountain. Nearest city: Salisbury. Directions: Contact Barton W. Blair, (203) 267-8980. Terrain: Running takeoff. Winds: Southwest. Skill required: Hang 2 through Hang 3.

Meriden Mountain. Nearest city: Meriden.

Directions: Contact Barton W. Blair, (203) 267-8980. Terrain: Cliff, short ridge. Winds: Northwest. Skill required: Hang 2 through Hang 4. Special instructions: Must be a member of USHGA and Connecticut Hang Gliding Association. Long cross-country ride logged at 26 miles, 5 hours and 6 minutes.

West Rock. Nearest city: New Haven. Terrain: 350 feet. Contact Barton W. Blair at (203) 267-8980 for more information.

FLORIDA

Key Biscayne. Nearest city: Miami Beach. Terrain: Lake. Winds: 5–12 mph in all directions. Skill required: Beginners limited to smooth winds up to 12 mph, and 500 feet of tow line. Novices limited to smooth winds to 16 mph, and static pulls only. Intermediate and advanced flyers limited as conditions permit, and winch pulls. Special instructions: Must register with Florida Free Flight Association. Club officers are generally available on site.[81]

Lake Alfred. Location: 20 miles northwest of Lake Wales. Terrain: Lake with long beach; trees at east end, railroad tracks along south side. Winds: 5–15 mph from 315°–45°. Towing: Static and winch pulls.[82]

Lake Jackson. Nearest city: Sebring. Terrain: Wide beach with few obstructions; several large apartment buildings on east side are soarable in moderate west winds. Winds: Best winds 5–12 mph in any direction. Towing: Winch pulls.[83]

Lake Wales. Location: At crossroads of routes 27 and 60. Terrain: Lake. Winds: 0–12 mph from 45°–135°. Towing: Primarily static-line pulls.[84]

Land Tow Site. Nearest city: Homestead. Location: 1 mile south of Kendall Glider Port. Winds: In all directions. Towing: Land tow.

Mandalay Marina. Nearest city: Rock Harbor. Directions: Go with local flyers. Winds: East, south, and west. Towing or motorized pontoons.

ILLINOIS

Boyle's Hill. Nearest city: Hennepin, 10 miles away. Directions: Go with local flyers. Terrain: 150 feet. Winds: West, northwest. Skill required: Hang 1.

Mark Dump. Nearest city: Granville. Directions: Go with local flyers. Terrain: Mine slag pile; 150 feet. Winds: Can fly in all directions. Skill required: Hang 1.

The Bluffs. Directions: Go with local flyers. Terrain: 300-foot vertical cliff launch. Winds: Southwest, 10–25 mph. Skill required: Intermediate and supervised novice. Special instructions: Watch for covey of rare water moccasins in landing zone.

INDIANA

East Cliff. Nearest city: New Albany. Directions: South on Highway 111 from New Albany, right on 211, first road to left, left at the T, stay on main road to takeoff. Terrain: 320-foot cliff. Winds: 90° easterly; flyable at 70°–120°. Skill required: Hang 3. Special instructions: For information, call Dennis, (812) 944-0530, or Rich, (812) 288-6597.

Floyd Cliffs. Nearest city: New Albany. Directions: South of New Albany off Highway 111. Terrain: 400-foot cliff. Skill required: Hang 3 and 4. Special instructions: Contact local pilots for specific regulations.

Lake Monroe. Nearest city: Bloomington. Directions: Southeast of Bloomington. Winds: 0°–270° north through west. Boat towing. Special instructions: Contact Central Indiana Hang Gliding Club, Indianapolis, (317) 291-9079.

Lake Raccoon. Nearest city: Rockville. Directions: 9 miles east of Rockville on Route 36. Winds: 45°–270° northeast to west. Boat tow. Special instructions: Contact Central Indiana Hang Gliding Club, Indianapolis, (317) 291-9079.

Mount Baldy. Nearest city: Michigan City. Location: National Lakeshore Park. Directions: Go with local flyers. Terrain: 100-foot dune, 2 miles long, soarable above 15 mph winds. Winds: Northeast, north, northwest. Skill required: Dependent on conditions, Hang 1–4. Regulated site—contact ranger station or New Horizons, 940 Western Ave., Geneva, Ill., (312) 232-6822, regarding rules. Borders Michigan.

Rushville. Nearest city: Metamora. Directions: West of Metamora on State Route 52. Winds: Primarily southwest; back side northeast. Special instructions: Contact Central Indiana Hang Gliding Club, Indianapolis, (317) 291-9079.

IOWA

Crestent Ski Hills. Nearest city: Crestent. Directions: 2 miles north of Crestent, signs show way. Terrain: 400-foot dirt hill cliff. Winds: Southwest to south. Skill required: Hang 3. Special instructions: Contact owner of Ski Hills.

Murray Hill. Location: Little Sioux. Directions: 2 miles northeast of Little Sioux, can be seen from town. Terrain: Dirt hill, 500-foot cliff. Winds: Northwest, best are westerly. Skill required: Hang 3. Special instructions: Keep gate closed at road to top because of cattle.

KENTUCKY

Sparta. Nearest city: Sparta. Directions: Call Richard Sacher at (812) 288-6597, or Dennis Loughmiller at (812) 944-0530. Winds: Northwest, flyable at 300°–340°. Terrain: Slope 35°. Skill required: Hang 2.

MARYLAND

Cumberland Gap. Directions: Contact Sport Flight, 9041 B Comprint Ct., Gaithersburg, MD 20760, (301) 840-9284. Terrain: Cliff launch. Winds: Southwest. Skill required: Hang 3 and 4.

High Rock. Nearest city: Pen Mar. Directions: Contact Sport Flight, 9041 B Comprint Ct., Gaithersburg, MD 20760, (301) 840-9284. Terrain: Cliff launch; 1,100-foot vertical drop. Winds: 225°–315°, thermals. Skill required: Hang 3 and 4.

Oregon Ridge. Nearest city: Baltimore. Directions: Off I-83; contact Sport Flight, 9041 B Comprint Ct., Gaithersburg, MD 20760, (301) 840-9284. Terrain: 150-foot slope. Winds: East to northeast. Skill required: Training on up.

MICHIGAN

Arcadia Bluffs. Nearest city: Arcadia. Location: 10 miles south of Frankford on M-22. Winds: West-northwest to north-northwest. Skill required: Good Hang 3 with soaring experience. Special instructions: If soarable, can fly to landing area. If not, it's a 2-mile walk down the beach.

Casco. Nearest city: South Haven. Location: 117th Street, Casco. Directions: Secret spot —contact New Horizons, 940 Western Avenue, Geneva, IL 60134, (312) 232-6822. Winds: Southwest to west-northwest. Skill required: Hang 3 to 4. Special instructions: Site on private property. Please go with local flyers or personnel of New Horizons.

Empire Bluffs. Nearest city: Empire. Directions: Go with local flyers. Terrain: Coastal sand bluff, 400 feet high. Winds: Southwest to northwest. Skill required: Hang 3. Special instructions: Must register with national park ranger.[85]

Green Point. Nearest cities: Frankfort and Elberta. Directions: 2 miles south of Elberta on M-22. Winds: Southwest, west, northwest; acceptable in winds. Skill required: Hang 2. Special instructions: Must register with Jim Nelson at Eco-Flight Hang Gliding Shop, P.O. Box 188, 826 Michigan Avenue, Benzonia, MI 49616, (616) 882-5070.[86]

Mount Baldy. Nearest city: Michigan City. Location: National Lakeshore Park. Directions: Go with local flyers. Terrain: 100-foot dune, 2 miles long, soarable above 15 mph winds. Winds: Northeast, north, northwest. Skill required: Dependent on conditions, Hang 1–4. Regulated site—contact ranger station or New Horizons, 940 Western Ave., Geneva, IL, (312) 232-6822, regarding rules. Borders Indiana.[87]

Pyramid Point. Nearest city: Glen Arbor. Directions: Inquire when registering. Terrain: 400-foot vertical sand bluff; flyable March through November. Winds: Soarable over 10 mph, 350°–045°. Skill required: Hang 3 and 4. Special instructions: Register with National Park Service office in Frankfort, or D. H. Day Campground in Glen Arbor. Landing 1/2 mile behind ridge next to access road or on narrow beach below.[88]

Sleeping Bear Dunes. Nearest city: Empire. Directions: Go with local flyers. Terrain: Dunes; land at launch or at Empire Beach 2 miles south; soarable over 485 feet. Skill required: Hang 3 or 4. Special instructions: Must register with National Park Service in Frankfort or D. H. Day Campground in Glen Arbor.[89]

Warren Dunes. Location: Warren Dunes State Park. Nearest city: Sawyer. Directions: Off I-94 to park exit, follow signs. Terrain: 180-foot sand dunes. Winds: South, southwest, west, northwest (best direction for soaring), and north. Skill required: Hang 1–4, depending on conditions. Special instructions: Register with Park Service and obtain information on weather reports and rules from them.[90]

Goderich, Ontario-Drysdale, Ontario. Location: Ontario, Canada. Nearest city: Goderich or Drysdale. Directions: Go with local flyers. Terrain: Cliff and tree ridge, launch at water station in Goderich, 12-1/2 miles, 150-foot ridge. Winds: West, southwest, northwest. Beach landing at Goderich. Near Detroit; used by Michigan pilots. Skill required: Hang 2–3.

Point Bruce-Point Stanley. Location: Ontario, Canada, Lake Erie area. Directions: Go with local flyers. 12-1/2 miles between sites. Terrain: 150-foot vertical cliff, beach landing at Point Bruce, many landing areas on top. Winds: South-southwest, south-southeast. Near Detroit; used by Michigan pilots. Skill required: Hang 2–3.

Wheatly-Erie Beach. Nearest city: Leamington. Directions: Go with local flyers. Terrain: 60- to 80-foot cliff follows shoreline, small ridge. Winds: South-southeast, east-southeast, southeast; 20 mph wind a must. Skill required: Hang 3. Near Detroit; used by Michigan pilots.

MISSOURI

Sioux Passage. Nearest city: St. Louis. Directions: Go with local flyers. Terrain: 50-foot vertical-slope launch. Winds: Northwest and north, 0–25 mph. Skill required: Beginner.

Sugarbowl-Leadwood. Nearest city: Leadwood. Directions: Go with local flyers. Terrain: Man-made sand dune. Skill required: Beginner and intermediate.

MONTANA

Johnson's. Nearest city: Livingston. Directions: Off Highway 89 (check map) south of Livingston. Terrain: Elevation 6,000 feet ASL; vertical descent; steep grassy slope. Winds: 0–25 mph and thermals; May through October best. Skill required: Hang 2.[91]

Mount Sentinal. Nearest city: Missoula. Location: On the University of Montana campus. Terrain: 5,000 feet ASL; vertical descent 1,960 feet; landing in golf course 1 mile away. Winds: West 270°, gliding 0–10, 260°–045°, soaring 12 and up, 270°–090° and in thermals. Skill required: Hang 3 with USHGA insurance. Special instructions: Must follow posted rules; direct contact with airport flight control via radio at launch.[92]

Red Mountain. Nearest city: Butte. Location:

South of Butte on Highway 15. Winds: Need 5 mph wind to make landing 4–5 miles away. Don't fly when wind is from the south. Late June through mid-October best. Skill required: Hang 4. Special instructions: Contact Dennis Sitton, Anaconda, (406) 563-2758, or Fred Darland, Butte, (406) 494-3778. Watch for bears![93]

The Hogback. Nearest city: Livingston. Location: South of Livingston on Highway 89 (see map). Terrain: 3-1/2 mile ridge; 300- and 500-foot vertical descent on north; 300- and 800-foot vertical descent on south. Winds: 0–25 mph and thermals. Skill required: Hang 2. Special instructions: Contact Dan Gravage at (406) 222-1559, or Barney Hallen at (406) 222-1780.[94]

NEBRASKA

Blair. Nearest city: Grave Yard, NE. Contact Don Pierce, 11009 "R" Plaza, No. 6, Omaha, NE 68137, (402) 339-3211.

Lake 11. Location: 84 State Street. Nearest city: Omaha. Terrain: Grass hills and dam. Winds: South, west, northwest, east. Skill required: Hang 1. Special instructions: Must sign waiver; contact Don Pierce, 11009 "R" Plaza, No. 6, Omaha, NE 68137, (402) 339-3211, or Omaha Parks and Recreation.

Lake 16. Location: 144 Fort Street, NE. Contact Don Pierce, 11009 "R" Plaza, No. 6, Omaha, NE 68137, (402) 339-3211.

NEW JERSEY

Turkey Hill. Nearest city: Newton. Directions: George Washington Bridge to Route 80 into Route 15 to Lafayette, then to Route 94 south till Route 206 south, through Newton. After Newton, look for Route 94 and the VFW hall on your right. A side reference is Don Bosco College, which is located across from Turkey Hill. For parking, use VFW hall lot. Terrain: 200-foot ridge, 30° angle, huge landing area, one large tree. Winds: North, northwest. Skill required: Hang 1–3. Special instructions:

Bring waiver and put in farmer's mailbox. If winds are hard, only Hang 3 flyers allowed.[95]

NEW MEXICO

La Bajada Ridge. Nearest city: Santa Fe. Directions: Go with local flyers from Santa Fe or Albuquerque. Terrain: 5-mile ridge; 600–1,200-foot vertical. Winds: Northwest to southwest, less than 20 mph. Skill required: Hang 3.

Sandia Crest/Sandia Peak. Nearest city: Albuquerque. Directions: From Albuquerque, east on I-40 to State Road 14, north to Sandia Crest turnoff, or go to Sandia Peak Tramway. Terrain: Rugged mountain flying, 4,000-foot vertical. Winds: Northwest to southwest, less than 20 mph. Skill required: Hang 3 or 4. Special instructions: Contact local pilots.

San Pedro Mountain. Nearest city: Albuquerque. Directions: Go with local flyers. Terrain: 1,200-foot vertical. Winds: Northwest or southeast. Skill required: Hang 3.

NEW YORK

Calhoun's. Nearest city: DeRuyter. Directions: Go with local flyers. Terrain: 2-stage, shallow hill, lots of thermal action. Landing areas controlled by land owners (crops and pasture). Wires at all landing areas. Winds: North and northwest. Skill required: Hang 2. Special instructions: Very controlled site.

Ellenville. Nearest city: Ellenville. Directions: 3 miles east of Ellenville on Route 52. Terrain: Mountain with four launch points: 1,100, 875, 800, and 600 AGL. Winds: Ridge lift and thermals—winds range from calm, stable, to strong, unstable high winds. Skill required: Advanced Hang 3 and up. Special instructions: Site of 1980 U.S. Nationals. One of most popular eastern sites.[96]

Farmingdale Pitts. Nearest city: Farmingdale. Directions: Right behind Farmingdale University. Winds: All except northwest. Skill required: Novice-beginner. Special instructions: Site is posted. Flyers must leave when asked to do so.

Labrador Pond. Nearest city: Truxton. Directions: Contact Condor Hang Gliding Club, 73 Hunting Street, Cortland, NY 13045. Terrain: 700-foot hill with ridge 1-1/2 miles long. Landing area is field. Winds: Westerly. Skill required: Advanced. Special Instructions: Must be USHGA and Condor Hang Gliding Club member to be covered by insurance required by state. State-owned site.

Leather Hill. Nearest city: Dover Plains. Directions: Take Route 22 north to town of Dover. Park is approximately one mile north of Harlem Valley [Wingdale] Psychiatric Center. 20-minute walk up. Terrain: 500 feet. Winds: Northwest. Skill required: Hang 2–4. Special instructions: Must be USGHA member with rating of intermediate or advanced. Novice pilots may fly under supervision of an advanced pilot. All nonresident pilots must be accompanied by a Dover resident pilot. Contact: Jim Wise, (914) 877-3319; Rich Dwy, (914) 832-6763; or George Weigel, (914) 855—1139.[97]

Mattituck. Nearest city: Mattituck. Directions: Call V. Matassa, (516) 681-8738. Terrain: Dune-type 40° slope. 1-mile-long ridge. Landing zone is narrow beach. Winds: Best soaring northwest, 18–22 mph. Skill required: Hang 3–4. Special instructions: Follow all posted rules. Call V. Matassa for guest passes—$10 for 10 days' rights, or charter membership.[98]

Port Washington. Nearest city: Port Washington, Long Island. Directions: Go with local flyers. Terrain: 35° slope. Winds: Northeast, southeast. Skill required: Beginner-intermediate. Special instructions: Site is posted. Flyers must leave when asked to do so.

Note: Many of the ski areas permit hang gliding. Check with local flyers' organizations and the ski areas themselves.

NORTH CAROLINA

Buzzard's Rock. Nearest city: Weaversville. Directions: Turn off Blue Ridge Parkway where Forest Service sign says "Weaverville—Vance's Birthplace."

Grandfather Mountain. Nearest city: Boone. Directions: Off Blue Ridge Parkway. Terrain: Cliff launch, 1,500-foot vertical drop; landing area has some trees and water. Winds: Soarable from northwest. Skill required: Hang 4. Site of the 1976 U.S. National Hang Gliding Championship and the 1976 Masters Championship.

Hibriten Mountain. Nearest city: Lenoir. Directions: Off Highway 18. Terrain: 900-foot ridge facing north; ramp launch. Skill required: Advanced Hang 2 with caution, and Hang 3. Special instructions: Talk to local pilots about landing approaches. Contact John Smith at (704) 754-5735, or Charles Pierce at (704) 758-9238 for key to the gate.

Jockey's Ridge. Nearest city: Nags Head. Location: Near Route 158. Terrain: Sand dunes. Winds: 10–20 mph, soaring possible. Skill required: Excellent for beginners and better. Special instructions: Contact Kitty Hawk Kites Hang Gliding Center at Jockey's Ridge, (919) 441-6247.

Lake Norman. Nearest city: Charlotte. Location: 15 miles north of Charlotte. Terrain: 550 miles of shoreline. Winds: Best in the summer. Towing.[99]

Lake Wylie. Nearest city: Charlotte. Location: 15 miles southwest of Charlotte. Terrain: 250 miles of shoreline. Towing.[100]

Tator Hill. Nearest city: Boone. Directions: 8-1/2 miles west of Boone off Highway 421. Terrain: 2,200-foot-long ridge. Winds: 0–20 mph. Skill required: Hang 3 and 4. Special instructions: Tight landing; ask local pilots about alternate area for inexperienced pilots; 30–45 minute ride to top over *rough* road.

Walker Top. Nearest city: Morganton. Directions: South of I-40, off U.S. 64. Terrain: 1,400 feet. Winds: Northwest. Skill required: Restricted Hang 3. Special instructions: Contact Dennis Walker, (704) 584-0770; talk to local pilots about landing areas.

White Lake. Directions: Ask local pilots. Terrain: White-sand lake, 2–3 miles in diameter. Towing. Special instructions: Only two good launch sites, both privately owned, but usually accessible.[101]

OKLAHOMA

Buffalo Mountain. Nearest city: Talahina. Directions: Go with local flyers. Terrain: Good road to top; cliff with ramp. Winds: South. Skill required: Good Hang 2. Special instructions: $5 fee per year required, payable to landing-area owner.

Cavanal Mountain. Nearest city: Poteau. Location: Overlooks city of Poteau. Terrain: 1,950-foot vertical. Winds: East and southeast. Skill required: Hang 3 and 4. Special instructions: See locals for landing instructions.

Red Clay Chat Pile. Nearest city: Cardin. Location: 15 miles north of Miami. Terrain: 200-foot vertical. Winds: All directions. Skill required: Hang 2 and better. Flyable all year.

Rich Mountain. Nearest city: Mena, Arkansas. Directions: Contact Gerry Kiefer, 12700 Hillcrest Rd., Suite 240, Dallas, TX 75230. Terrain: West end of ridge forms north wall of valley viewed from Three Sticks launch; 18-mile bowl. Winds: Southeast, south, southwest; soarable in 12 mph, blown out over 25 mph. Skill required: Advanced Hang 4. Special instructions: No landing area below launch. Do not fly unless soarable. Must land on top (abundant landing sites). Good cross-country site. One can easily fly to Heavener from here. Sailplanes towing up from Mena, Arkansas, have gained 14,500 feet of altitude here in mountain-wave conditions. Strong, smooth ridge and thermal lift encountered here. An A+ site for expert pilots. 2,000-foot average vertical.

Round Mountain. Nearest city: Heavener. Location: 2 miles north of Runestone. Terrain: 350-foot vertical. Winds: Southwest. Skill required: Hang 2 minimum. Special instructions: Notify Rufus Montgomery, property owner. $1 fee per day.

Runestone Mountain. Nearest city: Heavener. Directions: Go with local flyers. Terrain: Good road, cliff. Winds: Southeast. Skill required: Hang 2. Special instructions: Don't land on Mr. Ward's property!

Three Sticks Monument. Nearest city: Heavener. Directions: 3 miles south of junction of highways 63 and 259 (where 259 crosses Kiamichi Mountain). Terrain: 44-mile, 1,500-foot ASL ridge faces north. Skill required: Advanced Hang 3 and Hang 4. Special instructions: Landing fields are 11 to 1. Must thermal out to fields. Many regulars land in tree-lined Highway 259 directly under launch. Many tree landings have occurred. Slight changes in wind direction cause bad rotors behind the smaller knots and finger ridges in front of main ridge. Only a handful of regular Quachita Mountain pilots fly here. Most are intimidated by this site. Excellent valley and ridge thermals available here. Best during October through April.

OREGON

Anderson's. Nearest city: Oceanside, 5 miles south. Directions: Go with local flyers. Terrain: Ocean frontage; 800 feet high; 3,000-foot gains. Winds: Northwest. Skill required: Hang 3 and up. Special instructions: Gully launch, one-step takeoff.

Cape Kiwanda. Nearest city: Pacific City. Location: South of Tillamook off Highway 101. Terrain: Sand dunes. Winds: Off ocean. Skill required: Beginner on up.

Coburgs. Nearest city: Eugene. Location: 10 miles northeast of Eugene. Terrain: 1,700-foot ridge. Winds: West to south, thermals. Skill required: Hang 2. Special instructions: $2 fee per day for visitors.

Mount Harris. Nearest city: La Grande. Location: North of La Grande. Terrain: Vertical descent 1,400 feet. Skill required: Hang 3 and up.

Mount Tom. Nearest city: Eugene. Directions: Go with local flyers. Terrain: 2,700-foot inland mountain. Winds: North and northwest. Skill required: Hang 3 with sponsor and Hang 4. Special instructions: $2 fee per day.

Oceanside. Nearest city: Oceanside. Location: Off Highway 101. Winds: Off ocean. Skill required: Hang 4. Special instructions: Talk with local pilots and follow regulations.

OHGA Flight Park. Nearest city: Portland. Directions: Go with local flyers. Terrain: 360-foot vertical drop; landing in pasture. Skill required: Advanced Hang 2 and up. Special instructions: Must be a member of OHGA, Box 5592, Portland, OR 97228.

Parkdale. Near Mount Hood. Directions: Go with local flyers; four-wheel drive needed. Winds: Thermal; light westerly; best with sunshine. Skill required: Hang 3. Special instructions: Conditions can change quickly, so should be monitored.

Prairie Mountain. Nearest city: Eugene. Directions: Go with local flyers. Terrain: 3,000-foot coastal range. Winds: Thermals, north and south. Skill required: Hang 3. Special instructions: Should ask local pilot for instructions.

Yaquina Head. Nearest city: Newport. Location: Off Highway 101. Directions: Go with local flyers. Terrain: Cliff launch, 260-foot vertical drop. Winds: Usually soarable. Special instructions: Fly north side early spring through fall; south side fall through March.

PENNSYLVANIA

Brady's Bend. Nearest city: East Brady. Location: 50 miles northeast of Pittsburgh. Directions: Go with local flyers; site locked. Terrain: 530-foot vertical; 1 to 1 landing area; 3/4-mile ridge; cliff launch. Winds: Northwest. Skill required: Hang 3. Special instructions: Site maintained by Daedalus Hang Gliding Club—contact club member Monty Edgar at (412) 283-8891.

Templeton. Nearest city: Templeton (10 miles north of Kittaning). Location: Western Pennsylvania; 50 miles northeast of Pittsburgh. Directions: Go with local flyers; site locked. Terrain: 490-foot vertical; 5 to 1 glide to landing area; 3/4-mile ridge; cliff launch. Winds: Northwest. Skill required: Hang 3. Special instructions: Site maintained by Daedalus Hang Gliding Club—contact club member Monty Edgar at (412) 283-8891.

The Pulpit. Nearest city: McConnellsburg. Directions: Ask Ron Higgs, Box 77, Cascade, MD 21719. Terrain: 1,100 feet ASL. Winds: Northwest. Skill required: Hang 3 with cliff launch. Special instructions: Must check in with Ron Higgs, (301) 241-3508, before flying.

SOUTH CAROLINA

Big Glassy. Nearest city: Greenville. Directions: Go with local flyers. Special instructions: Must join SCHGA; yearly dues $30. Contact Connie Goff, Secretary of SCHGA, Rt. 7, South Rockview Drive, Greenville, SC 29609, (803) 834-9338.

Little Glassy. Nearest city: Greenville. Directions: Go with local flyers. Terrain: 400-foot sloping cliff launch; large pasture landing. Winds: Northwest 330°. Skill required: Hang 2. Special instructions: Contact Ashley Davis, (803) 233-4088.

TEXAS

Elephant Mountain. Nearest city: Marta-Alpine. Location: Big Bend area. Approximately 30 miles south of Alpine on Highway 118. Terrain: 2,000-foot mesa (road to top); 400- to 600-foot vertical cliffs on all sides. Winds: Prevailing, southwest; soarable 350 days a year; can launch in any direction. Skill required: Hang 3 and 4. Special instructions: Check in at Elephant Mountain Ranch with foreman, or contact Houston Hang Gliding Association. Private site—must be a member.

Hippie Hollow. Nearest city: Austin. Location: Northwest end of Lake Travis. Directions: Go with local flyers. Terrain: 400-foot cliff to water; two southeast bowls; one tight landing zone or water landing; evergreen bushes and rock. Skill required: Hang 3 or 4, depending on landing. Special instructions: Nude swimmers in area.

Lake Travis. Nearest city: Austin. Directions: Go with local flyers. Terrain: Small landing area; flying over water. Winds: Smooth, soarable off lake. Skill required: Hang 3.

Murchion. Nearest city: Austin. Location: Near 2222 in Austin. Terrain: Grass, 40-foot training hill. Skill required: Hang 1 or 2. Very good for beginners.

Pack Saddle. Nearest cities: Llano and Kingsland. Location: North of Kingsland on Highway 71. Terrain: Rocks, scrub brush, and trees; power lines east and west. Winds: South. Skill required: Hang 2 to 4. Special instructions: Members only ($100 per year) or owner will throw you in jail (he's a city judge)! Contact Pack Saddle Flying Club in Houston or San Antonio.

TENNESSEE

Crystal Flight Resort. Nearest city: Chattanooga. Directions: Route 4, Cummings Highway to ridge. Terrain: New 180-foot training hill. Skill required: Training and up. Special instructions: Phone (615) 825-1995.

Henson Gap Northwest. Nearest city: Dunlap. Directions: Go with locals. Terrain: 1,500-foot vertical ridge, over forest, faces northwest. Skill required: Hang 3 or equal. Special instructions: Must get pass from Tree Toppers Club.

Henson Gap Southwest. Nearest city: Dunlap. Directions: 4 miles by dirt four-wheel-drive road from Northwest site (above). Terrain: 1,500-foot vertical. Forested. Faces southwest. Skill required: Hang 4 only. Special instructions: Must be USHGA member and get pass from Tree Toppers Club.

Lookout Mountain. Nearest city: Chattanooga; Trenton, Georgia. Directions: Go with local flyers. Terrain: 1,500-foot ridge. Winds: From the southwest, 10–20 mph. Skill required: Hang 3. Special instructions: Contact Crystal Flight Resort, (615) 825-1995, Chattanooga. [102]

Clinch Mountain. Nearest city: Knoxville. Directions: 22 miles northeast of Knoxville on U.S. Highway 11W a few miles southwest of Rutledge—contact Taylor Watkins (615) 828-5543. Winds and terrain: Two sides—Southeast 1,500-foot vertical, 3 to 1 to large landing area. Some thermals. Northwest side—1,250-foot vertical at launch; averages 1,000 feet vertical for 20 miles. Skill required: Intermediate. Special instructions: Site of many record cross-country flights. If muddy, a four-wheel-drive is needed. [103]

Racoon Mountain. Nearest city: Chattanooga. Directions: contact Crystal Flight Resorts (615) 825-1995. Winds and terrain: 835 feet vertical. Flyable in 0–12 mph winds, from 0°–180°. Soarable in winds from 45° to 135° and thermals. 5 acres landing area with power lines or trees on two sides. Skill required: Novice. Special instructions: $2–$5 ground pass. $1.25–$1.50 lift fee for tram. Register with Crystal Flight Resort office in landing field. [104]

UTAH

Brigham City. Location: Brigham City. Directions: Go with local flyers. Terrain: Rough four-wheel road. Winds: Variable. Skill required: Hang 3 or 4.

Camel Pass. Location: Springville. Contact Wasatch Wings, 700 E. 12300 South, Draper, Utah 84020.

Dead Horse Point. Nearest city: Moab (45 minutes away). Directions: Go with local flyers. Terrain: Vertical-cliff launch. Skill required: Hang 4. Special instructions: Talk with local pilots before attempting to fly here.

Francis Peak. Location: Farmington. Directions: North of Salt Lake City 15 miles. Nice road to top. Go with local flyers. Terrain: 5,000-foot vertical fly; large landing area. Winds: Under 20 mph, northwest or southwest. Skill required: Hang 3 or 4, depending on conditions. Special instructions: Make sure you know proper flight path before flying; rotors are fairly common.

Heber City. Location: Heber City. Contact Wasatch Wings, 700 E. 12300 South, Draper, Utah 84020.

Inspiration Point. Nearest city: Oum. Location: Approximately 10 miles south of Draper. Directions: Go with local flyers. Terrain: Small landing area; 2,000-foot drop. Winds: Northwest or southwest. Skill required: Hang 3 or 4. Special instructions: Watch out for power lines.

Point of the Mountain. Nearest city: Draper (20 miles from Salt Lake). Directions: East of I-15, south of Draper. Terrain: 1,500 feet; 300-foot ridge. Winds: Up to 30 mph north or south. Skill required: Hang 2 to 4 depending on conditions. Special instructions: Daily fee for flying south side.

Willard Peak. Location: Ogden. Contact Wasatch Wings, 700 E. 12300 South, Draper, Utah 84020.

VIRGINIA

Big Walker Mountain. Location: Near Bland. Nearest city: Wytheville. Directions: Where Route 52 crosses Big Walker, turn east on Forest Service road toward Big Bend picnic area; follow approximately 6 miles. Note: Launch site cannot be seen from road; ask for help before you go. Terrain: Ridge over 30 miles long. Winds: Prevailing northwest. Skill required: Hang 2 in light winds; Hang 3 in turbulent winds. Special instructions: Landing fields occasionally change as farmers plant crops.

East River Mountain. Nearest city: Bluefield. Directions: On U.S. 52 where 52 crosses top at craft-shop parking lot. Terrain: Take-off in gap, long ridge (52-mile flights have been logged). Winds: Northwest. Skill required: Hang 3. Special instructions: Best landing field is Bluefield High School, two miles down the ridge; small landing field available in front; this site not recommended if not soarable. Borders West Virginia.

High Top. Nearest city: Standardsville. Directions: Go with local flyers. Terrain: 1,400-foot vertical ramp launch. Winds: East. Skill required: nonrated hill, should be Hang 3. Special instructions: Check with locals for site protocol.

Roanoke Mountain. Nearest city: Roanoke. Directions: Located on Blue Ridge Parkway, milepost 120. Terrain: 1,000-foot vertical ridge, 2 miles long. Winds: East, also flyable northeast. Skill required: Hang 3. Special instructions: Pilots must obtain a permit from any ranger station on Blue Ridge Parkway first. Hang 3 required.

Sutphins Farm. Nearest city: Flint Hill or Warrenton. Directions: Obtain from Sport Flight, 9041 B Comprint Ct., Gaithersburg, MD 20760, (301) 840-9284. Terrain: 300-foot vertical running launch. Winds: South to west. Skill required: Hang 2. Special instructions: Check with Sport Flight; rented hill.

WASHINGTON

Badger Mountain. Nearest city: Wenatchee. Location: North of East Wenatchee. Winds: South, thermals. Skill required: Hang 3 or better.

Barr's Mountain. Nearest city: Monroe. Location: South of Monroe on Highway 203. Terrain: Cliff launch; field landing at base of mountain. Winds: Smooth. Skill required: Hang 3.

Dog Mountain. Nearest city: Morton. Directions: Highway 12, five miles east of Morton, turn right at railroad overpass. Terrain: Cliff launch. Winds: 0–15 mph from southwest. Skill required: Hang 3. Special instructions: Logging area; flying restricted to weekends. 1976 U.S. National Hang Gliding Championship held here.

Eagle Butte. Nearest city: Kennewick. Location: Five miles west of Kennewick. Winds and terrain: 500-foot butte facing into west winds. Skill required: Hang 2, mild conditions; Hang 3, heavy thermals or strong wind. Thermals very strong.

High Drive. Nearest city: Spokane. Location: High Drive is off Maple Street in Spokane. Terrain: Steep hill, vertical drop, 500 feet, narrow landing next to freeway. Skill required: Hang 3. Special instructions: Winds over 20 mph cause turbulent conditions.

McBee Grade. Nearest city: Kiona. Directions: Go with local flyers. Terrain: Ridge flying. Winds: 10–20 mph. Skill required: Hang 3. Special instructions: No flying in winter.

Mount Spokane. Location: Northeast from Spokane. Terrain: Mountainous with trees. Winds: East to northeast best, good thermals. Skill required: Intermediate and advanced because of surrounding trees.

Step Toe Butte. Nearest city: Colfax. Directions: Call shop in Lewiston (see Yellow Pages). Terrain: 800-foot vertical. Winds:

360°. Skill required: Beginner. Special instructions: Narrow lift band; top of mountain is pointed; lots of landing area; good intermediate site.

Teako Mountain. Nearest city: Teako. Directions: Follow a road map; mountain is visible and obvious from Main Street. Terrain: Smooth face; wide lift band. Winds: South, west. Skill required: Novice. Special instructions: Watch out for power lines.

Ten Mile. Nearest city: Asotin. Directions: Call local shop (see Yellow Pages). Terrain: On breaks of Snake River. Winds: Canyon winds. Skill required: Intermediate. Special instructions: Lots of rotors, waves, and thermals, related turbulence; cross-country potential.

Wills Hill. Nearest city: Coupeville (Whidbeg Island). Directions: Go with local flyers. Terrain: 180-foot training hill, soarable at times. Winds: Southeast through southwest. Skill required: Beginner through advanced.

WEST VIRGINIA

East River Mountain. Nearest city: Bluefield. Directions: On U.S. 52 where 52 crosses top at craft-shop parking lot. Terrain: Takeoff in gap, long ridge (52-mile flights have been logged). Winds: Northwest. Skill required: Hang 3. Special instructions: Best landing field is Bluefield High School, two miles down the ridge; small landing field available in front; this site not recommended if not soarable. Borders Virginia.

WISCONSIN

Hagar City. Location: Hagar City. Directions: Go with local flyers. Terrain: 250-foot cliff, can be soarable depending on winds. Skill required: Hang 2 and up.

Omnibus Ski Area. Nearest city: Sturgeon Bay. Directions: North from Sturgeon Bay on Highway 42. Terrain: Bluffs and steep hills. Skill required: Hang 2 and up. Special instructions: Contact local flyers.

Spring Green. Nearest city: Spring Green. Directions: Located on bluff north of Spring Green. Winds: South and southwest. Skill required: Hang 2 with less than 10 mph; Hang 3 over 10 mph. Special instructions: Don't land in corn or crops.

WYOMING

Big Horn's West Side. Directions: Follow U.S. 14A to Yellowstone. Terrain: Mountains to desert; 1,200 to 5,000 feet. Winds: Northwest. Skill required: Hang 3 or better. Special instructions: Watch for radar domes and 800-foot ridge; need 500 feet of altitude before attempting to land on desert floor, otherwise you will land in parking lot. Contact Big Horn Hang Glider in Dayton, (307) 655-9230.

Red Grades. Nearest city: Sheridan. Location: Off U.S. 90 in northern Wyoming. Directions: U.S. 90 north toward Big Horn, follow road; need four-wheel-drive. Terrain: Mountain and plains; 1,200 feet vertical. Winds: Southeast and north; thermals. Skill required: Hang 2 or 3. Special instructions: Launch shallow and long, but easy. Contact Big Horn Hang Glider in Dayton, (307) 655-9230.

Sand Turn. Nearest city: Dayton. Location: U.S. 14. Directions: U.S. 90 north to U.S. 14 to Yellowstone. Terrain: Plains at base of mountain; vertical 1,200 feet; 1- to 2-hour flights possible. Winds: North and southeast; 0–20 mph, ADV 10; thermals. Skill required: Thermal ability; advanced Hang 2 or 3. Special instructions: Soaring hours 11 A.M. to 3 P.M., early morning and late evening. Sled rides good for advanced beginners. Contact Big Horn Hang Glider in Dayton, (307) 655-9230.

AUSTRIA

Hafelekar, Innsbruck. Ask local pilot for information, as you have to call the Innsbruck Airport if you want to fly here. Super flight —5,700 feet.

Hinterhornalm, Innsbruck.

Patscherkofel, Innsbruck. Ask local pilot for information, as you have to call the Innsbruck Airport if you want to fly here. Super flight—5,700 feet.

Reither Kogel, Brixlexx.

BRAZIL

São Conrado, Rio de Janeiro.

Bocaina, between Rio de Janeiro and São Paulo.

BULGARIA

Mount Witosha. Approximately 1,200 meters from takeoff to landing. Nearest city: Sofia.

Mount Chepen. Approximately 600 meters from takeoff to landing. Nearest city: Dragoman.

CANADA

Agassiz, Vancouver, British Columbia

Athabasca Tower, Hinton, Alberta

Big Hill Springs, Calgary, Alberta

Bruce Peak, Saltspring Isle, Victoria, British Columbia

Camrose, Edmonton, Alberta

Cape Anguille, Newfoundland. Contact Carroll Redden, Box 276, Corner Brook, Newfoundland, for more information.

Cochrane Hill, Calgary, Alberta

The Escarpment, Hamilton, Ontario

Fly Hills, Salmon Arm, British Columbia

Georgian Peaks, Collingwood, Ontario

Glen Mountain, Montreal, Quebec

Grizzly Ridge, Calgary, Alberta

Grouse Mountain, Vancouver, British Columbia

King Eddy, Vernon, British Columbia

King Mountain, Ottawa

Mount Blackstrap, Saskatoon, Saskatchewan

Mount Buchanan, Kaslo, British Columbia

Mount St. Hilaire, Montreal, Quebec

Mount St. Pierre, Matane, Quebec

Mount Swansea, Invermere, British Columbia

Mount Sykes, Newfoundland. Contact Carroll Redden, Box 276, Corner Brook, Newfoundland, for more information.

Mount Vernon, Vernon, British Columbia

Mount Yamaska, Granby, Quebec

Saddle Mountain, Lumby, British Columbia

Sicamous, Sicamous, British Columbia

Stoney Creek, Vernon, British Columbia

St. Veronique, Montreal, Quebec

Thornhill Mountain, Terrace, British Columbia

Vedder, Vancouver, British Columbia

Westbluff, Calgary, Alberta

CYPRUS

Staurovouni, Nicosia

Curium, Limassol

ENGLAND

Contact the following clubs for flying sites:

Avon Hang Gliding Club. Secretary: John Clark, 11 Bramley Close, Olveston, Avon. Telephone: Almondsbury 613778.

Pennine Hang Gliding Club. Secretary: John Wood, 4 Daffodil Close, Helmshore, Rossendale, Lancashire. Telephone: Rossendale 28669.

Southern Hang Gliding Club. Chairman: Tony Fuell, 74 Eldred Avenue, Brighton, Sussex. Telephone: 502952.

Thames Valley Hang Gliding Club. Chairman: Bill Nunn, Old Post Office, Peasmore, Near Newbury, Berkshire. Telephone: Chievely 288.

ITALY

Campo Tures, Bolzano

Colle Delle Finestre, Torino

Cornizzolo, Como

Frabosa, Mondovi

Monte San Gloroio, Torino

Monte Sumano, Vicenza

Piancavallo, Pordenone

JAPAN

Kurumayama, Chino City

Sugadira, Ueda City

Tanna, Atami City

Tsurumi Dake, Beppu City

LUXEMBOURG

Kanfen, Dudelange

Michelau, Diekirch

MEXICO

Joco, Mexico City

Valle Bravo, Mexico City

Jocotitlan, Toluca

Valle Del Bravo, Valle del Bravo

Iguala, Iguala

Tapalpa, Guadalajara

NORWAY

Bondalseide. Nearest cities: Ørsta/Volda, Ålesund.

Egge. Nearest cities: Oslo/Drammen.

Keiservarden. Nearest city: Bodø.

Meraker Skicenter. Nearest city: Trondheim.

Tromsø. Nearest city: Tromsø.

Vågå Hang gliding center. Nearest city: Lillehammer

RUMANIA

Moorea. Nearest city: Arad.

Ozun. Nearest city: Sf. Gheorghe.

Sinpetru. Nearest city: Braşov.

Poiana Braşov. Nearest city: Braşov.

SOUTH AFRICA

Barberton-White Rocks, Barberton. Elevation: 2,200 feet.

The Dam-Hartebeespoort, Johannesburg. Elevation: 900 feet.

One Gum Hill, Durban. Elevation: 1,400 feet.

Table Mountain-Africa Face, Cape Town. Elevation: 4,000 feet.

NOTES

1. Jean-Bernard Desfayes, *Delta: The Hang Gliding Handbook* (Newfoundland, New Jersey: Haessner Publishing, Inc., 1975), p. 13. By permission of Pierre M. Favre, Publishers.
2. Ibid. pp. 14–15.
3. Leonardo da Vinci, manuscript on the flight of birds, as printed in *The Journal of the Royal Aeronautical Society*, Vol. XXVII (1923), p. 314. Courtesy Smithsonian Institution.
4. Sir George Cayley, "Sir George Cayley's Aerial Carriage," *Mechanics' Magazine* (April 8, 1843), p. 278.
5. Beril Becker, *Dreams & Realities of the Conquest of the Skies* (New York: Atheneum, 1967), p. 74.
6. Otto Lilienthal, quoted in "The Flying Man," by Vernon, *McClure's Magazine* (September 1894). From the William J. Hammer Scientific Collection.
7. Otto Lilienthal, *Birdflight as the Basis of Aviation* (London: Longmans, Green, and Co., 1911).
8. Otto Lilienthal, "Practical Experiments in Soaring," *Ground Skimmer*, No. 10 (May 1973), p. 15.
9. Otto Lilienthal, "The Problem of Flying," *Ground Skimmer*, No. 8 (January–April 1973), p. 17.
10. Ibid. p. 15.
11. Lilienthal, *Ground Skimmer* (May 1973), p. 19.
12. Lilienthal, *Ground Skimmer* (January–April 1973), pp. 15–17.
13. Lilienthal, *Ground Skimmer* (May 1973), p. 18.
14. Ibid.
15. Ibid. pp. 19–21.
16. Michael A. Markowski, *Hang Glider's Bible* (Blue Ridge Summit, Pennsylvania: TAB Books, 1977), p. 40.
17. Neville Duke and Edward Lanchberry, *The Saga of Flight* (New York: John Day Co., 1961), pp. 27–29.
18. Markowski, op. cit. pp. 28–29.
19. Ibid.
20. Duke and Lanchberry, op. cit. pp. 22–23.
21. Coles Phinizy, "I'm Icarus—Fly Me," *Sports Illustrated*, Vol. 39, No. 24 (December 10, 1973), p. 114. Reprinted courtesy of SPORTS ILLUSTRATED. © 1973 Time Inc.
22. Michael Mendelson, *The Complete Outfitting and Source Book for Hang Gliding* (Sausalito, California: Great Outdoors Trading Co., 1977), p. 33.
23. Martin Hunt and David Hunn, *Hang Gliding* (New York: Arco Publishing Inc., 1977), p. 77. © 1977 by Martin Hunt. Originally from *Alphabook*, designed and produced by Alphabet & Image, Sherborne, Dorset, England.
24. Mendelson, loc. cit.
25. Jack Lambie, "In the Beginning . . . The First Hang Gliding Meet," *Hang Gliding*, No. 71 (December, 1978), p. 15.
26. Ibid. pp. 16–17.
27. Ibid. p. 17.
28. Ibid.
29. Ibid. p. 18.
30. Ibid.
31. Taras Kiceniuk, Jr., *Icarus V* (Palomar Mountain, California: Taras Kiceniuk, 1974), p. 2.

32. Lambie, op. cit. p. 18.
33. Ibid.
34. Ibid. p. 19.
35. Ibid.
36. Ibid.
37. Ibid.
38. Ibid.
39. Ibid.
40. R. V. Wills, "Annual Report to Shareholders, Creditors, Benefactors, Patrons, and Perplexed Observers," California, 1972, p. 3.
41. Phinizy, op. cit. p. 120.
42. Ibid.
43. Bill Allen, "Flying Bull," *Hang Gliding*, No. 55 (August 1977), p. 67.
44. Carol Boenish Price, "And the Race Goes On . . . ," *Hang Glider*, Vol. I, No. 1 (Summer 1974), p. 10.
45. Ibid.
46. Ibid. p. 11.
47. Ibid. p. 12.
48. Ibid.
49. Ibid.
50. Ibid. p. 14.
51. Ibid. p. 15.
52. Ibid.
53. Desfayes, op. cit. p. 43.
54. Phinizy, op. cit. p. 116.
55. Peter Brock, from a letter to the author.
56. Chris Wills, "In Greece With 20th Century Fox," *Hang Gliding*, No. 39 (April 1976), pp. 23–25, 46–51; No. 41 (June 1976), pp. 42–45.
57. "Ultralight News," *Hang Gliding*, No. 49 (February 1977), p. 12.
58. Ibid.
59. Jan Case, from a letter to the author.
60. Carol Boenish Price, "Women and Hang Gliding," *Hang Gliding*, No. 91 (August 1980), pp. 22–23, 45–47.
61. Bryan Allen, "The Gossamer Dream," *Guideposts*, (July 1980), pp. 13–16. Copyright 1980 by Guideposts Associates, Inc. Used by permission from *Guideposts* magazine.
62. Ibid.
63. Ibid.
64. Ibid.
65. Ibid.
66. Ibid.
67. Ibid.
68. Ibid.
69. Ibid.
70. Ibid.
71. Ibid.
72. Ibid.
73. Ibid.
74. Ibid.

75. Ken de Russy, from a letter to the author.
76. John Harris, from a letter to the author.
77. Earl Gustkey, "Hang Gliding: For Those Who Like Flights of Fancy," Los Angeles *Times* (July 11, 1980), Sports section, p. 1.
78. Phinizy, op. cit. p. 120.
79. Terry Ferrer, *Whole Air Magazine* (July–August 1980), p. 39.
80. Ibid. p. 38.
81. Ed Quirk, *Whole Air Catalog* (January–February 1980), p. 41.
82. Ibid.
83. Ibid.
84. Ibid.
85. Don Baker, *Whole Air Catalog* (November–December 1979), p. 30.
86. Ibid. p. 23.
87. Ibid. p. 30.
88. Ibid. p. 23.
89. Ibid.
90. Ibid. p. 30.
91. Dan Gravage, *Whole Air Magazine* (May–June 1980), p. 38.
92. Ibid.
93. Ibid. p. 39.
94. Ibid.
95. Robert Chapel, *Whole Air Magazine* (May–June 1980), p. 37.
96. Ibid. p. 37.
97. Ibid. p. 37.
98. Ibid.
99. Scott Lambert, *Whole Air Magazine* (March–April 1980), p. 36.
100. Ibid.
101. Ibid.
102. Tim Cocker, *Whole Air Magazine* (September–October 1979), p. 20.
103. Ibid. p. 21.
104. Ibid.

Note: All direct quotes by Volmer Jensen, Bill Bennett, Francis Rogallo, Willi Muller, Donnita Kilbourne, Tracy Knauss, Gil Dodgen, Chris Wills, Rich Grigsby, Chris Price, Bob Wills, Don Partridge, Jack Lambie, and Paul MacCready are from direct personal interviews by the author, unless otherwise stated.

BIBLIOGRAPHY

BOOKS

Becker, Beril. *Dreams and Realities of the Conquest of the Skies.* New York: Atheneum, 1967.

Carrier, Rick. *Fly: The Complete Book of Sky Sailing.* New York: McGraw-Hill, 1974.

Dedera, Don. *Hang Gliding: The Flyingest Flying.* Flagstaff, Arizona: Northland Press, 1975.

Desfayes, Jean-Bernard. *Delta: The Hang Gliding Handbook.* Newfoundland, New Jersey: Haessner Publishing, Inc., 1975.

Dickens, Peter L. *Hang Gliding—The Natural High of Self Launched Flight.* New York: Warren Books, 1977.

Doyle, Lorraine M. *Hang Gliding: Rapture of the Heights.* National City, California: Lion Press, 1974.

Duke, Neville and Edward Lanchberry. *The Saga of Flight.* New York: John Day Co., 1961.

Halacy, D. S., Jr. *The Complete Book of Hang Gliding.* New York: Hawthorn Books, Inc., 1975.

Hunn, David and Martin Hunt. *Hang Gliding.* New York: Arco Publishing Co., Inc., 1977.

Kiceniuk, Taras, Jr. *Icarus V.* Palomar Mountain, California: Taras Kiceniuk, 1974.

Lilienthal, Otto. *Birdflight as the Basis of Aviation.* London: Longmans, Green, and Co., 1911.

Markowski, Michael A. *The Hang Glider's Bible.* Blue Ridge Summit, Pennsylvania: TAB Books, 1977.

Mendelson, Michael. *The Complete Outfitting and Source Book for Hang Gliding.* Sausalito, California: The Great Outdoors Trading Co., 1977.

Mrazek, James E. *Hang Gliding and Soaring.* New York: St. Martin's Press, 1976.

Olney, Ross R. *Hang Gliding.* New York: G. P. Putnam's Sons, 1974.

Poynter, Dan. *Hang Gliding: The Basic Handbook of Skysurfing*, rev. ed. North Quincy: Massachusetts: Daniel F. Poynter, 1976.

Siposs, George. *Hang Gliding Handbook: Fly Like a Bird.* Blue Ridge Summit, Pennsylvania: TAB Books, 1975.

Wills, R. V. "Annual Report to Shareholders, Creditors, Benefactors, and Perplexed Observers." California, 1972.

ARTICLES

Allen, Bill. "Flying Bull," *Hang Gliding*, No. 55 (August 1977), p. 67.

Allen, Bryan. "The Gossamer Dream," *Guideposts* (July 1980), pp. 13–16.

Cayley, Sir George. "Sir George Cayley's Aerial Carriage," *Mechanics' Magazine* (April 8, 1843), pp. 277–278.

Gustkey, Earl. "Hang Gliding: For Those Who Like Flights of Fancy," Los Angeles *Times* (July 11, 1980), Sports section, pp. 1, 18, 20.

The Journal of the Royal Aeronautical Society, Vol. XXVII (1923), pp. 289–317. Courtesy Smithsonian Institution.

Lambie, Jack. "In the Beginning . . . The First Hang Gliding Meet," *Hang Gliding*, No. 71 (December 1978), pp. 14–20.

Lilienthal, Otto. "Practical Experiments in Soaring," *Ground Skimmer*, No. 10 (May 1973), pp. 15–21.

_____. "The Problem of Flying," *Ground Skimmer*, No. 8 (January–April 1973), pp. 15–18.

Phinizy, Coles. "I'm Icarus—Fly Me," *Sports Illustrated*, Vol. 39 (December 10, 1973), pp. 102–122.

Price, Carol. "And The Race Goes On," *Hang Glider*, Vol. I, No. 1 (Summer 1974), pp. 8–15.
_____. "Women . . . And Hang Gliding," *Hang Gliding*, No. 9 (August 1980), pp. 22–23, 45–47.
"Ultralight News," *Hang Gliding*, No. 49 (February 1977), p. 12.
Vernon. "The Flying Man," *McClure's Magazine* (September 1894), pp. 323–330. From the William J. Hammer Scientific Collection.
Wills, Chris. "In Greece With 20th Century-Fox," *Hang Gliding*, No. 39 (April 1976), pp. 23–25, 46–51; No. 41 (June 1976), pp. 42–45.

Index